Go ye therefore teach all nations
Thou shalt love thy neighbor as thyself

MISSIONAL REFORMATION
FOR DISCIPLING NATIONS

CHURCHSHIFT:
A MODEL FOR THE 21ST CENTURY CHURCH

ABI OLOWE, Ph.D.

MISSIONAL REFORMATION

PUBLISHED BY
OMEGA PUBLISHERS
HOUSTON, TEXAS, U.S.A.

All scripture quotations are taken from the King James Version
www.scripturegroup.net

Copyright © 2009 Abi Olowe, Ph.D. *All Rights Reserved*
First Printed: 2009

This book may not be reproduced, stored in a retrieval system, or transmitted in any form, in whole or in part, without the express permission of the author.

ISBN 978-0-9795299-4-8

Cover Design: B-Links, Inc (www.b-links.com)

Printed in United States of America

For further enquiries, please contact
Omega Publishers USA
Tel.: 281-744-5033

TO God our father, Jesus our savior, and the Holy Spirit our comforter

MISSIONAL REFORMATION

PREFACE

SOMETIME in March 2008, I received a revelatory prophecy from Evangelist Elizabeth Owoeye; after a prayer session, she said: "pick up your pen and get ready to be taking notes of revelations". I thought it was about a crisis I was having then. I didn't understand the prophecy until I started to receive revelations in August, 2008 during my first visit to the Embassy of God Church in Ukraine. These revelations continued in Houston, Texas and necessitated my second trip to the Ukraine in April, 2009. I have been overwhelmed by revelations on the Gospel of the Kingdom of God, doctrine of grace, triune man (body, spirit, and soul), and the Embassy of God Church. The first three books that are coming out of these revelations are:
1. Missional Reformation: Theological Background
2. Missional Reformation: Practical Application

MISSIONAL REFORMATION

3. Grace Theology

The first two are compiled in a single book – this book. All these three books, written in parallel, give a clear understanding of the difference between a classical church and a Missional Church, and God's plan for the new generation church. Reading through the books will clearly suggest that most of the writings are not from my wisdom. I am an engineering scientist and a computer programmer. I have no formal education in theology.

> For though I preach the Gospel, I have nothing to glory of: for necessity is laid upon me; yea, woe is unto me, if I preach not the Gospel! (I Corinthians 9:16)

FOREWORD

I AM absolutely impressed and in awe with the writing gift that the Lord has given to Dr. Olowe. His writing style makes you want to read and read without putting the book down. Dr. Olowe makes the church history an easy-reading, sweet as honey. Unlike many other accounts that provide a boring reading. It's even more amazing when you think of the fact that Dr. Olowe did not study theology or church history in the university, he actually studied science and engineering, which goes along to prove that the revelation he received on this subject and his writing style are God-given gifts.

Dr. Olowe is an ardent student of his chosen subject. He came over here to Ukraine and delved into studying absolutely everything at the Embassy of God church. The result is the historic work you are holding in your hands. Almost everybody who has been to Kiev, Embassy of God church, has exclaimed in disbelief that such a revolutionary work will be taking place in Ukraine. Many have said that they have never seen a church like this before. Some call it the first true Apostolic Church they have ever seen; others call it the Model Church for the 21st century, but none has been able to put a comprehensive expression into what God is doing in Kiev. Even though many books and articles have been written about the phenomenal work God is doing here at the Embassy of God, no doubt Dr. Olowe's work has proved to be by far the most comprehensive and complete study of the events that have taken place here.

Indeed, God has dug a well of life for the 21st century church in the most unexpected of all places. The Church is no doubt in need of a new reformation. As the founder of the Embassy of God church, I have attempted to, by the grace of God, build on the solid foundation of the Apostles and church history. My biggest passion is to make God popular again. I believe with the ChurchShift model, we can definitely bring the rain of God into all spheres of the society, as it has been done before, so it can still be done today. I therefore congratulate Dr. Abi Olowe for this book, *Missional Reformation*, which is a monumental gift to the Body of Christ. It is my prayer that this book will spark another reformation for the people of the 21st century and beyond. "Jesus Christ the same yesterday, and today, and for ever." (Hebrews 13:8, KJV). If He did it in the early years of Christianity, He will definitely do it again in our time.

To all the readers of *Missional Reformation*, I wish to encourage you to take the time and the pain to actually study this book with all the care and attention as possible. This could be the most important journey of your life. Your faith will be revitalized; the fire of God will come upon you. God's passion will consume you again; you will have a better understanding of your faith and the Church of Christ more than ever before. But above all, you will discover that God uses ordinary people and that you can as well be the next history maker and revolutionary of your generation.

May the Lord bless you as you read!

Yours faithfully in Him,
Sunday Adelaja
Senior Pastor, The Embassy of God
Kiev, Ukraine

MISSIONAL REFORMATION

NOTES

This book actually opened my eyes to so many theological issues and new way of discipling nations, new move of Pentecostalism at the same time, very theological.

This book will propel you to join the new chariots of ideas on Churchshift and how to reach our community. Its emphasis is on the new methodology of reaching out to the lost.

I strongly recommend the book to Bible scholars, students, and Church Pastors who are thirsty for ways of reaching out to the lost but do not know the methodology. It is a new move of God in this 21st century.

Pastor Gabriel Dada, Th.D.
District Superintendent
Christ Apostolic Church, Central Florida

ACKNOWLEDGEMENTS

I THANK our Lord Jesus Christ, the author of our Faith and the Good Shepherd who orders my steps and who counts me worthy of this project.

Of course, my gratitude goes to Pastors Sunday and Bose Adelaja who allowed me access to their personal life, both public and private. They welcomed me into their house and trusted me to review valuable documents.

Also, I express my gratitude to the Embassy of God's ministers and staff who were very cooperative; I specifically thank the guest department leader, Ludmila Kulitenko, who coordinated many of my meetings; Valeriya and Rodion, my valuable interpreters, and the drivers.

MISSIONAL REFORMATION

I must also thank the editorial staff, especially LaTonya Pegues and my reviewers for their special interest in this project.

CONTENTS

Preface v
Foreword vii
    Notes x
Acknowledgements xi
Contents xiii

VOLUME 1: THEOLOGICAL BACKGROUND

Introduction 25
1. Reforms 29
    Definitions 29
        Church and Society 30
        Culture 30
        Reform and Reformation 31
    Types of Reforms 32

  Direction and Source *32*
  Impact *33*
 Social Reforms 33
 Church Reforms 36
 Points in Chapter 1 38
2. History of Church Reforms 39
 Ancient (30–590) 40
  The Apostles *40*
  Apostolic and Church Fathers *41*
  Persecutions *42*
  Corruption *43*
  Heresies *43*
  End of Persecution *46*
  Emperors and the Church *47*
  Doctrine of Grace and Free Will *49*
 Medieval (590-1648) 49
  Islamic crusades and slavery *50*
  Scholasticism *51*
  Schism *52*
  The Protestant Reformation *53*
  Church of England Reformation *58*
 Modern (1648-1970) 59
  Revival Movements *59*
  Missions *61*
  Pentecostal Movement *64*
 Points in Chapter 2 70
3. Postmodern Movements 71
 General Overview 72
  Postmodernism *72*
  Common Name *78*
  Common Values *80*
  Common Theology *81*
 Church Planting Movement 83

  Classification of Models *84*
  Non Cell-Based Church Planting *86*
  Cell-Based Church Planting *90*
 Church Cell Movement 98
  Microscopic Characteristics of church cells *98*
  Macroscopic Characteristics of church cells *101*
 Seven-Sphere Movement...110
  Theological Bedrock *111*
  Implementation *112*
  Criticism *113*
 Stewardship Movement 115
  Purpose of the Movement *116*
  Implementation *117*
  Criticism *117*
 Churchshift Movement 118
 Dominionism 119
  Anti-Dominionism Movement *120*
  Kingdom on Earth *121*
 Points in Chapter 3 124
4. The Gospel of The Kingdom 125
 Clarification..125
 Revelation of the Gospels..127
  Scriptural Revelation *127*
  Pictorial Revelation *130*
 Security of the believer..132
 Full Gospel 133
 Other names of the Gospels...135
 The Two Gospels...136
  Gospel of Salvation *136*
  Gospel of Discipling Nations *138*
 Grace 143
  Grace and Good Works *143*
  Universal Grace and Special Grace *147*

Points in Chapter 4 152
5. Theology of Good Works 153
Discipling 154
Go ye *154*
Therefore *154*
Teach *155*
All Nations *155*
Stewardship 158
General Material Resources *159*
Personal Non-Material Resources *160*
Promised Land *162*
Giving 164
Forms of Giving *164*
Giving to God *165*
Giving to Man *168*
Peace 171
Purpose of peace *172*
Responsibility of the Church *173*
How do we make peace? *174*
Light 175
Principles *175*
Consequences *177*
Points in Chapter 5 178
6. The Seven Spheres 179
The Concept of Spheres 179
Sphere Models 180
William Carey Model *180*
Abraham Kuyper Model *181*
Cunningham and Bright Model *183*
Coalition on Revival Model *184*
Landa Cope Model *186*
Sunday Adelaja Model *187*
Standard Model *187*

- Points in Chapter 6 190
- 7. Illustration of Reforms 191
  - Graphical Illustration 192
    - *Guidelines* *192*
    - *Hypotheses* *193*
    - *The Model* *194*
  - Examples of Mixed Reforms 196
    - *Socio-Spiritual (Syncretic) Reforms* *196*
    - *Spiritual Social (Missional) Reforms* *200*
    - *Religion Based Reforms* *203*
  - Points in Chapter 7 206
- 8. Principles of Churchshift 207
  - Overview of Churchshift 207
    - *The Concept* *207*
    - *Definitions* *208*
    - *Rationale for Churchshift* *209*
  - Kingdom Principles 214
    - *For the Church* *214*
    - *For the Leader* *216*
    - *For the Believer* *217*
  - Points in Chapter 8 220
- 9. Components of Churchshift 221
  - Graphical Model 221
  - The Church 223
    - *Role of the Church* *223*
    - *Layer 1: Leadership Ladder School* *225*
    - *Layer 2: Churchshift Ministries* *229*
    - *Layer 3: Expansion of Church wall* *230*
  - The Spheres 231
    - *Business and Finance* *232*
    - *Government* *233*
    - *Family* *234*

Church and Religion *235*
Points in Chapter 9 236

VOLUME 2: PRACTICAL APPLICATION

Introduction to Volume 2 239
10. The Model Church 241
    History of the Embassy of God 242
    Liturgy 246
        Praise and Worship *247*
        Prayer *249*
        The Word of God *251*
        Sacrament *252*
    Activities 253
        Church Anniversary *253*
        March of Life *254*
    Church Growth 255
        Myles Munroe Effect *255*
        Home Group System *256*
    Points in Chapter 10 262
11. Structures 263
    Spiritual Governance 265
        Apostolic Council *265*
        Spiritual Council *266*
    Administration 267
        Management *267*
        Missions *270*
        Finance *274*
    Points in Chapter 11 276
12. Daughter Churches 277
    Kiev Region 278
        Sergey Pyshnny *278*

  Bose Adelaja *279*
  Vladimir Dzuba *281*
  Tatiana Maksimenko *282*
  Galina Korobka *283*
 Ukraine 285
  Igor Tomchenko *285*
 United States of America 287
  Vasily Biletsky *287*
  Yuri Binder *288*
  Andrei Kuksenko *290*
 Germany 291
  Natalia Potopayeva *291*
 Russia 294
  Aleksandr Dzuba *294*
 Malawi 296
  Yevgeniy Peresvetov *296*
 Points in Chapter 12 298
13. Church Ministries **299**
 Direct Service 300
  Praise and Worship *300*
  Banner Ministry *302*
  Prayer Ministry *305*
  Beginners Ministry *306*
 Indirect Service 307
  Publishing Houses *307*
  Joshua Bible Institute *309*
  Press Center *310*
 Points in Chapter 13 312
14. Missional (Churchshift) Ministries **313**
 Overview 314
  Parachurch Organizations *314*
  Churchshift Pastor *315*
  Equipping for Ministry *315*

 General Method of Soul Winning *317*
 Administration *317*
 General Statistics *317*
Arts, Entertainment, and Sports 319
 Arts and Entertainment Ministries *320*
 Design - Living Gospel Ministry *325*
 Sports Ministries *327*
Business and Finance 331
 Club 1000 .... *331*
 Fitness Health Ministries *335*
Church and Religion 339
 Education *341*
Distribution and Media 344
Education 346
 Evangelizing *346*
 Educating *349*
Family and Home 354
 Rehabilitation Centers *354*
 Stephania Soup Kitchen *358*
 Embassy of Life Orphanage *365*
 Handicapped Ministry *370*
 Youth Ministries *373*
 Children Ministries *377*
 Family Ministries *381*
 Healing *383*
 Trust Hotline Ministry *384*
Government and law 388
 Organized Righteousness *389*
 Orange Revolution *390*
Points in Chapter 14 392

15. Testimonies 393
 Transformation 394
  Off Prostitution *395*

Off Gang	*402*
Off Addiction	*405*
Off Jail	*412*
Healing	415
Blood Disease	*415*
Cancer and Tumors	*415*
HIV/AIDS	*416*
Points in Chapter 15	418
Conclusion	419
Bibliography	421
Internet by subject	432
Index	435

VOLUME 1

THEOLOGICAL BACKGROUND

MISSIONAL REFORMATION

INTRODUCTION

IN the editorial of the September 2008 issue of the *Australian Presbyterian*, Peter Hastie asks the following vital questions:

> How far can we absorb contemporary culture? Should Christians adopt some of the values of the present age, and if so, which ones? Alternatively, should believers become counter-cultural and divorce themselves entirely from everything that modern society approves?

Peter Hastie continues:

> The world has invaded the Church to an alarming degree. Indeed, the world's values have become so commonplace among believers that we are in danger of losing our identity as a "holy people". We have capitulated to the world in what we think about worship, leadership, life-style and sexuality, to mention just a few areas… Un-

MISSIONAL REFORMATION

> less Christians are vigilant, the world conquers the church by stealth. (Peter Hastie)

The Church has gone through generations, like in any other history, following certain identifiable patterns. The first generation of Christians, the Apostolic Fathers, provided initial reforms and doctrines to jumpstart the Faith. Then another generation rose, and another, and another. The last generation was the Pentecostal and Charismatic Movement. We are in a new generation, and many people have been talking about it. The signs are written all over and God is the one in control. The signs noted above by Peter Hastie are some of the indications of the new generation. The Church must get out of the closet and engage the society.

> And also all that generation were gathered unto their fathers: and there arose another generation after them. - Judges 2:10

This we have seen occurred repeatedly in the history of Israel; they forsook God period after period. The same phenomenon has occurred in the history of the Church from time to time when it goes through a period of spiritual lethargy. God has always revived the Church through Great Reforms or Great Revivals. Great Revival has been covered in a previous book: *"Great Revivals, Great Revivalist"* (Olowe 2007). Today, it appears that the Church is found in a situation where it is not having the necessary impact on the society and many are wondering why.

For almost 2000 years, the Church focused on the Gospel of Salvation which deals with how to relate to God. Almost the entire Chapter 2 of this book is about the development of the Gospel of Salvation. We have entered a new generation in Church history, a generation of discipling nations. The Gospel of Salvation alone has been difficult to master and we are still learning. But God is now telling us that He is satisfied with the level we have attained on this Gospel and it is time to move to the next level. He is now telling us that it is time to understand the Gospel of the Kingdom which is the ultimate goal. God has used several individuals independently to usher our attention to this Gospel. One of the powerful revelations from God was His response to a missionary, Landa Cope. She explains how God revealed to her the devastating fruit of preaching Salvation alone in Africa.

Many have written on the relationship between the Church and the society (for example Rod Parsley's *Culturally Incorrect*), many are wondering and asking questions why the Church is not imparting values to the society. There are many other people and organizations that God has used to bring a new revived energy into it. A 1998 book titled *"Missional Church: A Vision for the Sending of the Church in North America"* written by a group of Professors and missiologists was the first work to introduce the concept of a *Missional Church*. Since its publication, we have been inundated with missional books, missional websites, missional groups, and missional speakers. The Church is now in a state

MISSIONAL REFORMATION

of trying to fully understand what a Missional Church is supposed to be. In this book, the missional reformation is named "Churchshift" after a book published by Sunday Adelaja of the Embassy of God Church. As God used the nation of Israel to demonstrate his relationship with people, so also He has used the Embassy of God Church in the Ukraine, led by Sunday Adelaja, to demonstrate the Gospel of discipling nations. The Embassy of God Church is truly a model Missional Church.

This book, *Missional Reformation,* is written in two volumes for the edification of all, layman, clergy, and theologian. Volume 1 is written to provide the theological background of a Missional Church and Volume 2 focuses on our model church, the Embassy of God Church. Every one should read Volume 2 (Chapters 10 to 15), but before that, you may want to follow the following study guide:

If you are the curious type and want to quickly set your mind in focus, read Chapter 4 first. That is what jumpstarted this project resulting in three books written in parallel. It contains important revelations about the Kingdom of God that I received for all believers and non-believers. If you are a clergy seeking to flow into the new direction of the Church, you should read Chapters 3, 1, and 7 first. Theologians should read all the books. Get ready to disciple nations.

1. REFORMS

IT is pertinent to say upfront that what we are dealing with in this book is the much talked about relationship between the Church and the Society. The Church and the secular world have gone through reforms that shape both worlds. In this Chapter, we will define specific terms useful to understand all kinds of reforms that are shaping both worlds.

DEFINITIONS

The underlining guideline in this book is found in Romans 12:2 which states in part: "be not conformed to this world".

With this statement, Apostle Paul has defined two worlds, and this will be critical in our definitions.

CHURCH AND SOCIETY

Based on the text of Romans 12:2 stated above, the entire world will be divided into two, (1) the Church (or Spiritual world) and (2) the Society (or Secular world). The Society will refer to the entire human race excluding Christians (or simply the Church). The Society can further be divided into segments, called spheres, which represent different areas of influence, such as arts, education, science, government, business, and so on.

The following adjectives will be used to qualify human society: "social" or "societal".

CULTURE

Culture is a significant term in this study. Culture can simply be defined as *a way of life of a group* of people. Culture can be applied to both the society and the church. So we have *church culture* and *social culture*. Social culture can be inherited or developed over time. Culture shapes a person's worldview. The culture of a society (social culture) includes behaviors and symbols such as language, musical style, dressing, food, customs (or traditions), gestures, and so on. Culture is the dominant element of the Society that the

Church battles with because it virtually defines the human society. Culture can be applied to a specific segment of the Society, for example arts culture, science culture, and so on. Consequently, we have worldviews specific to segments (or spheres) of the Society like arts worldview, education worldview, and so on.

REFORM AND REFORMATION

A reform will be defined as *an act that is intended to influence a specific culture.* The act could be behavior, belief, value, or symbol. Synonyms of reform are: improvement, reorganization, restructuring, transformation, development, restoration. A reform can produce a negative influence, a positive influence, or no impact to the target culture.

Reformation

In order to distinguish positive reforms from negative reforms, the term "Reformation" will be used when a reform produces a positive influence.

Reformer

A Reformer will be defined as a leader or someone who executes a specific reform.

TYPES OF REFORMS

In the context of our definitions of Church and Society, there are four principal types of reforms based on the source. We will offer the following terms and definitions for the purpose of understanding the thesis in this book:

DIRECTION AND SOURCE

The four types of reforms from Church and society are:

- **1. Church (or Spiritual) Reform**; this is a reform implemented within the walls of the Church. Many Church reforms have themselves been reformed over the years.
- **2. Social (or Secular) Reform**; in the context of our definitions, this is any reform outside the walls of the Church. It could be governmental, legal, educational, sportive, and so on.
- **3. Spiritual Social (or Missional) Reform**; this is a reform emanating from the Church intended to influence the Society.
- **4. Socio-spiritual (or Syncretic) Reform**; this is a reform emanating from the society to influence the Church.

Cases 1 and 2 will be termed as *"pure reforms"* and 3 and 4 will be termed as *"mixed reforms"*. As will be shown in Chapter 7, a socio-spiritual (Syncretic) reform does not support the principle of the Kingdom of God. The four types of reforms are summarized in Table 1.1.

Table 1.1: Types of Church-Society Reforms

Reform	Source	Target	Name
Church	Church	Church	Spiritual
Society	Society	Society	Social
Socio Spiritual	Society	Church	Syncretism
Spiritual Social	Church	Society	Missional

IMPACT

Based on impact on the society or church, there are three types of reforms:
1. Positive Reforms (Reformations)
2. Negative Reforms
3. Transparent Reforms (no impact)

Examples of spiritual reforms that produce negative impacts are heresies and false prophecy. We will study examples of pure reforms in this Chapter (for social) and in Chapter 2 (for spiritual), and study mixed reforms in Chapter 7.

SOCIAL REFORMS

Social reforms could be positive (social reformations) or negative or transparent. Examples of negative social reforms are racism and fascism. Most social reformers are philoso-

MISSIONAL REFORMATION

phers or civil rights leaders; many civil rights leaders, such as Desmond Tutu, have religious background.

Born on October 2, 1869 and died on January 30, 1948, Mahatma Gandhi could be regarded as the most popular social reformer. Known as Father of the Nation, he played a key role in winning freedom for India; he introduced the concept of non-violence and holding fast to truth or firmness in a righteous cause, in achieving goals. Even Martin Luther King Jr. traveled to India to learn his footsteps. Some known social reformers are given in Table 1.2.

Table 1.2: Some known Social Reformers

Granville Sharp, England, 1735-1813 Scholar and abolitionist who won a case establishing the principle that any slave would become free upon reaching British territory in 1772; Sharp continued his abolitionist activities, notably the promotion of a colony of former slaves in Sierra Leone, which was unsuccessful. He founded a Bible society and wrote many pamphlets on political questions.
Harriet Beecher Stowe, USA, 1811–1896 Abolitionist who exposed the cruelty of slavery through her 1852 novel, *Uncle Tom's Cabin*. The message reached millions as a novel and play, and became popular in the U.S. and Britain. It energized anti-slavery forces in North America, embittered the South, and influenced the war.
Susan Brownell, USA, 1820-1906 Leader of the woman-suffrage movement. Together with Elizabeth Cady Stanton, she worked for women's suffrage for over 50 years. She was the first woman arrested, put on trial, and fined for voting on November 5, 1872. She wrote an Amendment in 1878 which later became the 19th Amendment giving women the right to vote. She founded the International Council of Women (1888) and the International Woman Suffrage Council (1904).

Klas Pontus Arnoldson, Sweden, 1844-1916
Journalist, pacifist, peace advocate, and proponent of Scandinavian unity; in the union crisis in 1905, he opposed war with Norway. He won the 1908 Nobel Peace Prize.

Mahatma Gandhi, India, 1869-1948
Developed the concepts of Ahimsa (non-violence) and Satyagraha (holding fast to truth); dedicated himself completely to the service of humanity. He fought for social and moral regeneration and for India's freedom.

Rosa Parks, USA, 1913-2005
Stood against bus segregation in Montgomery in 1955; she refused to give up her seat on a city bus. She became known as "the mother of the civil rights movement."

Andrei Dmitriyevich Sakharov, Soviet Union, 1921-1989
One of the Soviet leading nuclear physicist and human-rights advocate; he received the 1975 Nobel Peace Prize. He helped to develop the USSR's hydrogen bomb between 1948 and 1956. An outspoken critic of Soviet repression, he was exiled to Gorky in 1980; the banishment inspired worldwide protest before he was pardoned by Gorbachev in 1986.

Nelson Rolihlahla Mandela, South Africa, 1918
An anti-apartheid activist, his opposition to apartheid made him a symbol of freedom and equality worldwide. He spent 27 years as a political prisoner before becoming the first black president in South Africa in 1994. Mandela has received more than one hundred awards over four decades, most notably the Nobel Peace Prize in 1993.

Martin Luther King Jr., USA, 1929-1968
His philosophy and commitment to the method of nonviolent resistance earned him worldwide recognition; his years of leading blacks in nonviolent protest and direct action helped to desegregate the South. He was assassinated in 1968.

Benazir Bhutto, Pakistan, 1953–2007
After being an advisor of her father, she became the first woman, at 35, to be elected to lead an Islamic nation having been Prime Minister twice. She was assassinated on December 27, 2007. In 2008, she was named one of seven winners of the United Nations Human Rights Prize.

MISSIONAL REFORMATION

Social reforms are not limited to political or human rights activities. Nations have produced millions of reforms in all sectors (spheres) of the society such as family (charity, rehabilitation), education, arts, sports, business, government, science, technology, entertainment, and so on. These spheres will be more elaborated in Chapters 3 and 6.

CHURCH REFORMS

In strict theological sense and in the worldview of the Reformed Church, "Church Reformation" is defined as the movement in history, beginning in 1517, which broke up the institutional unity of the Roman Catholic Church and established the third great branch of Christianity (after Catholicism and Orthodoxy), called Protestantism (Ritchie).

But in the real biblical sense, Church reformation dates back to the first century when the Church was trying to find her footing. And in recent times, there has also been the rise of Pentecostal and Charismatic Movements and Postmodern Movements which have not been considered when the definition was provided. So, we will open up the definition to include all reforms that have positive impact on the Church.

Church reformation can be seen as Church restoration. Early Church reformations have been applied strictly within the Church walls and these have led to the development of various denominations because of differences in doctrines.

These reformations will be discussed in Chapter 2. As the Church continues to grow, God is teaching us new and common reformations that reunite the Church. Postmodern reformations are uniting Catholics with Protestants as seen at www.emergentvillage.com, the emergent village website.

POINTS IN CHAPTER 1

Reforms are acts that influence cultures. A reform that produces a positive influence to a culture is termed reformation.

Between the Church and the Society, there are four kinds of reforms: Church (Spiritual), Social (Secular), Socio-spiritual (Syncretic), and Spiritual Social (Missional).

Spiritual and Secular are pure reforms while Syncretic and Missional are mixed reforms.

Reforms exist in all sectors of society, such as family, education, science, arts, and so on.

2. HISTORY OF CHURCH REFORMS

THERE are certain aspects of the Church history which are needed to be grasped in order to follow some arguments in future Chapters. It is difficult to squeeze the entire church history in one Chapter whereas others write it in volumes of books. That is why it is better to focus on a specific angle of history. We are focusing on reforms that have shaped the Church till present day. There are several history books out there for further reading; some of them are listed in the bibliography section. A good source is Philip Schaff's book, *History of the Christian Church*, written in 8 volumes.

MISSIONAL REFORMATION

History is no doubt a very important tool. Many parts of the Holy Bible itself are historical. History helps us to look back and identify some errors that were made and some corrections that were made in error. Church history will equip us with theological tools that will enable us to evaluate and understand the issues of our day; it will enable us to be knowledgeable of where some church traditions came from. Besides all these, Church history can uplift us spiritually. The history of the Church can be divided into four eras, namely: Ancient (30–590), Medieval (590-1648), Modern (1648-1970), and Postmodern (1970-Now). Historians in the Reformed Faith usually say that the Modern era starts in 1517 when the reformation started. But for the purpose of this book, the year 1648, when the reformation ended, is more appropriate as the start of the Modern era. The end of the Modern era (1967 to 1980) is blurring; it is pegged at the period of Catholic Charismatic Renewal movement.

ANCIENT (30–590)

THE APOSTLES

The first great church reformers were the Foundational Apostles. The Apostles including Paul, the masterbuilder (1 Cor. 3:10) wrote most of the epistles that laid the foundation of church organization. They created the first two principal church offices: bishops and deacons (Phil. 1:1; I Tim. 3:1-13). Bishops are the same as elders or overseers (1 Tim. 3:1-7, Tit. 1:5-9; Acts 20:17, 28; 1 Pet. 5:1); the terms are used interchangeably. There were many bishops in a church, Phil. 1:1; Acts 20:17, but soon (in 110-150) a bishop became the chief elder, and not long after (around 180) only one bishop became in charge of all the churches in a city or region.

APOSTOLIC AND CHURCH FATHERS

The term "Apostolic Fathers" is used to apply to those who are known, or are considered, to have had personal relations with some of the Apostles and who contributed to the reformation of the early church up to the 2nd century. Actually, only the Apostle John lived long enough to be acquainted with some of the 2nd century Fathers. Among them were Clement of Rome (96-97), Ignatius (arrested at Antioch and martyred around 110-115 in Rome), and Polycarp, bishop of Smyrna, martyred in 155 after refusing the urge of the Proconsul for him to curse Christ in exchange for freedom.

After the demise of the Apostolic Fathers, the term "Church Fathers" became the term used for those who contributed to the development of the church, especially before persecution ended in 313 AD. The teachings of the Apostolic and Church Fathers were valuable to provide initial doctrines, especially in Church administration. Well known Church Fathers were Tertullian (155-220), considered the founder of western theology, Clement of Alexandria, the first major scholar in Alexandria to mix Christianity with Greek philosophy, Origen (185- 254), the first to write biblical commentaries, Cyprian (200-258), Bishop of Carthage, who set the tone for the Catholic view, and Anthony (251-356), the first major Christian monk, father of Christian monasticism, who went to the deserts in Egypt around 271. Many of these Church Fathers were bishops in North Africa (Egypt, Algeria, and Tunisia). Their writings are made available by New Advent (Catholic Encyclopedia) on the Internet (newadvent.org).

PERSECUTIONS

Between 30 and 260 AD, persecution of Christians was very rampant. Persecutions started with the Sanhedrin after a lame man was healed and Peter preached at the temple (Acts 3 and 4). The Romans followed in the persecution of Christians. They perceived the Christians as a threat and levied several frivolous and false accusations against them, such as cannibalism (because the Romans would not understand "partaking in the body of Christ" in Communion), disruption of business (Acts 19:21-40), incest (because they "loved" each other), atheism (for refusing to honor Roman gods), and so on (Gospelcom.net). Most notable among the frivolous charges was that Christians caused disasters.

Satirizing the prevailing view, the church father Tertullian put it this way: "If the Tiber reaches the walls, if the Nile does not rise to the fields, if the sky doesn't move or the earth does, if there is famine, if there is plague, the cry is at once: 'The Christians to the lion'." (Gospelcom.net)

CORRUPTION

In 250, Emperor Decius issued an edict to suppress Christianity; he commanded all bishops and church officers to sacrifice to the gods before a magistrate and to obtain certificates certifying that they had done so. Many professing Christians rushed to obtain their certificates, some by sacrificing and others by bribing officials or obtaining forged certificates. That was when corruption in large scale crept into the Church. Some, like Cyprian, Bishop of Carthage, went into hiding, some others like Paul of Thebes fled to live in caves in the desert as hermits. That command also saw many bishops, like Fabian (Rome), Babylas (Antioch), and Alexander (Alexandria), martyred. Decius died in 251 after 2 years of reign and the persecution ended then.

HERESIES

As the church grew, several kinds of error, known as false teachings or heresies, started to creep in as early as in the first century. The apostles wrote much of the epistles to combat one error after another. False teachings were popular among gentiles, especially outside Israel.

MISSIONAL REFORMATION

> For there must be also heresies among you, that they which are approved may be made manifest among you. 1 Cor. 11:19

> But there were false prophets also among the people, even as there shall be false teachers among you, who privily shall bring in damnable heresies, even denying the Lord that bought them, and bring upon themselves swift destruction. 2 Pet 2:1

Gnosticism was one of the first early heresies. The letter to the Colossians reflects the tension within the early church with the emergence of Gnosticism.

> And this I say, lest any man should beguile you with enticing words. Col. 2:4

After the deaths of the apostles and their immediate successors, falsehood found it easier to take root. There were no eyewitnesses left to repudiate false claims. At a certain point, heresy became a tool used by the Church to persecute themselves, even leading to martyrdom. Whoever brought a doctrine that was against the popular view of the Church would be labeled as heretic. During their time, the emperors (read below) flip-flopped; some doctrines that were already condemned as heretic, would later be cleared, and then re-condemned, and on and on. The Eastern Church itself became the center of heresies. Heresies were one of the causes of progressive rift between the Eastern and Western Churches. The churches of Rome and Constantinople were often separated for long periods of time between the fourth and the ninth centuries mainly due to heresies, held in the capital of the Eastern empire (Arianism, 335-381; Monotheletism, 533-680; Iconoclasm, 723-787; 815-842) and strictly rejected by Rome. In our context, heresies would be regarded as NEGATIVE Church reforms.

There were several early heresies during the growth of Christianity, many apocryphal "Gospels" were written to propagate hidden agenda, and claimed to be "secret", but on many occasions, the real false doctrines were recognized and the Church stood firmly against them all, gradually improving its hold on the truth. This was an era of fundamental doctrines and theology.

Gnosticism

The Gnostics were several groups with similar philosophies.

> The Gnostic doctrine must have been one of the strangest ever believed by rational people. (Mark Ritchie)

Dualism was the most basic principle of Gnosticism. The Gnostics identified matter as evil and spirit as good. Because matter was evil, the God who created the earth must also be evil. Jesus was seen as the spiritual being who had brought Salvation; therefore, He must not be the son of the God of the Old Testament. Orthodox writers battled many, especially the Gnostics, who claimed to have "secret" traditions, passed down by their leaders straight from the Apostles that were not written down in the Scripture.

END OF PERSECUTION

Christians suffered the worst persecution between 303 and 313, with churches and scriptures destroyed. The persecution in the West ended after Diocletian voluntarily resigned in 305 due to sickness, but the Eastern emperor, Galerius, continued, trying to wipe out Christianity; he died in 311. In 313, Constantine from Gaul defeated Maxentius at Rome and became the new western emperor; it was claimed that he saw the cross of Christ in the sky which he claimed helped him in his victorious fight against Maxentius and as a result, he converted to Christianity. He persuaded the eastern emperor then, Licinius, and they issued the Edict of Milan which finally legalized Christianity. In 320, Licinius reneged on the Edict of Milan which granted religious freedom and began another persecution of Christians. It became a challenge to Constantine who fought and defeated Licinius. Constantine then became the sole emperor of the Roman Empire, and Christian persecution in the East and West ended for good. David Barrett reports that more than 410,000 believers from the time of Christ till 2009 had given their lives as martyrs for the Christian Faith. According to Beverly Pegues (2007), more Christians were martyred in the 20th century than in previous centuries combined.

EMPERORS AND THE CHURCH

When persecution ended, the emperors started to reform the Church and this created elitism. Mark Ritchie writes:

> Excessive favor began to be shown to "Christian" emperors. This started almost immediately, with Eusebius' favorable biography of Constantine. Constantine is still regarded as something of a "thirteenth apostle" in the Eastern Orthodox churches. Politicians began to interfere into Church affairs, with Constantine setting the example.

Emperor Constantine summoned the first Ecumenical Council at Nicea in 325 to resolve a number of issues, including a controversial Arian heresy in the East. In 330, Constantine created a new capital at Byzantium, renamed Nova Roma ("New Rome"); the city later became known as Constantinople. The Arian heresy was problematic; it held the East and West bound for 46 years (335-381). The second Ecumenical Council in 381 was held at Constantinople and the fourth at Chalcedon in 451. It was at this Council of Chalcedon, with 150 bishops in attendance, that the two natures (divine and human) in Christ were defined against Eutyches thesis; Eutyches was excommunicated. Proceedings and Canons released at the Ecumenical Councils are made available on the internet (newadvent.org) by New Advent (Catholic Encyclopedia). It is worth noting that the Council of Chalcedon created a major setback to the Church; the Church of Alexandria in Egypt became divided into two branches. Those who accepted the terms of the Council became known as Chalcedonians or Melkites; those others in majority were labeled non-Chalcedonians or Monophysites (because they proclaim the one nature of Christ after His incarnation). Some historians claim that this disunity weakened the Church and contributed to the downfall of Christianity when the Muslim invasions began in the medieval age (Ritchie).

From one emperor to another, the church gradually grew from legality to establishment as the state religion. The emperors interfered more and more in the church, deposing and exiling whichever bishops did not tow their line. Emperors always wanted to control all of their territories using a universal religion as a tool; they believed a united Church would be useful for this purpose. They tried so hard to silence all heresies, but it was difficult. They eventually became sympathetic to some of them, for example, Constantine himself ended up being Arian. The Orthodox Church was in favor of the government controlled church, a view still held till the present day (see Chapter 7). Certainly, Constantine deserves credit for turning the Empire from persecuting Christians to defending the Christian Faith. He abolished crucifixion and gladiatorial activities and encouraged liberation of slaves (Schaff). However, those abuses which were so prominent during the time of the Protestant Reformation got their start in the 300's.

DOCTRINE OF GRACE AND FREE WILL

The debates on free will, grace, faith, and good works, which are still prominent today, developed gradually from the fifth century. They started with Augustine bringing up controversy on Pelagius teaching of Free Will. In 405, Pelagius had some concerns about a statement in Augustine's writings in "Confessions", which says *"Give what you command, and command what you choose."* Pelagius argued that man has free will and is able to choose good from evil. He also claimed that each person is born new without inheriting Adam's sin. Augustine responded with five major points: original sin, total depravity, unconditional election, irresistible grace, and perseverance of the saints. John Cassian developed a middle ground which later came to be called Semi-Pelagianism. The development of the doctrine of grace is fully discussed in *"Grace Theology* (Olowe 2009)".

Future doctrines such as Calvinism or Arminianism were a follow up of Pelagian controversies. Calvinism was more or less Augustianism while Arminianism was a revival of Semi-Pelagianism.

MEDIEVAL (590-1648)

Islamic crusades, slavery, Christian Arts, schisms, reformations, ideologies, and wars dominated the medieval age. It is safe to mention that most of the doctrines in present day Christianity were developed in the medieval age.

ISLAMIC CRUSADES AND SLAVERY

After the end of persecution in 313 AD, the first blow to Christianity was Islamic jihad. In 610, Mohammed, leader of the movement, supposedly heard the call of "Allah" and began a jihad. By 750, Islamic armies had conquered North Africa, Arabia, part of Europe, Palestine and Mesopotamia, and were spreading eastward. Europeans then viewed Muslim as the Antichrist, the heretic, and a military threat. It was during this medieval age that the capital of the Eastern Empire, Constantinople, was captured by Turks (led by Fatih Sultan Mehmet II) on May 29, 1453; the city was renamed Istanbul.

When Islam presented a serious military threat to Italy and Central Europe, Pope Nicholas V tried unsuccessfully to unite Christendom against Muslims. On the other hand, in order to compete against the Muslims and to legitimize its slave trade activities, Portugal ran to the Catholic Church and the Pope fell for it because the Church needed to control increasing Muslim invasions into Europe. In 1452, Pope Nicholas V issued the papal bull *Dum Diversas*, granting Afonso V of Portugal the right to subdue and even to enslave Muslims, pagans and other unbelievers. This approval of slavery was reaffirmed in his *Romanus Pontifex* bull of 1455. These papal bulls legitimized slavery and slave trade and eventually paved way to European colonialism. This was the first ever NEGATIVE *Missional Reform*. Many saw it as against biblical principles and humanity. Catholic writers have claimed that several Popes, between 1591 and 1839, condemned the act. There were debates on whether they condemned only slave trade and not slavery itself. Slavery and slave trade are subjects of debate up till today. Some pro-slavery clergies cite biblical "tolerance" of servitude as a justification.

On May 21, 2001, France legally recognized slavery as a crime against humanity. On February 25, 2007, the state of Virginia, USA, apologized for its role in the institution of slavery, and on August 24, 2007, Mayor Ken Livingstone of London, UK apologized publicly for Britain's role in colonial slave trade. The Catholic Church, however, has been widely criticized for being silent. In a Catholic press release on November 23, 2008 at a public debate in Liverpool, Archbishop of Accra, Ghana, Palmer Buckle, on the importance of public apologies for slavery, said: *"My great grandfather was kept as a slave, and saw freedom. In that context he got education. It's come out positive. My duty is to help others to begin to look more positively."* He did not apologize.

SCHOLASTICISM

The period of early scholasticism coincided with the growth of early Islamic and Jewish philosophies. From the 8th Century, the Muslims used rational theology, a form of scholasticism. In the 11th century, this new style of study, called Scholasticism, began to replace the old way of simply quoting the early church fathers. Argumentation became more rigorous. Aristotle was a well known figure in this new way of learning. Scholasticism reached its highest development when theologian Thomas Aquinas released his book written 1265-1274, *Summa Theologica*, which was a synthesis of Greek philosophy and Christian doctrine. The full text of the book is made available by New Advent (Catholic Encyclopedia) on the Internet (newadvent.org).

SCHISM

For the first thousand years of her history, the Church remained as one with five historic Patriarchal centers: four in the East, Jerusalem, Antioch, Alexandria, and Constantinople; and one in the West, Rome. The relationship between East and West wore down gradually. Intermittent schisms occurred under many Popes (Cleenewerck). Disputes on theology, jurisdictional rights, and heresies in the East that were rejected by Rome, led to long period of separation between the Eastern Orthodox and Western Roman Catholic Christianity for 37 years from 482 to 519 (Acacian Schism), and for 13 years from 866-879 (Photian schism). In spite of these sporadic schisms, the Church was still unified until 1054 when the Great Schism occurred. The primary issue then was disputes over conflicting claims of jurisdiction, in particular,

Rome's claim to a universal papal supremacy. The addition of the *Filioque* clause by Rome in 1014 to the Nicene Creed was a secondary issue. The Orthodox and Roman Catholics went their separate ways. In 1204, Rome's sack of Constantinople sealed the separation. In 1453, Turks overrun Constantinople and ended the Byzantine Empire.

On October 31, 1517, Martin Luther nailed his 95 Theses to the door of the Roman Church in Wittenberg, the debut of another schism, the Protestant Reformation. From 1529 to 1536, the Church of England under Henry VIII also pulled away from Rome.

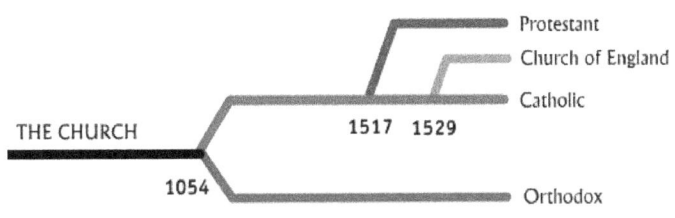

Figure 2.1: Major schism in medieval age

THE PROTESTANT REFORMATION

The crisis of theology began in the fourteenth century with the breakdown of the philosophical foundations of scholasticism. Newly derived theology of "nominalism", legitimizing the church as an intermediary between man and God, did not go well with many. New thinking favored the moving away from philosophical arguments laid out by Thomas Aquinas. There were heated debates, unrest (1378–1416), uprising, and wars. The first of a series of new perceptions came from John Wycliffe at Oxford University, and then from Jan Hus at the University of Prague. The Catholic Church eventually silenced Wycliffe and Hus and their supporters through the Council of Constance (1414–1417); Jan Hus was executed by burning and Wycliffe was condemned as a heretic.

The protests against Rome and the Pope were reopened about the same time in Germany and in Switzerland. In 1517 Martin Luther, an Augustinian monk and professor at the University of Wittenberg, called for a reopening of the debate. Parallel to events in Germany, Ulrich Zwingli was leading a movement in Switzerland. The two movements agreed on most issues except that the Zwingli movement, some of which are modern day Anabaptists, wanted a more radical approach. They spread both ideas rapidly from place to place through the printing press, including Luther's 95 Theses.

These movements criticized the Church on the practice of selling indulgences and on purgatory. Other practices under attack included particular judgment, devotion to Mary (Mariology), the intercession of and devotion to the saints, most of the sacraments, the mandatory celibacy requirement of its clergy (including monasticism), seeking spiritual benefit from so-called relics of dead saints, treating the dead saints with divine honor, and the authority of the Pope. Of major controversy was the practice of buying and selling church positions and corruption within the Church's hierarchy, even reaching the position of the Pope. Also, Luther attacked Augustine's doctrine of Grace. The Pope condemned the Reformation and Martin Luther was excommunicated from the Catholic Church.

Reason for Reformation

Before the reformation, there was a great decline in the Church for several reasons, some of which are (Baker 1994, Ritchie) elitism (many elites came to the church because of prestige and influence of the local bishop), assimilation of false doctrines, and making alliances with worldly rulers due to rivalry and battle for territorial gains. These behavioral traits were still manifested by the Catholic and Anglican Missionaries in the 19th century in Africa (Olowe 2007).

Theologically, one major contention is the issue of "Justification" for which the Catholic proclaims is by faith and good works. This issue is of major significance in this book and in another: "*Grace Theology*" (Olowe 2009). Also before the reformation, it was believed that a monastic life and vows of celibacy were the only ways to escape sin and to attain sanctification; this led several people into the monasteries and convents thinking that that would please God and ensure their eternal Salvation. The reformers also refused to accept that the clergy are to hold the keys of Heaven and to be practically the mediators between God and man.

> He who desired to obtain forgiveness had to seek it through a jungle of priests, saints, Mary worship, masses, penances, confession, absolution and the like, so that there might as well have been no throne of Grace at all. (J.C. Ryle, quoted by Hammond)

Development of Doctrine of Salvation

After the excommunication of Luther, the movements started to split along certain doctrinal inclinations. The Church now entered the second stage of Reformation producing tenets and doctrines. Luther, Calvin, and Zwingli were prominent leaders of the movements of that era. Certain doctrinal disagreements between Luther and Zwingli, and later between Luther and John Calvin, led to the emergence of rival Protestant churches. Radical Reformers from Zwingli movement often referred to the Lutherans as the "new papists". The reformation soon developed into a series of wars between the Catholics and the Protestants. The Protestant Reformation is considered to have ended with the Peace of Westphalia in 1648. The major denominations to emerge directly from the Reformation were the Lutherans and the Presbyterians. Subsequent denominations usually trace their roots to the initial movements. English Reformation gave rise to Anglicanism.

Calvinism

John Calvin, a French reformer, became the most influential among reformed theologians. Both Luther and Calvin thought along lines linked with the theological teachings of Augustine of Hippo. Calvinism stresses the sovereignty or rule of God in all things in Salvation but also in all of life. The five points of Calvinism (TULIP), also called the doctrines of grace, serves as a summary of the differences between Calvinism and Arminianism; they were a point-by-point response to the five points of the Arminian Remonstrance's defense in 1619, written by Calvinists. TULIP was based on the writings and teaching of Calvin. TULIP stands for Total depravity, Unconditional election, Limited atonement, Irresistible grace, and Perseverance of the saints. The Calvinists doctrines of predestination and of election are highly debated up till now. It is discussed in more detail in *"Grace Theology"* (Olowe 2009).

Arminianism

Arminianism and Calvinism share some doctrines in common; however, they are viewed as rivals because of their differences over the doctrines of predestination and free will, a spill over of the debate between Augustine and Pelagians. Jacobus Arminius (1560-1609), a Dutch theologian, was a student of Theodore Beza, Calvin's successor. Arminius rejected several tenets of the Calvinists doctrine of Salvation but he died before he could defend his views before a national synod. The Remonstrants (who revised Arminius' doctrine) replied in his stead with the five articles of Remonstrance. The Remonstrants' doctrine was rejected at the Synod of Dort (composed of mainly Calvinists) held in Dordrecht, Holland, in 1618. However, many evangelical Christians adopted the Remonstrants' doctrine. The historic debate

MISSIONAL REFORMATION

between Calvinists and Arminians led to the emergence of new movements and heated discussions and divergence in these new movements. For example, fellow Methodists, John Wesley and George Whitfield, differed between Arminianism and Calvinism. Wesley was a defender of Arminian teachings. He brought Arminius' system to live again during his revivals and today, it is prominent in the Methodist movement.

CHURCH OF ENGLAND REFORMATION

The separation of the Church of England from Rome was incomplete and more conservative than that of the Protestants. Reformers in the Church of England built a compromise between Catholic tradition and Protestantism. The Puritan movement, a protest group within the Church of England; sprang up during the reign of Elizabeth I. By the end of Elizabeth's reign, the Puritans constituted a major group within the Church of England. Some remained in and some (the Separatists) left the Church of England. Later (in the 16th and 17th centuries), Puritanism extended to other denominations and countries. The Puritans were ejected from the Church of England in the Great Ejection of 1662. They established their own denominations in 1662-1690s; some were Presbyterians, but most were Congregationalists.

MODERN (1648-1970)

After the period of developments of doctrines, the Church then started to witness a period of movements, more movements, awakenings, discovery (missions), and revivals. All these led to the multiplicity of denominations created by doctrinal differences. Today, it is estimated that there are up to 40,000 church denominations (Barrett 2009) in 238 countries; however, each country is treated separately; for example, there would be 238 catholic denominations, one from each country.

REVIVAL MOVEMENTS

The Church witnessed a series of revival movements, starting in early 18th century till mid 20th century.

Methodism

John Wesley had an experience on May 24, 1738, at a Moravian meeting on Aldersgate Street, London, in which he felt his heart "strangely warmed"; that became his source of renewed energy. John Wesley and George Whitefield were friends at Oxford. When Whitefield returned to UK from USA in 1739, he started to preach at Kingswood village, near Bristol, to miners in the open air. At Whitefield's invitation, Wesley preached his first sermon in the open air in April of that year. There, the Wesley Methodist Movement began. Wesley continued as itinerant Evangelist for fifty years teaching in the open air and in churches; he adopted what was to become known as Arminian Evangelical Methodism. Methodism was effectively divided into Arminian and Calvinistic groupings when George Whitefield departed later in 1739 to Savannah to found the Bethleham Orphange. Methodism in both forms was a very successful evangelical movement in the United Kingdom. Methodists, under Wesley's direction, became leaders in many social justice issues of the day including prison reform and abolitionism movements. Wesley's greatest theological achievement was his promotion of what he termed "Christian Perfection," or holiness of heart and life.

Great Awakening and Evangelicalism

The first Great Awakening started as early as 1733 and lasted till 1750s; it occurred in parallel with the rise of the Methodist movement. It was therefore an Anglo-American revival movement. Jonathan Edwards and George Whitefield were prominent leaders of the first Great Awakening. The revival spread from Britain to Connecticut River Valley, Northampton, USA and back to Britain. The Great Awakening gave birth to the Evangelical Movement.

In the second great awakening (1790s -1850s), preachers like Charles Finney, Lyman Beecher, Barton Stone, Peter Cartwright, and James Finley were involved. The revival swept through USA, Canada, England (1849), and Scotland

(1858-59). The emphasis of the awakening was renewed personal Salvation and unrestricted submission to the will of God. There were massive gains in Baptist and Methodist attendances. The awakening also led to a rise of new denominations and a rise of abolitionism.

MISSIONS

Missions existed right from the first century (Paul's Missionary journeys for example); also the Catholic Mission and the Orthodox Mission existed. However, like Pentecostalism which was visible in the early churches but later disappeared, missionary activities became unnoticeable for centuries; there were no organized missionary societies and there was no real missionary interest. William Carey (1761 – 1834) is regarded as the Father of modern missions; he prepared a missionary plan and co-founded the Baptist Missionary Society in 1792, the first of its kind; in 1793, he was already on a mission to India until his death. Other missionary societies, such as Church Missionary Society in 1799, sprang up, with missions to South Africa and West India. Missions to West Africa became a global activity in the 19th century when slave trade was becoming unpopular. Slave trade became noticeable during the Age of Exploration in the 15th century.

Exploration

Portugal started exploration of the world in the 15th century. Its first great wave of expeditions was launched by Prince

MISSIONAL REFORMATION

Henry the Navigator. Led by the 21-year-old Prince in 1415, the Portuguese task force sailed from Lisbon to attack the Muslims on the African coast in a convoy of about 200 ships. Reaching there, the Portuguese found the slave trade, practiced by the Islamic North Africans, lucrative, and the idea of joining in the trade developed. They ran to the Pope as discussed above for legitimacy. Soon, Spain, Portugal, and the Islamic North Africa became rivals in slave trade. Because of their difficulties with North African Muslims in traversing the Western Sahara to explore West African coasts, the Portuguese decided to bypass them by sailing through the Atlantic Ocean, carrying their Bibles with them. They carried the Bible as a tool for creating Christian allies against the Muslims in the Maghreb (North West Africa). The first group of islands the Portuguese ship sighted was the Azores in 1427. Prince Henry started to send settlers there from 1432. The Portuguese were the first Europeans to trade in West Africa and this lasted for centuries before other Europeans eventually came. For example, they started trade with Benin in Nigeria in 1486 and built the first church in 1515; the first British Missionary came in 1842, that is, 356 years after the Portuguese. The Portuguese had the opportunity to evangelize all of Africa, but their Mission collapsed because it was based on a faulty principle, and that was hiding behind the Bible to trade in slaves. Portugal was the first to build a huge empire through exploration. Portugal established trade with Japan, India, China, and Africa. The European discovery of the Americas by Christopher Columbus did not occur until 1492.

Colonization and Missions

Britain started to pass a series of legislations against slave trade and soon they took to the sea, hunting to intercept the Portuguese slave vessels. Whenever there was an interception, the human cargo would be emptied at Freetown in Sierra Leone. There, the British founded the Fourah Bay Institute to educate the freed slaves in Christianity. Samuel Ajayi Crowther, who became the first African Anglican Bishop, was a product of the institute. Orthodox Churches already existed right from the first century in North Africa, including Carthage (Tunisia), Alexandria (Egypt), and Hippo (Algeria), and in East Africa in Ethiopia and Eritrea. Using Freetown as a hub, the British started to spread Christianity to West, Central, and South African nations, chasing out the Portuguese as well as establishing trade with England. In order to consolidate their hold on these countries, the British started to annex them to Britain. Other European countries, especially France, rushed with their Bibles to divide the remaining parts of Africa among themselves. The Portuguese Mission in Africa (and even in Asia) finally died.

Various Missions came to Africa in the 19th and 20th centuries and maintained close relationship with the colonial governments who took over the rulership from the Africans. The colonial governments and missionaries worked hand in

MISSIONAL REFORMATION

hand. It should be admitted that missionaries brought to Africa benefits that come with Christian civilization such as hospitality, healthcare, love, and education. However, they battled for territorial gains and compromised the Christian Faith with local rulers. They did not preach Christ with enough vigor and spirituality to combat the evils in the land as done by the native prophetic movements that arose.

PENTECOSTAL MOVEMENT

The first decade of the 20th century was greeted by the Pentecostal Movement. Pentecost commemorates the day the Holy Spirit descended in fulfillment of the promise of Jesus (Acts 2: 1-4). While there is evidence of early Christians being filled with the Holy Spirit and speaking in tongues, this seems to have come to an end in the third century while the Church was preoccupied with heresies and debates on doctrines dominated by a mixture of philosophy and faith. Many Christians began to wonder why the Acts 2 Holy Spirit baptism couldn't happen again. This wondering did not originate in the 20th century, it started before then.

> The impulse to the prayer movement in the 1820s was given (among others) by the Anglican priest James Haldane Stewart. He made an appeal to this by means of more than half a million pamphlets which were spread throughout Great Britain, the U.S.A. and on the Continent. They longed for renewed spiritual power, as had been visible in the first century after the outpouring of the Holy Spirit in the young church. This movement was

by no means restricted to the British Isles, similar investigations and prayers being offered in France, Germany and elsewhere. – Wikipedia

In fact, Pentecostalism was observed before the 20th century:

> In 1830 prophetic utterances were recorded in Port Glasgow, Scotland among Dissenters and Karlshuld, Bavaria among Roman Catholics. These took the form of prophecy, speaking in tongues and miraculous healing. They were regarded as the answer to the prayers that many had been making. - Wikipedia

Edward Irving (1792–1834), Scottish Presbyterian clergyman, continued in the new Pentecostal trend of that era. Today, *Irvingism*, the main doctrine behind the foundation of the Catholic Apostolic Church, is associated with Edward Irving. Although some consider Irving as the John the Baptist (forerunner) of Modern Pentecostalism (McGee), actually, James Stewart seems to be (from the quotations above).

However, Pentecostalism began in full force in the first decade of the 20th century with William Seymour's Azusa Street Mission; it started with Charles Parham's renewed preaching of Pentecostalism, after another period of silence. Towards the last decade of the 20th century, Pentecostalism had become the world's fastest growing Christian Movement. Although it is embedded in postmodern movements, Pentecostalism ended the Modern era of Church history. Today, there are variants of Pentecostalism.

MISSIONAL REFORMATION

Classical Pentecostal Movement

Charles Parham (1873–1929) founded Bethel Bible School in Topeka, Kansas, on January 1, 1901 with a small group of students consciously seeking to recover the gift of speaking in tongues; on that day, Agnes Oznam became the first of Parham's students to speak in an unknown tongue. In 1905 Parham preached at a revival in Houston, Texas. William Seymour, a black holiness evangelist attended, but because of segregation could only sit in the hallway. After a few obstacles, Seymour carried the message to Azusa Street in Los Angeles. At the Azusa Street Mission, a run down section of the city, a revival commenced that would last several years and spread around the world. Hundreds received the gifts of the Holy Spirit. The press learned of this revival and told the story to the world. Since then, Seymour is for ever remembered for this great Azusa Street Mission.

Pentecostalism appeared simultaneously in other parts of the world, such as in Wales (1904–1905), India (1905-1907), and in Korea (1907–08). Before the Azusa Street revival, Evan Roberts conducted a series of "Higher Life" revival meetings in Keswick, Wales. There were evidences of speaking in tongues, revelatory visions, and prophecy.

Prophetic Movements

These movements are the origin of most African Indigenous Pentecostalism, which had its beginnings independent of the Azusa Street movement. There was an outpour of the Holy

Spirit in the first half of the 20th century, also in West and Central Africa, and many Prophetic Movements arose due to the Lord's calling of individual native prophets. The prophets exhibited the same features across the continent of praying and healing; they garnered large followers for the healing miracles that accompanied their ministries. The prophets recognized the powers of the indigenous worldview and subdued idol worship with the power of Christ (Kalu). Some of the Prophetic Movements were eventually silenced by the colonial governments through the influence of the Mission Churches; some of them survived persecution and became what are today the Indigenous Movement Churches. For example, Christ Apostolic Church that was led by Apostle Joseph Ayo Babalola (Olowe 2007) is the first indigenous Pentecostal Church in Nigeria, independent of the classical movement.

Some of the notable prophets the Lord raised up during this period were Wade Harris (Liberia, 1913), Garrick Braide (Nigeria, 1914), Moses Orimolade (Nigeria, 1919), Simon Kimbang (Congo, 1921), Josiah Ositelu (Nigeria, 1925), and Joseph Ayo Babalola (Nigeria, 1928), to mention a few.

Neo-Pentecostal and Charismatic Movement

More than a half century after its lowly beginnings, the gifts of the Holy Spirit spread to the mainstream churches. The "Neo-Pentecostal" movement started in an Episcopalian congregation in Van Nuys California in 1960, under the ministry of Dennis Bennett and spread to other Protestant churches.

The Catholic Charismatic Renewal movement had its beginnings in Pittsburgh, Pennsylvania, in 1967 among students and faculty of DuQuesne University (Synan); this marks the final phase of penetration of Pentecostalism into the mainline churches. By 1993, the Pentecostal movement had become the fastest growing Christian movement in the world, with the number of both Pentecostals and Charismatics at well over 420 million people.

Other Movements

There are other phenomena that have occurred (controversial though) in the facet of Pentecostalism. One of them is the phenomenon known as "holy laughter"; it started at a revival meeting at the Toronto Airport Vineyard Church in January 1994. Within months, the church had become a spectacular international attraction. Groups visited the church from around the world to witness and perhaps participate in this unusual expression of praise featuring a manifestation of uncontrolled laughter; it has been labeled the "Toronto blessing", or "holy laughter". There are other manifestations besides laughter, such as rolling on the floor, shaking, jerking, uttering animals sounds, and so on. Of course, this new expression of worship has generated controversy, especially among Pentecostals; the behaviors have no scriptural backing, they say.

2. HISTORY OF CHURCH REFORMS

Another phenomenon is the Brownsville revival in Florida that started in June 1995. Many people frequently tie this with the "Toronto blessing".

> A number of people who question the methods and theological fundamentals of the Brownsville Revival see indications that it was planned and modeled after what is going on in Toronto. (Crann)

POINTS IN CHAPTER 2

The first great Church Reformers were the biblical Apostles, followed by the Church Fathers. They provided the initial doctrines especially in Church administration and combating heresies.

Christians were persecuted and martyred. Emperor Constantine finally put an end to persecution in 313 AD and took over reforming the Church.

The great schism between Eastern Orthodox and Western Roman Catholic occurred in 1054. Subsequent schism of the Protestants and Church of England followed in 1517 and 1529 respectively.

The development of doctrines of Salvation started with the teaching of Pelagius, which was debated by Augustine. Calvinists and Arminians later resumed on the debate. These doctrines and variants of them are spread across the various denominations today.

Pentecostalism and its variants emerged fully in the early 20th century and became the fastest growing movement until recently when the postmodern movements took over.

3. POSTMODERN MOVEMENTS

THIS Chapter covers the development of the Church in the 20th and 21st centuries. A new generation of movements arose from Christians with initial background from various denominations, Catholic, Protestant, Anglican, and Evangelical, and these movements are gradually breaking denominational boundaries. The movements have initially been called Church Growth Movement (CGM) and then Great Commission Movement (GCM). According to statistics provided by David Barrett, the population of those affiliated with these postmodern movements surpassed the Pentecostals by the year 2000. He gives the number affiliated with Pentecostals and Charismatics as 523.8 million while the Great Commission Christians numbered 647.8 million. The figures in both cases include the doubly-affiliated which are difficult to pull out. Double affiliation comes from many who still pledge allegiance to the traditional mainstream churches. Also, almost all these postmodern churches are charismatic in nature. However, it is important to see the growth of these new generation movements which are predicted to surpass the Catholics by 2025, or even before then.

GENERAL OVERVIEW

POSTMODERNISM

The term *postmodernism* first entered the philosophical glossary in 1979, when Jean-François Leotard published *The Postmodern Condition*. Since then, the term has been used in various aspects of life making it difficult to have a clear definition. Postmodernism is highly debated even among postmodernists themselves. We can view Postmodernism as a general term used to describe a set of intellectual ideas that appears in a wide variety of disciplines, including art, architecture, music, film, sociology, communications, fashion, technology, fiction, cultural and literary criticism, among others. Two important terms frequently used to describe postmodernism are "cultural shift" and "intellectual".

Postmodernism is largely a reaction to the assumed certainty (or objective) efforts to explain reality. In the postmodern philosophy, the concept of absolute truth or objective reality is moot; reality only comes into being through individual interpretations. This is subjective truth: what is "true" for me is just true for me. Jimmy Long says:

> Instead of human reason that leads to truth, postmodernism posits multiple truths that lead only to preferences.

Jake Bouma (2007) highlighted four characteristics of postmodernism, namely, subjective truth, virtual reality, micronarratives, and communities. Of these, "subjective truth" is the most alerting for the Church to worry about.

Origin of Postmodernism among Youth

In his book, Jimmy Long (2004) traces the connections between postmodernism and the emerging generations:

> The church today is at a critical junction in regard to two major societal changes. The first societal change is the generation transition from the Baby Boom generation to Generation X

Postmodernism is predominant in the Western world, especially in the USA among the youth of this generation. The term has been used by Jimmy Long for the Generation X (those born between 1964 and 1984) in the USA. The source of postmodernism is a combination of the following reasons:

o Youth's insatiable appetite for choices in music, movies, clothing, internet, electronics, and books (Bouma 2007);

- The increase in the number of information sources, especially on the internet, makes postmodern youth more likely to mix fact and fiction. (Bouma 2007)
- Confusion of what is taught in sciences at school against what is taught in Church (Ham and Beemer 2009). There is where the subjective truth sets in.

Origin of Postmodernism in the Church

In the year 2000, statistics from Barna Group showed that 61% of young adults who were regular church attendees were "spiritually disengaged" from the traditional churches. They were not actively attending church, praying, or reading their Bibles anymore. Ham and Beemer, in another study, highlighted in their book, *"Already Gone: Why your kids will quit church and what you can do to stop it,"* that youth are already "lost" in their hearts and minds in elementary, middle and high school. The book reveals that 20–29 year olds who regularly attend Sunday school are actually more likely to be pro-abortion, pro-gay marriage, and defend premarital sex. The book also reveals that those who faithfully attend Sunday school are more likely to leave the Church than those who do not and are more likely to believe that the Bible is less true. In an interview, Ham says:

> The church opened a door for the exodus of youth, beginning in the 19th century, when it began teaching that "the age of the earth is not an issue as long as you trust in Jesus and believe in the resurrection and the Gospel accounts." (WorldNetDaily.com)

Although theologians started to teach about creation and of "the age of the earth" using common grace through "general revelation" of God (see Hanko, October 2009), this could only have been exposed to few of the young people. Simply put, the youth are confused with what science is teaching about evolution theory and what the Bible teaches about creation. Ham provides a better explanation below:

> In previous generations, young people could live with this inconsistency, he [Ken Ham] said, but with an increasingly secular and atheistic public education system – where some 90 percent of church-going youth are trained – today's youth [in the USA] find it hard to see a connection between what they are taught in church and what they learn at school. "Because of the way in which they've been educated," Ham said, teens come to believe "that what they are taught in school is reality, but the church teaches stories and morality and relationship. (Ken Ham's interview on WorldNetDaily.com)

Ham holds church leaders and parents accountable for not providing the youth with adequate teaching on creation.

Many of the youth who ran away from the Church found home in the emergent movement which surfaced after the publication of *"The Emergent Church"* by Dan Kimball in 2003. The emergent movement allowed some of the philosophies of the social postmodernism.

Postmodernism classified

We need to understand the context of the term as it applies to this book. As defined in Chapter 1, we have the Church culture and the Society culture. The root of the postmodernism as it is being currently applied is from the Society culture. The accommodation of some of the philosophies of "social postmodernism" into some movements such as the emerging church is syncretism as briefly described in Chapter 1; this topic will further be covered in Chapter 7. However, there are several other movements which are not syncretic and it seems that even the emergent movement is making adjustments. We know that there are cultural shifts in this new generation churches. But, because of the concept of "subjective truth", many are distancing themselves from the term "postmodernism". This is noted by Stetzer and Putman:

> Lots of people throw terms around to describe the [cultural] shift. The term that receives the most attention is "postmodernism." However, since postmodernism is an art form, a literary category, an academic discipline, and even a cultural force, even that fails to describe the situation... Many are now running away from the term postmodernism. (Stetzer and Putman)

However, the term "postmodernism" is still the best term to describe all the new generation movements for the mere fact that there is cultural shift one way or the other in a new era. For this, we will define four types of postmodernism:

o *Social postmodernism*: deals with the shift in the social culture by social philosophies;

- *Spiritual postmodernism*: deals with the shift in the church culture by church reformations;
- *Syncretic postmodernism*: deals with importing the social philosophies into church culture;
- *Missional postmodernism*: deals with influencing social culture by church culture.

The Church is at a crossroad and it needs to decide whether to allow syncretism or to culturally engage the society. Missional postmodernism is the interest of this book. Spiritual postmodernism is implied in order for Missional postmodernism to be effective.

> Evangelicals have struggled with responding to these new realities, finding reasons not to respond. It is important to note that the shift to postmodernism has not happened everywhere – it has not yet impacted the church culture because the church culture acts as a protective shield, unmolested by the secular culture's music, literature, and values (Stetzer and Putman)

What Stetzer and Putman are saying above is that Syncretic postmodernism can not survive time. It is rightly said. According to Url Scaramanga, the name "Emerging" or "Emergent" is about to disappear because it seems many are misusing the term to introduce Syncretic postmodernism.

> The Emerging Church is officially dead...at least, the name is dead. Dan Kimball says of the term, "I can't defend or even explain theologically what is now known broadly as 'the emerging church' anymore, because it has developed into so many significantly different theological

strands. Some I strongly would disagree with." (Url Scaramanga)

COMMON NAME

The ever growing new generation movements have witnessed several shifts in popularly accepted models so also is the general name to describe the movement. Much has been said about the *Emergent Movement* under *Postmodernism*. The emergent movement is being promoted by "Emergent Village", with people such as Brian McLaren, Tony Jones, Marc Scandrette and Tim Conder.

Other leading movements are *Purpose Driven* (purposedrivenchurch.com), *Churchshift* (churchshift.org, churchshiftusa.org), and *Missional*. Each of these movements is a product of books written by different people. Rick Warren published *"The Purpose Driven Church"* in 1995. A 1998 book titled *Missional Church,* edited by Darrell Guder, was written by a group of Professors and missiologists. Sunday Adelaja published *"Churchshift"* in 2008 and the Churchshift movement is just kicking off.

All these movements share a belief that missions are the heart of the Church, and that the traditional methods of carrying out missions are no longer effective. The most suitable general name that has been adopted for the postmodern church is *"Missional Church"*. We will stick to that name in this book and in future references. The name has been used since Chapter 1. The choice of the name is irrespective of the original intentions of Darrell et al's book; it is the best name to be used as the umbrella for all Missional Postmodern Movements. Three of the dozens of websites on Missional Church are: missionalchurch.org, missionalpeople.com, and friendofmissional.org. Lois Barrett et al have suggested patterns of a Missional Church and have also given examples of churches in the USA that are "Missional". The term has also been used to describe the "Emergent Church" as follows:

> Emergent is a growing generative friendship among missional Christian leaders seeking to love our world in the Spirit of Jesus Christ. (emergentvillage.org)

The term "emerging church" isn't new, confesses Dan Kimball on his blog; it was used for a book called *"The Emerging Church"* in 1970 by Bruce Larson and Ralph Osborne. Dan Kimball wrote, in September 2008, an article, titled *Emerging and Emergent Distinctions,* that a new network, *"Origins Project"* (theoriginsproject.org), was in the works that would try to make a fresh start in the direction he originally intended when he wrote his book *"The Emerging Church"*:

> Scot [McKnight] is going to be part of shaping a new network being formed right now. (Dan Kimball 2008)

What most of these postmodern movements lack are theological backings to support their models of "new way of doing church". This book and *Grace Theology* (Olowe 2009) will provide the necessary theological background for *Churchshift* movement and for Missional Church in general.

MISSIONAL REFORMATION

The term *"Classical Church"* will be used to describe contemporary churches up till the modern era while *"Missional Church"* will denote the church in the postmodern era. This book will also stress the differences between Classical Church and Missional Church (see introduction to Volume 2). The term *"Missionary Church"* is not to be confused with *"Missional Church"*. Missionary churches send missionaries to foreign countries to perform missionary work as it is done in the classical church. As such, the missionaries are a few members of the congregation who desire to engage in mission work. A Missional Church, however, does not necessarily need to send missionaries to foreign countries, missional works are done right there in the city or town where the church is. In addition, every member of the congregation is regarded as a missionary and church life is oriented around that view.

The three basic categories of postmodern movements are church planting, church cell, and seven-sphere. The fourth, the stewardship movement, perhaps not included in David Barrett's statistics, has traits geared towards the same goal. Churchshift has ideologies of all the movements combined.

COMMON VALUES

A long list of common characteristics of a Missional Church is given at friendofmissional.org. The central aim of a Missional Church is *cultural engagement and transformation*.

Another common characteristic that can be used to describe a Missional Church is *"Kingdom minded"*. The postmodern movements instill energy into evangelism to execute the Great Commission. Some Christians have criticized them with a general label of "market churches". Troubled by the wave of these "militant" movements, here is a comment quoted in Sarah Leslie's article *"Dominionism and the Rise of Christian Imperialism"*:

> Christ never intended that His Gospel should be propagated by fire and sword or His righteousness wrought by the wrath of man. When the high praises of God are in our mouth with them we should have an olive-branch of peace in our hands. - Matthew Henry, circa 1700

We shall see in future discourse that if these postmodern movements execute their programs in honesty of the purpose, it is God's design for this generation. One other general criticism of the postmodern churches is that aggressive discipling does not necessarily produce proper conversion:

> In order to ensure the flood of new converts that they expected, adding new members to the church became of overriding importance. – Tricia Trillin

COMMON THEOLOGY

The doctrine of *special and universal grace* is the theological bedrock of a Missional Church. This doctrine has a wider scope (see *"Grace Theology"* (Olowe 2009)) than the *common grace* doctrine articulated by Dutch Abraham Kuyper

(1837-1920). Vincent Bacote also captured the idea of *common grace* doctrine serving as a theological base for Missional Church. In his lecture at Princeton in 1898, Kuyper stated that

> Common grace is by which God maintains the life of the world, by relaxing the sins, and allows the untrammeled development of our life to glorify Himself as Creator.

Kuyper teaches that all humans, whether saved or not, receive common grace as part of God's purpose to build His Kingdom. Kuyper notes that if God is Sovereign, then his Lordship must remain over all life and cannot be closed up within church walls. The secular world has not been given over to Satan or to fallen humanity. Man is required to make use of the common grace to perform his stewardship duty. Kuyper applied Christian principles to different sectors (spheres) of the society and reiterates that it is part of the duty of an Elect to do so in order to glorify God. This is what Missional Church is all about. Kuyper's doctrine of *common grace* is more applicable to the seven-sphere movement and thus will be discussed further under that section below and in greater details in Chapters 4. References will be made to *common grace* throughout the rest of the book.

In Kuyper's analysis, he divided the world into three (as against the two we defined in Chapter 1): Government, Society, and Church:

> A primordial Sovereignty which eradicates in mankind is a threefold deduced supremacy, viz., 1. The Sovereignty

in the State; 2. The Sovereignty in Society; and 3. The Sovereignty in the Church. (Kuyper)

However, in our analysis, we will stick to the two-world model; the government is part of the society. Kuyper was involved in politics through Guillaume Groen van Prinsterer from 1864, and he eventually became the Dutch Prime Minister in 1901 (Wikipedia). Having been involved in politics certainly influenced Kuyper's analysis.

CHURCH PLANTING MOVEMENT

As mentioned previously, Church Planting Movement is one of the four basic postmodern movements that we will be discussing. Church planting is a process by which new churches are established within a community by a planter which could be an individual, a denomination, a church planting center, a network, an association, or other church planting resources.

Church planting has existed since the early church formation in the first century and has been used by the missionaries to fulfill the Great Commission. Leading church growth writer, C. Peter Wagner, famously observed that Church Planting is the most effective evangelistic strategy on earth. However, Jim Thomas sounds a note of caution:

> While this may be true for some churches subscribing to the church growth philosophy and practices, there are some aspects of the church growth school that run con-

trary to Missional Church philosophies and practices. For one, Missional churches focus on Kingdom growth rather than church growth. They are more likely to focus on planting new churches than in enlarging themselves (though they do not shun numerical growth as a by-product of being missional), and to measure growth by "the ability to release rather than retain.

CLASSIFICATION OF MODELS

This ideology of planting churches is not different from the classical reason of carrying out missions. The widely accepted definition of a Christian mission (since the Lausanne Congress of 1974) is: "*to form a viable indigenous church-planting movement.*" The scriptural base and justification is the Great Commission of Matthew 28. There are several methods of church planting which are currently very dynamic and developing. New methods are devised at a fast rate like car models. Perhaps by the time this book is published a new model will be out. It makes it more difficult to find a unique way of categorization. Right now, there is no universally accepted method of classification; it varies from author to author. Pastor John Iuliano wrote:

> One of the reasons that there are so many methods is because the Bible doesn't dictate that there is only one way it can be done. This, I believe, is because God has made us creative and innovative and the last word on church planting has still not been written.

I will try to provide an acceptable classification method. Most of the current popular models can be classified in two ways: by the planter and by the structure.

1. Classification by the Church Planter (or accountability):
    a. Pioneering – accountable to an individual
    b. Modality – accountable to a mother church
    c. Sodality – accountable to a denomination or network
2. Classification by Structure
    a. Cell-based
    b. Non cell-based

Structure-based provides the best way of classification because not all cell-based church models depend on the characteristics of a planter. In the Church Planting Movement, only the non cell-based models depend on the characteristics of the Church planter. However, both classifications will be merged with structure-based being the major classification method and the planter-based being the minor. Here, we will examine different methods in the pioneering, modality, and sodality models in the non cell-based models of church planting. Each method has its advantages and disadvantages and we may not be able to cover them all; in some cases, they are self revealing.

NON CELL-BASED CHURCH PLANTING

Pioneering

The only method available to an individual church planter is termed the *"parachute drop"*. The individual and his family will move into a new location to start a church from scratch. The planter and his family are "pioneering" the new territory. This method is suitable only for a person particularly gifted in personal evangelism or who is already known. The parachute drop method is also available in the sodality model (discussed below). The church plant may have flexibility in its own mission, vision, and programs, but it may also suffer from isolation and financial support. The pioneered church may grow into a mega church, depending on the leader; Winners Chapel in Ota, Nigeria, or the Lakewood Church in Houston, Texas, for example. When a pioneered church grows, it could adopt any of the other models discussed below to plant more churches.

Modality

The term "Modality" denotes a "daughter church" having relationship with, accountability to, and receiving nurture and covering from a "mother church". In the modality model, an existing church (mother) provides the initial leadership and resources (finance and people) to get a new church (daughter) started. The existing relationship allows for a close working relationship between the "mother" and "daughter" churches. Although the new church eventually becomes autonomous, the mother church often has significant influence in the new church, especially on programs. The ultimate goal is to see the daughter grow to enough maturity so that she is also able to reproduce. The advantage of this model is the immediate availability of initial resources, finance and a nucleus of experienced Christians to give the church initial momentum. There are different methods of this model.

Branching

This method entails the breaking up of a nucleus of the mother church that lives in the geographical vicinity of the new daughter church plant. This nucleus of people moves their allegiance from the mother church to this branch church. This method was successfully implemented by David Yonggi Cho's Full Gospel Church (FGC) in Korea. In 1984, Pastor Cho sent out a nucleus of 5,000 people and a budget of $4 million (US) as a branch church in another suburb of Seoul, Korea, with one of his associates as the assembly pastor. By 1990 this branch grew to over 100,000 members. The purpose of branching is to grow the church with an initial boost in a new community.

Satellite

In the satellite method, small churches are planted around a geographical area and are connected to a central church during the weekly celebration by satellite. In this model, the government of the central church is the same for the satellite.

This model tries to give people the feel of a large congregation with the warmth and at the same time getting personal attention of a local church leader. The satellite method is somehow similar to branching except the satellite church is designed to stay connected to the mother church whereas the branch church is designed to eventually become autonomous. This method is available to both non cell-based and cell-based models. The satellite and the central church have the same government.

Some of the world's mega churches, such as The Works and Mission Baptist Church, Ivory Coast, use the cell-based satellite method. The Methodist Pentecostal Church in Chile has planted over 40 satellite churches around Santiago. Even though the central church can only accommodate 16,000 people, Pastor Javier Vasquez ministers to over 350,000 through their satellite system.

Another common feature of satellite churches is their regular celebration services. This is where all the satellite churches and the central church join together for a huge celebration. In South America they have to hire parks and stadiums for these events because there are no buildings large enough to accommodate them.

Monosphere
This terminology is coined in this book to represent a homogeneous culture church, in terms of the composition of the members, which is mostly sphere-based. A sphere is defined

as an area of influence such as, science, education, business, family, arts, and so on. Some daughter churches of the Embassy of God Church in Ukraine are monospherical.

Adoption

This happens when an existing group or church comes under the spiritual coverage of a mother church or a denomination. This usually takes place because the adoptee feels that they can benefit from this new relationship. The existing church under the new coverage grows because of the reputation of the mother. From the mother church's point of view, adoption ought to be with no strings attached. The new group needs to flow with the vision and direction that the mother church has already established. The parent church usually releases gifting to the adopted church so that they can quickly come into the same stream and flow together.

Sodality

The sodality model is similar to the modality model except the mother here is a church planting organization or a denomination instead of a single church in the modality model. The advantage of the sodality model is that the new church gets better moral and financial support. In addition to adoption and monosphere discussed above, there are some other methods specific to sodality.

Collaborative Network

This is a rapidly growing trend where an organization (or many organizations) committed to church planting work together to plant churches. The alliances are referred to as collaborative or partnership networks or colonizing. The participating organizations often share common beliefs and a passion for starting new churches. Planters often get many of the benefits of the "sponsoring church" but with increased autonomy in decision making. This pattern often crosses denominational boundaries in a spirit of co-operation.

Parachute Drop

This method as discussed above is the only method available to an individual planting a church. It can also be used by an established organization; it is the model used mostly in the New Testament and the 19th century missionaries. A known evangelist or apostle of the organization has the ability to swiftly break through a locality and build a nucleus which becomes the foundation of the church. A pastor is dispatched to the new assembly and the evangelist and/or apostle moves to another location.

CELL-BASED CHURCH PLANTING

Before we can further classify cell based church planting, we have to understand the concept of a cell as it is being used today. From most of its usages so far, we can conveniently define a cell as follows:

> A group of 3 to 25 people meeting at least once a week in or outside a church building for one or more of the following reasons: worship, spiritual growth, leadership development, discipleship, fellowship, and evangelism.

From a very practical standpoint, there is common agreement among experts that a cell must be small enough so that all its members can freely contribute and share personal needs; the smaller the cell, the more the level of intimacy among members. It would be an exceptional case if there are more than 25 members in a cell.

Today, there are dozens of cell models, many of which are only different by names and by the basic structure in order to create uniqueness, but they can all be grouped under two broad categories:

1. Cell Church – a self running unit;
2. Church Cell – the cell is a unit of the church;

The *church cell* is usually a unit of multiplied cells, the agglomeration of which celebrates together in a church building. One of the purposes of church cells is multiplication. These types of cells will be discussed in the next section under "church cell movements". The cell churches will be discussed in this section.

Cell Church

From the discussion above, a cell church can be defined as:

MISSIONAL REFORMATION

> A small group of 3 to 25 people who meet at least once in a week in a location other than a church building but functioning as a church.

There are several models of cell churches; the points below differentiate one cell church model from the other:

1. Leader: each cell church may or may not have a leader;
2. Leadership development: It may have a leadership training program usually for the purpose of multiplication;
3. Autonomy: there might be interrelationships between various cell churches of the same model, but each may be self sustaining and self propagating;
4. Programs: may or may not have programs, formal liturgy, etc.
5. Franchising: similarity among the cells (with regard to teaching material, format, etc.)
6. Central Church: there might be a central church where all cell churches celebrate on a particular occasion;
7. Purpose: primary purpose is fellowship; there could be are others
8. Values: or doctrine if any

A cell church is usually called a *house church* or *home church*. It is a church that functions without a church building. There are several thousands of house churches in the world. They are easy to start and to maintain. There is neither a church building to maintain, nor salaries to be paid. There are two distinct house church movements today.

The first kind of movement is found in countries such as the USA, Australia, and the UK where Christianity already thrives. The main objective of this movement is to return to the New Testament style of gathering believers. A commonly held belief in the movement is that Jesus Christ alone is the Head of the Church, hence no need of a hierarchical leadership structure. Every member of a typical house church is free to contribute to the gathering.

> After all, homes are where most of the churches in the days of the New Testament met for worship, fellowship, teaching, and ministry. Led by laypersons like us, they were powerful—and changed their world by meeting God at home. (www.homechurchonline.com)

The second kind of house church movement is found in countries like China, India, and some Islamic states where Christians are in the minority. The house churches are heavily persecuted in these countries. The reason for persecution varies from country to country, but the common goal is to slow down the spread of Christianity. Many of these countries tolerate foreign churches (for diplomatic reasons) but discourage indigenous churches from being established. Because the house churches could not be granted permits, they operate underground. They are deemed illegal by the governments and as such they are subjected to frequent harassment and persecution.

In China, the official church, known as the Three-Self Patriotic Movement (TSPM), was founded in the 1950s to

MISSIONAL REFORMATION

free Chinese from foreign religious influence. However, TSPM is highly syncretized (see Chapter 7 on governmental syncretism). Many Chinese Christians would not align themselves with the official church, being under the authority of the Communist government, serving the Party first before God. These believers meet in house churches; some isolated, others form part of well-organized network of hundreds of thousands of home churches. Because house churches operate outside government regulations, their members and leaders are sometimes harassed by local government officials. A popular leader of the house church movement in China, Watchman Nee, was imprisoned in 1952 and died in 1972 in a labor camp farm.

> In May 2007, police in Aksu City, Xinjiang, arrested approximately 30 house church leaders who met with Christians from the United States. Four American Christians were interrogated in connection with the meeting and later expelled from China. (www.Win1040.org)

In spite of the persecutions, the house church movement is thriving in China.

> Figures released by house churches show there are 80 million to 100 million Christians in China. And 80% of them, i.e. 64 million to 80 million, are house church adherents. (Yanto Bi - GlobalVoices)

House churches also implement missional reformation. In 2008, house churches played a significant role in relief work after the May 12 earthquake in Sichuan province in China.

Also in Indian where about 80% of the citizens are Hindus, Christians are persecuted; even by the government. Many churches operate underground as home churches.

> Over four months after government authorities closed several house churches in Karnataka, India, the Karnataka High Court said they should reopen and can hold worship services ... Following attacks on several churches on August 17, 2008, the district administration issued notices seeking a survey of churches functioning without permission. In early September, several churches were sealed... Local Christian leaders say the problems were because extremist Hindutva groups influenced officials. (cbn.com, indianchristians.in)

Some house churches have a conventional leadership structure, while others have none. All cell churches can be classified into two: *structured* and *unstructured* cell churches.

Structured Cell Church

A Structured Cell Church is a fully functioning cell church; this means that it has a leader and programs. Many of them have strong leadership development programs for personal growth. Chinese house churches typically have a leadership structure. Some structured cell churches in the USA started as unstructured campus ministries. Notable among them are Xenos and the Great Commission Churches (GCC). Xenos started in 1971 as a campus ministry with several cell churches scattered in and out of the Ohio State University campus. The Great Commission Association of Churches started in 1970 by James Douglas McCotter, after meeting

Dennis Clark and Herschel Martindale. They started as a campus ministry. Today, over 60 churches in the USA are affiliated with GCC; there are also international affiliations in Europe, Asia and Latin America. GCA maintains an administrative support staff in Columbus, Ohio, the same city where Xenos lives. GCC has had its own dose of criticisms, especially on the rigidity of the leadership.

Some structured cell churches allow their cells to grow beyond the 25-member upper limit set for a cell because they operate like a church outside a real church building.

Unstructured Cell Church

Unstructured cell churches are the ones springing up at an amazing rate. People are trying to get away from cumbersome church administration and leadership hierarchy. There are dozens of models in this category; the most unstructured being what is called *"simple church"*. A simple church meets to facilitate relationship and discipleship without trained leaders, formal liturgy, programs or any structure at all for that matter. The group meets on any day of the week, in houses, apartments, public schools, barbershops, parks, taverns, or wherever people live. In fact, the meeting place really doesn't matter as long as people gather in the name of Jesus. It is called simple church because there is no need for a church building, professional clergy, budget, denominations or Sunday worship programs. The simple church is highly criticized for lack of trained leaders and development programs. Even some members of the group are complaining about this and say that the life span of the cell is usually short, between 6 months to 2 years. So, how do they carryout the Great Commission? Two variants of the group are popping up, "Black and White" Simple and "Grey" Simple (Dodson), but are not well defined. As will be discussed further in Chapter 9, a Missional Church must have a leadership training program. It can be deduced therefore that a simple church may not be a Missional Church.

Another model, developed by Neil Cole, is the *organic church*. The organic cell naturally emerges on its own (hence the emergent church) from people in the same community with common values. The word "natural" is important in the formation of an organic church; people are not forced to come together. The name "organic" has been used previously by Kuyper to define the church:

> Regeneration does not save a few isolated individuals, finally to be joined together mechanically as an aggregate heap. Regeneration saves the organism, itself, of our race. And therefore all regenerate human life forms one organic body, of which Christ is the Head, and whose members are bound together by their mystical union with Him.

The articulated values of the group, which have also been extended to other models of the unstructured cell churches, are: **D** - Divine Truth; **N** - Nurturing Relationships; **A** - Apostolic Mission.

CHURCH CELL MOVEMENT

According to Wolfgang Simson, six of the top seven largest mega churches in the world today use a *church cell* model. Although the church cell system has been used right from the inception of the Church, David Yonggi Cho, Pastor of Yoido Full Gospel Church (YFGC) can rightly be regarded as the father of modern cell movement. YFGC was founded in 1958 by David Cho in an old Marine tent with 5 members. Today, his central church is the largest in the world having over 830,000 members total, with an average of 253,000 in attendance at a worship service, and with over 100,000 elders and deacons (www.fgtv.com). Cho's cell system has been replicated and adapted by church leaders all over the world, most of them specifically for church growth. Church cell is sometimes referred to as home group or cell group.

MICROSCOPIC CHARACTERISTICS OF CHURCH CELLS

Joel Comiskey in his dissertation, categorized cell churches microscopically into Pure Cells and Meta Cells. This defines the nature of each cell. These models apply to the cells in a classical church. A third model, found at a Missional church (see Volume 2, Chapter 10), is added in this book. All models also apply to churches described under Church Planting.

Pure Cell Model

David Yonggi Cho's cell system is classified as Pure Cell; it is widely used in classical churches. Each cell group is similar in purpose, vision, and format. The vision and mission follow that of the central church. Multiplication of cells is strongly encouraged and promoted by this model.

Meta Cell Model

The Meta Cell model is an invention of Carl George. He tried hard in three books (Comiskey) to define what this model should look like.

> George (1994) says, "Cells include Sunday-School classes, ministry teams, outreach teams, worship-production teams, sports teams, recovery groups, and more . . . any time sixteen or fewer people meet together, you have a small-group meeting". (Comiskey 1997).

It seems that George's description is more of task oriented groups involving only church based tasks.

> For the Meta-Church any type of groups within the church constitute the cells. All these groups may have different agendas and purposes... Since the agenda of every group cannot be identical, the goal of the Meta-Church is accommodation (David Tan cited in Comiskey)

Missional Cell Model

The Embassy of God Church in the Ukraine has cell groups with microscopic characteristics similar in principle to the Meta model, but with tasks that are Churchshift-based instead of church-based; Churchshift will be more defined in this chapter and in future chapters. Basically, the mission of each group is to engage the society in a specific sector (sphere).

Common Characteristics

The following are the common characteristics of all church cell models:

1. Local Church: each cell must be part of a local church; those who attend the cell meetings are expected to attend the church services;
2. Leader: leadership is not optional; each cell church must have a leader; some cell churches plant geographical districts or zonal leaders, however, the fundamental leadership role is always given to the cell leader (Comiskey).
3. Leadership Development: there must be a leadership training program put in place, usually for the purpose of multiplication;
4. Multiplication: it is the primary focus of most cell churches; however, in the Meta or Missional model, multiplication is desired but not enforced;
5. Accountability: each cell leader is accountable to a superior, usually the geographical zonal leader (if it exists);
6. Uniformity of Lesson Material: all of the cell leaders cover the same lesson plan; in Meta model, there is flexibility in the lesson materials since it is task oriented;

7. Discipleship: every member is monitored and pastored; this is why a cell should not be too large; smaller is better for effective discipleship;
8. Programs: they must be limited in order not to loose focus; the local church already has most of the programs; however, in the Meta or Missional model, each cell has specific programs or tasks that do not conflict with the church;
9. Participation: each member of the local church must be committed to a church cell;

MACROSCOPIC CHARACTERISTICS OF CHURCH CELLS

Macroscopically, there are two basic models of cell multiplication: splitting and tree formation. This characteristic describes the global structure of the cell system.

Splitting Model

The pioneer of this model is David Yonggi Cho. Realizing that the work of leading his large congregation was too much for one person, he employed Jethro's advice to Moses; Cho branched (as discussed under church planting) his church into several locations in Seoul and grew each location by church cells. He trained the initial cell leaders, each of whom was required to train an assistant, and when cell membership reached a certain number, the assistant leader would form a new cell, taking about half of the old cell with him or her.

MISSIONAL REFORMATION

This model has also been used by some Nigerian churches. In Nigeria, a church cell is usually called *house fellowship*. Deeper Life Bible Church (DLBC) started as a house fellowship at the Lagos University campus by Pastor William Kumuyi. The DLBC house fellowship system is named House Caring Fellowship (HCF). When Pastor Enoch Adeboye took over the leadership of the Redeemed Christian Church of God (RCCG), he developed a house fellowship system called CARE (Contact And Relate Everyone). This system resulted in the initial rapid growth of the church through planting of several churches. DLBC and RCCG implement cell-based splitting model. The RCCG slogan is "plant a church at every 5 miles radius".

Method and Implementation

The basic idea of this model is to first plant a church at a particular location, and then grow it through church cells, starting with the pioneer members. In this model, a maximum cell size is set. Members of the cell recruit new members through evangelism and when the cell exceeds the maximum size, the cell splits into two and a new leader is released to lead the new cell.

In a 1993 interview, Cho explained how his cells do the recruiting, termed "net fishing" (Comiskey, 1997).

> We have 50,000 cell groups and each group will love two people to Christ within the next year. They select someone who's not a Christian, whom they can pray for, love, and serve. They bring meals, help sweep out the

person's store-- whatever it takes to show they really care for them. After three or four months of such love, the hardest soul softens up and surrenders to Christ (quoted in George 1994).

All the cell groups celebrate together on a weekly basis at the local church. The House Fellowship System of RCCG and DLBC are compared in Table 3:1.

Table 3.1: Comparison of House Fellowship Systems

	DLBC	RCCG
Optimum Size	15	8-12
Max Size	15	15
Release of Leaders	Size dependent	Size dependent

Tree Model

The most known (and I believe the only known) tree formation model is popularly called G12, meaning "Government of 12" or "Groups of 12". The G12 critics call it "market church" because of the similarity of its structure with multi-level marketing models. César Castellanos, the senior Pastor at the Misión Carismática Internacional (MCI) in Bogotá, Colombia, developed the G12 strategy after visiting the Yoido Full Gospel Church, Korea in 1986. He formed his church into groups of 12, while his brother-in-law, César Fajardo, did the same with the youth. From 1991 to 1994 the church grew from 70 to 1,200 members, and between 1994 and 1999, to 45,000 people in a regular weekly church celebration. By the year 2008, MCI had 55,000 church cells and approximately 550,000 members. In 2000, church leaders around the world, seeking to increase the size of their churches, traveled to Bogotá to learn about the G12 vision. Some churches follow the G12 model as is, others extract portions they like out of it and use it. This model is popular worldwide and a number of well-known people are involved in promoting it.

Method and Implementation

G12 is based on the methodology used by Jesus who selected 12 disciples in his ministry. In G12, the main leader would disciple 12 people to the level of leadership; they would instate Christian values, teachings, prayer and ministry on a weekly basis until their disciples were ready to lead their own cell groups. These cell leaders are each responsible for finding 12 people from the community to disciple in a cell group. After a specified time, and after certain strict requirements are met, these cell members then become leaders themselves, and start their own cells. Thus, the membership of the church is multiplied, and the message of the Gospel is taken into the community. This number 12 is considered significant as representing Government.

The G12 system in its original form has numerous strict standards. In order to be part of the vision, one is expected to be dedicated, attend cell group meetings once a week, go to retreats, go out to evangelize, go to the Sunday morning service, and also attend special meetings with one's leader's leader. Each week is loaded with these church activities and other social activities from within cell group members. The week is taken up with meetings and church activities as it is believed that they will make one a serious disciple. There are 4 stages of implementation called, *Ladder of Success*: Win, Consolidate, Disciple, and Send.

Winning: New believers are added to the church through personal evangelism, weekend celebration church services, and monthly "net" meetings.

Consolidation: This process is central to the success of the G12 strategy. Consolidation takes place in three stages.
 - Pre-Encounter: Members of the consolidation team are assigned to new members to help enroll them in a weekly cell meeting, guide them through a short Pre-Encounter course, and register them to attend an Encounter Retreat.
 - Encounter: Members are supposed to "encounter God" at the Encounter weekend retreat through teachings on repentance, forgiveness, breaking of curses, inner healing, deliverance, water baptism, baptism in the Holy Spirit, and the vision of the church.
 - Post-Encounter: After the Encounter, the new believers go through a ten-week Post-encounter course, which takes them deeper into the Word and further consolidates their commitment to Christ. During these teaching sessions, the new believer learns about spiritual warfare, the armor of God, how to resist and overcome temptation, and how to deal with the attacks of the evil one.

Discipleship: After completing the consolidation process, the new disciple enters the School of Leaders, which consists of three ten-week trimesters of study. Participants are taught how to become a leader, evangelism, courtship, abundant life, etc. During the second trimester, the students will open their own cells but will also continue meeting in their original cells, which now become their leadership, or G12, groups. The goal is to become a leader of a cell group.

Sending: As the disciple progresses through the School of Leaders, he opens his own cell and begins to develop his twelve, taking them through each step of the process of the vision and eventually sending them to make their disciples.

Criticisms

The G12 is highly criticized. I believe the rise to popularity contributed to it. It has been criticized for everything it stands for, everything under the sun.

1. *The Number 12*: G12 is criticized for the spiritualization of the number 12; the argument that it is not scriptural can be discarded as a non-issue. The first action taken by the 11 remaining Apostles was to re-establish a group of 12 by replacing Judas, but the Bible does not tell us what happened with each Apostle afterwards. This is not the first time the number is significantly used; one of the governing bodies in Mormonism is the "Quorum of Twelve". One could suggest that if anyone is interested in the G12 model and has a problem with the spiritual attachment to the number 12, a differ-

ent number can be used. Comiskey in his thesis has suggested an optimum 10-15 people for an effective and manageable cell.

2. *By their fruits*: Not to mention names, some of the initial carriers of G12 are deemed "controversial". This raised doubts and questions on the motives behind their moves. Some of them were accused of financial misbehavior.

3. *Franchising or too rigid*: The founder seems to hold a position that the model must be used as it was given for the expected results to manifest. By following the G12 model in its entirety, the adoptee inherits a covenant relationship with MCI with his/her church becoming part of the MCI network. This would require multiple trips to Bogotá. It was even reported that MCI asked people to sign a written agreement to follow the model exactly. This is franchising and it has caused divisions among adherents. Many churches still use the same basic strategy as the G12 Vision, but have severed themselves from the Bogotá leadership, changing the name and terminology. Comiskey (2002) has provided a logical rebuttal to the rigidity:

> Castellanos took Cho's cell system and totally adapted it to fit his circumstances. If Castellanos had the liberty to change and adapt at will, we should take the same liberty. Let's follow Castellano's example and never lock ourselves into one closed system!!.

This criticism is justified if by now the G12 is still not flexible to allow adaptation, although Ricardo Becerra says it is now flexible. The leaders of the G12 must understand that freely God has given the vision, freely it must be released (Matt. 10:8). They must understand that even the Gospel of Salvation is adapted differently to different cultures because of differences in worldview. For example, the practice of spiritual warfare, breaking generational curses, and deliverance, that are included in the G12 system, are entirely viewed differently in different cultures and cannot be enforced as they are in Colombia.

The G12 vision has been challenged for other reasons, such as pragmatism and creating a Catholic-style hierarchy among Protestants. The G12 model has a good structure of discipleship. However, one concern is that people do not disciple in their area of gifting (see Chapter 5).

General Comments

We can admit that none of the current cell church models is perfect to fully carry out the Great Commission. No doubt, they will constantly need refinement and adaptation to improve its overall quality and effectiveness and serve Christ's purpose. The G12 model has received sizable amount of criticism, mostly because of controversy over some of its forerunners and the insistent of adoption instead of adaptation. If greed or other motivations other than implementing the Great Commission do no set in, the G12 structure is suitable for today's church without the constraint of adoption. The model is the only one that makes it possible for every believer to become a cell leader and practice it; this is important for implementing the Great Commission. The G12 application should vary from culture to culture and church to church and not adopted as is.

Splitting vs. Tree

The top cell churches today are given in Table 3.2. The main advantage of the tree over the splitting model is that everyone is ministered to and everyone is a minister. The goal that every believer must become a leader is easier to achieve with the Tree model than with the Splitting model. The main advantage of the Splitting model over the Tree model is that it is not hierarchal; all cells are at the same level.

Table 3.2: The Top Cell Churches Today

	Worship attendance	Cell groups	Macro Model
1. Yoido Full Gospel, Korea	250,000	25,000	Splitting
2. Deeper Life Bible Church, Nigeria	120,000		Splitting
3. Grace and Truth, Korea	105,000	1,000+	Splitting
4. Kum Ran Methodist, Korea	50,000	2,700	Splitting
5. Nambu Full Gospel, Korea	47,000		Splitting
6. Elim Christian, El Salvador	35,000+	11,000	
7. MCI, Bogotá, Colombia	35,000+	14,000	Tree
8. Showers of Grace, Guatemala	25,000	1,000+	Tree
9. Embassy of God, Kiev, Ukraine	25,000		Tree
10. Family of God, Indonesia	12,000	1000+	Tree
11. Faith Comm. Baptist, Singapore	11,000	700	Splitting

Source: partially from Comiskey (2000) and current book

Satellite

The top satellite churches are given in Table 3.3. From a global perspective, the satellite model is not primarily a church cell model; it is church planting and as such has been discussed under that section. However, most satellite churches grow their local churches by a church cell model.

Table 3.3: The Top Satellite Churches Today

	Worship attendance	Central church	Satellites	Cells
Methodist Pentecostal Church, Santiago, Chile	350,000	16,000	40	
Works and Mission Baptist Church, Abidjan, Ivory Coast	200,000	6,000	100+	18,000
Igreja Mana, Lisbon, Portugal	60,000		400	
New Life Fellowship, Bombay, India	50,000		250	1,200
Igreja da Paz, Santarem, Brazil	25,000		450	1,400
Family of God, Solo, Indonesia	18,000		50	1,500

Source: partially from Comiskey (2000)

SEVEN-SPHERE MOVEMENT

Seven-sphere is also termed 7-M (seven mountains). The basic idea of this movement is to divide the society culture into seven sub-cultures, called spheres. Although, evangelizing in different areas of influence of the society can be traced back to William Carey's mission to India in the first decade of the nineteenth century, it only started to gather momentum from 1975 when Loren Cunningham and Bill Bright met in Colorado; they had similar revelation of discipling in seven spheres of the society. Landa Cope and Sunday Adelaja are two others who have developed this concept.

THEOLOGICAL BEDROCK

Kuyper's doctrine of common or universal grace provides the theological bedrock for Missional Churches in general, for seven-sphere movement in particular. Synopsis of this theology has been stated above under "common theology". Kuyper regarded every sector of the society, such as, education, business, law, politics, and so on, as unholy. Kuyper explains that every sector (sphere) of the society is sinful and it is the duty of Christians to reconcile these spheres to God.

> What follows from this is Christian responsibility for engagement in every area of life... Thus the church receded in order to be neither more or less than the congregation of believers, and in every department the life of the world was not emancipated from God, but from the dominion of the Church. Thus domestic life regained its independence, trade and commerce realized their strength in liberty, art and science were set free from every ecclesiastical bond and restored to their own inspirations, and man began to understand the subjection of all nature with its hidden forces and treasures to himself as a holy duty, imposed upon him by the original ordinances of Paradise: "Have dominion over them". Henceforth the curse should no longer rest upon the world itself, but upon that which is sinful in it, and instead of monastic flight from the world the duty is now empha-

> sized of serving God in the world, in every position in life. (Kuyper)

In Chapter 2, it is stated that history serves a check and balance of errors of the past. If we go back to Chapter 2 on the Augustine-Pelagius debate in the early 5th century on grace and free-will, we will see that Pelagius' teaching could have been more acceptable if he understood the concept of universal grace. Pelagius argued that man has free will and is able to choose good from evil. It is through common grace that man has the ability to choose good from evil. However, man is incapable of choosing God or Salvation and is incapable of not sinning. This theology is further discussed in Chapters 4 and 5 and in *Grace Theology* (Olowe 2009).

IMPLEMENTATION

In 1994, the Embassy of God in Ukraine, pastored by Sunday Adelaja, started to provide community services in one area of influence, and gradually they added more and more spheres as Adelaja followed the instruction of the Holy Spirit. By 2007, the church had provided community services in six of the seven spheres and also uses it for winning souls. Most churches, such as Faith Community Baptist Church in Singapore or Catholic churches, have community service programs, but the concept of winning souls in spheres has never been done as by Adelaja and his church. We can emphatically claim that, the Embassy of God is the first known church executing the Great Commission in the seven spheres and it is producing fruits that remain (John 15:16).

One of the strong proponents of the seven-sphere ideology is Peter Wagner and the Church Growth Movement.

> We all agree that the society to be transformed is not just one big conglomerate, but a unified whole that is made up of several vital pieces, each one of which must take its own path toward transformation. These segments of society should be seen as apostolic spheres. (Wagner)

Most members of this movement have expressed beliefs in dominionism. Peter Wagner wrote:

> Our theological bedrock is what has been known as Dominion Theology. This means that our divine mandate is to do whatever is necessary, by the power of the Holy Spirit, to retake the dominion of God's creation which Adam forfeited to Satan in the Garden of Eden. It is nothing less than seeing God's Kingdom coming and His will being done here on earth as it is in heaven.
> --C. Peter Wagner, letter, May 31, 2007.

One of the objectives of this book is to show how to disciple in different spheres of the society; it will be dealt with in detail in later chapters, starting with its history in Chapter 6.

CRITICISM

The only criticism of the seven-sphere movement is from anti-dominionists in connection with dominionism. The subject will be covered later. In one of their blogs titled: "*Neo-*

Kuyperian Spheres", the "Discernment Research Group" writes:

> Did Loren Cunningham and Bill Bright just happen to have corresponding spiritual experiences where God told them a new way to make disciples of all nations, as described in the previous post? Did God really give them a vision of "categories of society" that were to be the church's "seven spheres of influence"? Or, perhaps, were they exposed to the teachings of Abraham Kuyper? The latter is a more likely scenario since Kuyper is behind the modern concept of "spheres." Bright may have been exposed to Kuyper's teachings while a student at Princeton Theological Seminary, which now houses the Abraham Kuyper Center for Public Theology.

The concept of using spheres of influence to define nations is not unbiblical. Actually, Landa Cope has provided biblical references to each of the spheres defined and so did Kuyper. We cannot refute or doubt the claim that God gave Cunningham and Bright the vision on the basis that Kuyper mentioned something similar before. They may have been influenced by Kuyper, however, we can see in several instances in both the Old and New Testaments that God repeats His words to different messengers. Using spheres to define nations has been the most effective way of discipling nations. God has given this idea to different people. Everyone can now be a missionary and evangelize.

STEWARDSHIP MOVEMENT

The stewardship movement is a progressive development from three roots (Beebe 1994): church support, mission support, and a concern for Christian use of resources. The International Catholic Stewardship Council (ICSC) was founded in 1962 with its mandate to find solutions to financial development, mission interpretation, and stewardship education. The financial support system was primary because tax support was no longer available, and churches needed to find ways of supporting their ministries. Today, this movement is found among the Catholics and the Reformed Faith. Although it sprang up primarily in response to finance problems facing the church, the movement fits into the new wave of discipleship. Every church group gives this broad definition for a steward: *"trustee of what belongs to God."*

> Stewards are managers of the many gifts God has given to us (ICSC) (www.catholicstewardship.org)
>
> Stewardship is the free and joyous activity of the child of God and God's family, the church, in managing all of life and life's resources for God's purposes. (Lutheran) (www.lcms.org)
>
> The ministry of stewardship calls each of us to be good trustees of these gifts for God. Stewardship involves the use of our time, talent, and treasure in a way that honors God. (Presbyterian) (www.upc.org)
>
> Stewardship is the lifestyle of the one who accepts Christ's lordship and walks in partnership with God, acting as His

MISSIONAL REFORMATION

> agent in managing His affairs on earth. (Adventist) (adventiststewardship.com)

> Stewardship is about making choices, as individuals and in community. It is more than giving money to the church. Stewardship is about being faithful disciples, caring for and managing all that God has given us. Stewardship is not just one part of Christian discipleship; it involves every aspect of life in all the stages of life. (United Church of Christ)

> Christian stewardship is a grateful and responsible use of God's gifts in the light of God's purpose as revealed in Jesus Christ. (www.episcopalchurch.org)

Stewardship Movement believes in dominionism:

> When God created the earth, he gave mankind a special role. He gave us dominion over the earth.
> (www.upc.org)

> It was in Eden that humanity first became stewards, and acted as God's agents on earth
> (adventiststewardship.com)

The movement also develops ministries in evangelism, giving, family care, and so on. It provides social services, most often to its members.

PURPOSE OF THE MOVEMENT

The Standing Rules of the Ecumenical Stewardship Center (ESC) (www.stewardshipresources.org) provides an expanded definition and purpose of stewardship as follows:

Stewardship is lived out in:
- living and telling the Good News;
- sharing God in seeking justice, peace, and the integrity of creation in an interdependent universe;
- wisely employing God-given human resources, abilities, and relationships;
- sharing the material resources we hold and giving them in service, justice, and compassion;
- providing for future generations, sharing in the life, worship, and responsible stewardship of the Church and of its mission

IMPLEMENTATION

If well implemented, this expanded definition has encompassed all the principles of good works (Chapter 4). Some groups create outreach ministries and provide services, but mainly to its members.

CRITICISM

Most practices and rhythms of the Stewardship Movements do not reinforce the broad definition; they focus more on finances. Each year there is a budget to prepare as well as a strategy to meet the budget. Reverend William Avery of the Lutheran Church laments about this:

> This annual reality, for which the congregational stewardship committee takes major responsibility, keeps bringing

home the message that stewardship means the finances of the church members for the church. Within 99% of the congregations, stewardship means money — money for the church! (William O. Avery)

CHURCHSHIFT MOVEMENT

Churchshift can summarily be defined as *"discipling nations by stewardship"*. Stewardship in Churchshift is not as practiced by the mainstream churches in which finance dominates the programs. The "nations" in the definition of Churchshift is important because it represents spheres of the society. Therefore, in the Churchshift movement, stewardship is important in discipleship, reaching out to the society by providing services in specific areas of influence (called spheres). The movement combines the three basic ideologies of the Missional Church described above, that is, church planting, church cell, and the seven-sphere systems. Through the vision received by the leader, Sunday Adelaja, the movement formally started in 1994. Adelaja published a book on this ideology in 2008. The Churchshift (ideology, theology, and application) will be discussed in this book.

DOMINIONISM

At the beginning of the current Chapter, it was stated that the trend in the postmodern movements is to pursue the Great Commission through aggressive evangelism. As a result, dominionism came to the lime light in a more pronounced way. Many of the postmodern movements have subscribed to dominionism. Dominionism or Dominion Theology is derived from the following passages:

> So God created man in His own image, in the image of God created He him; male and female created he them. And God blessed them, and God said unto them, be fruitful, and multiply, and replenish the earth, and subdue it: and have dominion over the fish of the sea, and over the fowl of the air, and over every living thing that moveth upon the earth (Genesis 1:27-28)

These verses are interpreted by dominionists as God's mandate to mankind to take over the management of the Earth. God reaffirmed dominion of man even after the flood (Gen. 9:2). Other passages that echo dominionism are:

> Knowest thou the ordinances of heaven? Canst thou set the dominion thereof in the earth? Job 38: 33

> Thou madest him to have dominion over the works of thy hands; thou hast put all things under his feet: Ps. 8: 6

The development of dominionism stems from Calvinism and was elaborated by Kuyper's doctrine of God's common grace which mandates man to influence all aspects of life.

Genesis 1:28 is thus taken as granting of a "*cultural mandate*". Dutch Reformed theologian, Abraham Kuyper, is notably called the father of Neo-Calvinism.

ANTI-DOMINIONISM MOVEMENT

Some American anti-dominionists accuse dominionism as a continuation of Rushdoony's ideals. Rousas John Rushdoony (1916-2001), a Neo-Calvinist, founded Christian *Reconstructionism* in the 1970s. His formulation of Dominion Theology is known through a series of books, importantly, "*Institute of Biblical Law*". Rushdoony believed that both the civic laws and moral laws in the Bible should be relevant to man. Several statements credited to Rushdoony, especially on death penalty, seem to be the issue with anti-dominionists in the USA; it turned dominionism into a political controversy. It is agreed that many statements credited to Rushdoony are provocative, especially his comments on civil rights groups and slavery. However, if we put aside Rushdoony's proclamations, God's mandate to man to have dominion according to the passages still stands. Many postmodern dominionists would not subscribe to some of Rushdoony's rhetoric. Man can still have dominion and subdue the world with Christ's message of love and good works. Being a dominionist does not mean that one subscribes to Rushdoony's views.

Some religious fundamentalists and atheists who do not believe in the Bible call dominionists "Christianists" to mimic the term "Islamists". After reading most of the criticism of the Christian anti-dominionists, none provides credible alternative interpretation of the passages in Genesis besides mere calling dominionism a heresy and aberrant theology. The mandate in the passage cannot be disputed. However, man's mandate to have dominion is only on God's creations and not on other men. Jesus gives us the mandate to win other men unto God. Kuyper also firmly rejected the idea of "dominion" of Christians over others. The concept of dominionism on spheres of society means that we have the mandate to have dominion, for example, over science culture, and not over men in science; not to change the culture, but to influence the culture with Christian values.

KINGDOM ON EARTH

Since man's mandate is to manage the earth, the dominionists also believe in the Kingdom of God on Earth. Here are some quotations:

> The Great Commission includes saving souls and planting churches, but it is much more than just that. God's mandate to us is nothing less than taking dominion of His entire creation here on Earth. (Peter Wagner in Churchshift)
>
> The purpose of the church, therefore, is to prepare for the triumphant return of the King by completing the dominion mandate. This assignment will successfully increase throughout the world in the last days as God's Kingdom rule is extended in the hearts and lives of countless disciples in great number and in those who have

> headship in the main cultural spheres of influence throughout the nations of the earth. (Mark Pfeifer)
>
> Every thought and saying of Jesus was directed and subordinated to one single thing ..., the realization of the Kingdom of God upon the earth, and this one phrase [Kingdom of God] sums up his whole ministry and his whole life's work. (Michael Grant)

The way it is being interpreted by many believers is that the Kingdom of God on Earth signifies establishing Kingdom principles on earth.

> Jesus didn't leave the Kingdom of God in heaven when He came to earth. He brought it with Him. The born-again believer is in the Kingdom at the moment. (Sunday Adelaja: Churchshift)

Some Christians argue that the church culture is the Kingdom of God on earth. Kuyper in his lecture on *"Calvinism and Religion"* defines the church as follows:

> The Church is a spiritual organism, including heaven and earth, but having at present its center, and the starting-point for its action, not upon earth, but in heaven.

This could be understood to mean that the Church mimics heaven culture and represents the Kingdom of heaven on earth. Still, others have understood the Kingdom of God to be essentially an ideal pattern for human society.

> The Kingdom is not primarily concerned with individual Salvation or with the future but with the social problems of the present... The parables of the Kingdom make it

> clear that in some sense, the Kingdom is present and at work in the world - George Ladd

In summary, many Christians agree that the Kingdom of God exists in three realms:

1. in heaven (Matt 8:11);
2. on earth now (Matt 12:28, 21:31);
3. on earth in the future when Jesus returns (2 Pet 1:11);

Numbers 1 and 3 represent eternal Kingdom. Kingdom of darkness coexists with the Kingdom of God only in number 2, that is, on earth now (Col. 1:13). Since the Kingdom of darkness is spiritual (Eph. 6:12), one can say that the Kingdom of God on earth now is also spiritual, physically being populated by the Church through Kingdom principles. What are Kingdom principles? Kingdom principles are acts or beliefs that do not violate the Will of God.

> Not every one that saith unto me, Lord, Lord, shall enter into the Kingdom of heaven; but he that doeth the will of my Father which is in heaven. Matt. 7: 21

Doing the Will of God is important to reach His eternal Kingdom. So, what is the Will of God? This question will be answered in the next Chapter as revealed by the Holy Spirit. It is also discussed in *Grace Theology* (Olowe 2009). The definition of Kingdom principles will be more refined in Chapter 8.

POINTS IN CHAPTER 3

The general name that has been adopted for the postmodern church is "Missional Church".

The central aim of a Missional Church is *cultural engagement and transformation*. The postmodern movements instill energy into evangelism to execute the Great Commission.

Five postmodern movements have been identified; they are church planting, cell, seven-sphere, stewardship, and Churchshift.

Most postmodern movements believe in *dominionism*; and they are *Kingdom driven*.

4. THE GOSPEL OF THE KINGDOM

WE are in a new generation; a generation of discipling nations and many concepts are coming up. In the last Chapter, we learned about the different models. This Chapter contains revelations received from the Holy Spirit and follow-up deductive reasoning. It is the key to this book and *"Grace Theology"* (Olowe 2009).

CLARIFICATION

Because of their strong anti-dominionism stance, some Christians have almost denied the Gospel of the Kingdom. In a part of their conclusion, labeled "Truth", the "Discernment Research Group" (herescope.blogspot.com) criticized the "seven-sphere doctrine" thus:

> The effect of "spheres" doctrine on two leaders of two of the most prominent evangelical mission groups has utterly changed the face of modern evangelical missions. It has changed the focus from spreading the Gospel, to changing the culture and society of nations by operating within and upon the "spheres." No matter what the original intent of Kuyper might have been, this is the ultimate conclusion. The biblical Gospel of Salvation has been transformed into the "Gospel of the Kingdom."

No, the Gospel of Salvation has not been transformed into the Gospel of the Kingdom. The Kingdom of God is actually the central teaching of Jesus Christ and not Salvation (which is just a part of it). For almost 2000 years now, the Church has taken the Gospel of the Kingdom to be the Gospel of Salvation. The revelation I received that will be related later enlightens us more about the Gospel of the Kingdom of God. In fact, the Gospel of the Kingdom is the only one mentioned in the biblical Gospel books at several instances. The term "Gospel of Salvation" was conceived by the Apostles and only mentioned in the epistles.

> And Jesus went about all Galilee, teaching in their synagogues, and preaching the Gospel of the Kingdom, and healing all manner of sickness and all manner of disease among the people. Matthew 4: 23, 9: 35

And this Gospel of the Kingdom shall be preached in all the world for a witness unto all nations; and then shall the end come. Matthew 24: 14

Now after that John was put in prison, Jesus came into Galilee, preaching the Gospel of the Kingdom of God. Mark 1: 14

I must preach the Kingdom of God to other cities also; for therefore am I sent. Luke 4:43

REVELATION OF THE GOSPELS

When I started this project, the first revelation I received was on the Kingdom of God. The Gospel of the Kingdom of God has been given unto us right from the Old Testament (Rom. 1:2). When I sought to understand the Gospels, I received two revelations, one scriptural and the other, pictorial.

SCRIPTURAL REVELATION

First, the Holy Spirit did not give me a direct clue but instructed me twice to study the "Great Commandments". As I followed the direction, more revelations came; I searched through the literature and I couldn't find this revealed to mankind before, only debates, and I asked "Lord, why have you kept quiet on this for so long?" The Holy Spirit directed me to this passage:

MISSIONAL REFORMATION

> How by revelation he made known unto me the mystery; (as I wrote afore in few words, whereby, when ye read, ye may understand my knowledge in the mystery of Christ) which in other ages was not made known unto the sons of men, as it is now revealed unto his holy apostles and prophets by the Spirit;. – Eph 3:3-6

The essential message from the passage, I believe, is that the right time is now for us to know that the Commandments form the basis of the Gospels. This is a new generation, a generation of relating to ourselves, a generation of peace.

In the Old Testament, there are 613 laws or so which are usually distributed over three broad categories: civil, ceremonial, and moral laws. It is the moral laws that are relevant to the Church today because the civil laws are mostly taken care of by the government and culture. The ceremonial have been taken care of by the blood of Jesus; these are the laws of which Paul says "we are not under the law". In the Great Commandments, Jesus cited two passages where all the laws in the Old Testament have been summarized into two. Let us consider the Ten Commandments, the primary moral laws written by God; the first 4 commandments relate us to God (Deut. 6:5), and the last 6 relate us to people (Lev. 19:18).

> Jesus said unto him, Thou shalt love the Lord thy God with all thy heart, and with all thy soul, and with all thy mind. This is the first and Great Commandment. And the second is like unto it, Thou shalt love thy neighbour as thyself. On these two commandments hang ALL the law and the prophets. Matt. 22: 37-40

The Great Commandments are illustrated in Figure 4.1. All laws and Gospels hang on these two Great Commandments. These two commandments summarize God's Will for mankind (Salvation and good works); they are also the basis of John Wesley's theology of Christian perfection. The two times Moses received the 10 Commandments, God gave him on two slabs of stone (Ex. 34:1); it was intentional. God separated the laws relating to God from those relating to men. This means that the Gospel of God is two Gospels combined into one.

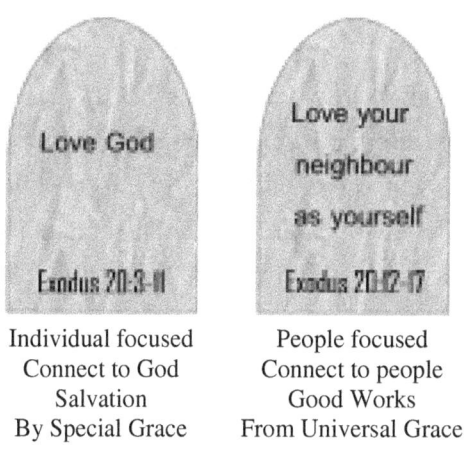

Individual focused / People focused
Connect to God / Connect to people
Salvation / Good Works
By Special Grace / From Universal Grace

Figure 4.1: The Great Commandments (Gospel of God)

The commandments are not optional:
> Whosoever therefore shall break one of these least commandments, and shall teach men so, he shall be called the least in the Kingdom of heaven: but whosoever shall do and teach them, the same shall be called great in the

> Kingdom of heaven. For I say unto you, That except your righteousness shall exceed the righteousness of the scribes and Pharisees, ye shall in no case enter into the Kingdom of heaven. Matt. 5:19-20

The Scribes and the Pharisees are known for their expertise in telling others what to do; they know the law but they don't obey them. But Jesus says we have to obey God. Also, at another occasion, Jesus says:

> Why callest me good? There is none good but one, that is, God: but if thou wilt enter into life, keep the commandments.

Also, Revelation 22:14 says those who do His commandments have right to the tree of life. So, to enter into eternal life, we must keep the commandments. The first Great Commandment is individual focused; so also is the Gospel of Salvation. The second Great Commandment is people focused; so also is the Gospel of Discipling Nations or of Stewardship. Stewardship and discipling nations are referred to as good works in the epistles.

PICTORIAL REVELATION

The illustration of Figure 4.2 is what I received in a vision as I ponder on Salvation and the Kingdom of God. I saw three images as shown in the Figure; in each there is a cross and a man at the arms of the cross. The "Kingdom" and "Salvation" labels are my interpretations.

4. THE GOSPEL OF THE KINGDOM

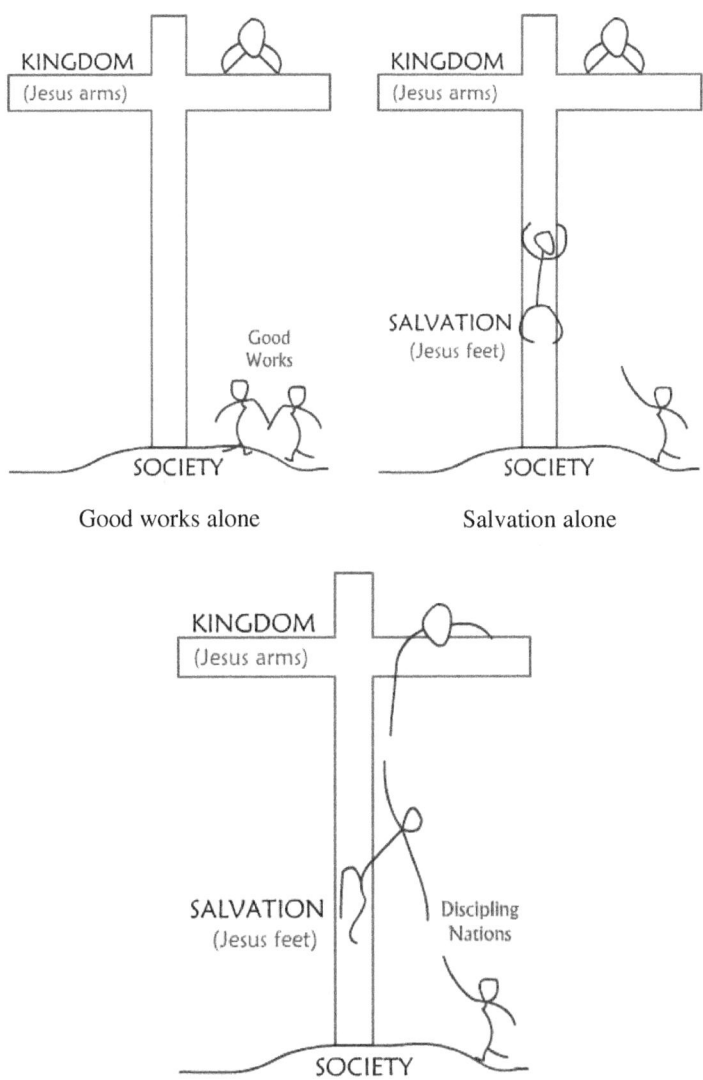

Figure 4.2: Reaching the Kingdom of God
WORK = With Others Reach Kingdom

1. In the first image, I saw two men, one helping the other, but both were on the ground. The man at the "Kingdom" stayed indifferent and was looking at them.
2. In the second image, I saw one of the men had climbed to where the feet of Jesus was nailed and which I label "Salvation"; he refused to help the other and was trying to climb the cross further, but the man at the "Kingdom" also refused to help him.
3. In the third image, I saw the man at "Salvation" helping the other man on the ground, then I saw the man at the "Kingdom" stretching his hand to help him climb.

My interpretation of the illustration is that one needs both Salvation and good works to enter into the Kingdom of God.

> Even so faith, if it hath no works, is dead, being alone.
> James 2:17

SECURITY OF THE BELIEVER

Somehow, the two Gospels, Salvation (love God) and Good Works (love others), as revealed are intertwined and both are needed for entrance into the Kingdom of God. The two Great Commandments instruct us to love God and others.
1. You cannot claim to love God if you don't love your neighbour (1 John 4:20). To see God you need to be holy and have peace with all men (Heb 12:14).

2. If we love one another, then God's love is perfected in us (1 John 4:12). If you seek the Kingdom of God by your good works and fail to seek "His righteousness" which connects you to God (Matt 6:33), your likelihood of getting to the Kingdom of God is slim.

The two premises above show that neither Salvation alone nor good works (or discipling nations) alone can get one into the Kingdom of God as also interpreted from the pictorial revelation. What God is telling us with this revelation is that we need to go back to the Old Testament and study His Will. The Church has focused on the Gospel of Salvation for so long. God's Will has always been for us to have a good relationship with Him and with our selves. In the second image of the pictorial illustration (Figure 4.2), refusing to help the other person is equivalent to *evil works*. The scripture clearly stipulates that Salvation with *evil works* (opposite of good works) will certainly debar one from the Kingdom of God. What of *no work* at all? This is covered in more details in *Grace Theology* (Olowe 2009).

FULL GOSPEL

The new revelation about the Kingdom of God now enlightens us on what full Gospel or a Missional Church is supposed to mean. A church that claims to be a full Gospel Church may not be in the biblical sense. A Full Gospel

Church must teach and practice both Salvation and good works. A full Gospel church must open its walls to the society. Once the walls are closed, the church is only concentrating on the Gospel of Salvation. In short, Full Gospel must mean to preach and practice the Gospel of the Kingdom of God which is in two parts.

Kingdom = Salvation + Good Works

In *"The Old Testament Template"*, Landa Cope indicated how she saw that though Africa was the most evangelized continent in the world, something had gone wrong and poor countries before the Gospel came had become even poorer. She explains how God revealed to her that *"the devastation you see is the fruit of preaching Salvation alone, without the rest of the biblical message."* She further wrote:

> The message that reformed Western cultures and built nations on solidly Christian values was not the Gospel of Salvation, but the Gospel of the Kingdom, which includes Salvation. The truths of the Gospel of the Kingdom are to transform us as they teach us how to live every part of life. Our transformed lives are then to be salt and light to our families, neighbourhoods, communities and finally, our nations, making them better places to live for everyone. Not perfect communities, not heaven on earth, but better because the influence of good is as great, if not greater, than evil.

Cope gets it right when she says "the Gospel of the Kingdom includes Salvation". Her further explanation in the text is what *good work* is about, "good is greater than evil". Good works, stewardship, and discipling nations will be used interchangeably in this book as the same Gospel. A Missional Church must be a Full Gospel Church.

OTHER NAMES OF THE GOSPELS

The Scripture sometimes refers to the Gospels by different names. For example, the term "Gospel of God" (Rom. 1:1; 15:16) also means Gospel of the Kingdom of God; it simply means it originated from God. The Ten Commandments are God's handwriting on two slabs of stone representing the Gospel of God in two parts. Acts 10:36 and 2 Cor. 5:18-19 seem to suggest that such a term as "Gospel of Peace" (Rom. 10:15, Eph. 6:15) could either be interpreted as the Gospel of Salvation or of good works. However, it is used in Rom. 10:15 to reflect good works. It is discussed further below. There are other specific terms such as "my Gospel" (Rom. 2:16; 16:25; 2 Tim. 2:8), "our Gospel" (1 Thess. 1:5), or "Gospel of the circumcision" (Gal. 2:7) used by Paul which could also mean Gospel of Salvation or of good works depending on how they are interpreted. The biblical names and references are provided in Table 5.1.

As we shall discuss in the last section of this chapter, the grace of God can also be categorized into two parts: *special grace* and *universal grace*; so, the Gospel of the grace of God could be more appropriately referred to as the Gospel of the Kingdom rather than the Gospel of Salvation. Common grace and universal grace will be used interchangeably in this book, though the term "universal grace" is preferred.

Table 4.1: Biblical Names and References of the Gospels

GOSPEL	OTHER NAMES	REFERENCES
Salvation	Gospel of your Salvation Gospel of Christ	Eph 1:13 Rom 1:16, 15:19,29; 1 Cor 9:12; 2 Cor 4:4, 9:13, 10:14; Gal 1:7; Philip 1:27; 1 Thess 3:2; 2 Thess 1:8
Good Works	Gospel of peace	Rom 10:15; Eph. 6:15
Kingdom of God	the Gospel Gospel of the grace of God Gospel of the blessed God Gospel of God	Numerous Acts 20:24 1 Tim 1:11 Rom 1:1, 15:16; 1 Thess 2:2-9

THE TWO GOSPELS

GOSPEL OF SALVATION

The Gospel of Salvation (Gospel of special grace) is derived from the first Great Commandment (Deut. 6:5; Matt 22:37):

> Thou shalt love the Lord thy God with all thy heart, and with all thy soul, and with all thy mind.

The love of God connects us to God. Because of sin, we can only receive Salvation by the mercy or special grace of God

(Gal. 1:6, 15; Rom. 3:24; Eph. 2:8). In the Old Testament, there are several instances when God shows His mercies if one repents according to the first four Commandments, which form the first Great Commandment. Even King Manasseh, one of the worst criminals in the Bible received God's mercy after repenting and connecting to God (2 Kings 21, 2 Chron. 33).

In the New Testament, by grace, God sent Jesus to the world as our Savior (John 3:16, 1 John 4:14), so that we might be reconciled to Him (2 Cor. 5:18). This shows that Salvation can now be received ONLY through Jesus Christ.

> Neither is there Salvation in any other: for there is none other name under heaven given among men, whereby we must be saved. Acts 4:12
>
> I am the way, the truth, and the life; no one cometh to the Father but by Me. John 14:6

The doctrine of Salvation (or doctrine of special grace), although has been developed from the early church fathers through the 16th and 17th century reformers, is still a subject of debate. However, the Gospel is to teach us how to:
o connect to God through Jesus Christ;
o maintain the connection (through prayers, fasting, worship, sacraments, and the word); this is where doctrinal differences come in; there are around 40,000 today;
o make repairs when the connection wears down;
o reconnect when there is a disconnection (backsliding).

MISSIONAL REFORMATION

These four cardinal principles are what the Church has been preaching and developing for almost 2000 years. The Gospel of Salvation is utilizing God's special grace. When Paul says in Galatians 1:6 there is no other Gospel of Christ, he means we cannot be saved by any other than Christ.

GOSPEL OF DISCIPLING NATIONS

The Gospel of Discipling Nations (Gospel of universal grace), also called Gospel of Good Works, is the implementation of the second Great Commandment (Lev 19:18; Matt 22:39).

> Thou shalt love thy neighbour as thyself.

It teaches us how to relate to people and our environment. The second Great Commandment also forms the basis of James' argument for good works (Jas 2:8). If you love your neighbor, you will provide services to him (Luke 10:30-37) and help him to reach his promised land (see Chapter 8).

What is Discipling Nations or Good Works?

It is using God's universal grace to serve and profit others.

> For we are his workmanship, created in Christ Jesus unto good works, which God hath before ordained that we should walk in them. Eph. 2: 10

> Well reported of for good works; if she have brought up children, if she have lodged strangers, if she have washed

the saints' feet, if she have relieved the afflicted, if she have diligently followed every good work. I Tim. 5: 10

The doctrine of universal grace will be elaborated further by the end of the chapter. However, we should note that man needs *special grace* for Salvation and *universal grace* for stewardship (good works). Special grace is the potential deposited on earth by the Lord Jesus Christ which is available to anyone who believes.

Purpose of Good Works

The purpose of good works is to please and glorify God.

> Let your light so shine before men, that they may see your good works, and glorify your Father which is in heaven. Matt. 5: 16

> That ye might walk worthy of the Lord unto all pleasing, being fruitful in every good work, and increasing in the knowledge of God; Col. 1: 10

> Having your conversation honest among the Gentiles: that, whereas they speak against you as evildoers, they may by your good works, which they shall behold, glorify God in the day of visitation. 1 Pet. 2: 12

How has it been implemented?

For so long, the Church has implemented this Gospel as an institution, in different forms, such as Parachurch organizations (engaging in social welfare and evangelism), charity or Non-Governmental Organizations (NGOs), Church Missions, and so on. There are close to 2 million non-profit organizations in the USA. Up till now, we have not really understood it as a Gospel and as a mandate for all believers. Missions have been implementing the Great Commission (Matt 28:18-20) which echoes the second Great Commandments, but in most cases, it is not being fully implemented. The Great Commission is more than making disciples; part of it reads: *"Teaching them to observe all things whatsoever I have commanded you (Matt 28:20)"*. Jesus Christ taught the disciples many things including, forgiveness, servanthood, peace, almsgiving, helping, loving, and so on. However, God has His plans. As we have seen in Chapter 3, in this new generation, God has been imparting knowledge and wisdom to mankind to develop this Gospel and implement it.

Benefits of Good Works

Reward in the Kingdom is in proportion of Good Works

> For the Son of man shall come in the glory of his Father with his angels; and then he shall reward every man according to his works. Matt. 16: 27
>
> Rejoice, and be exceeding glad: for great is your reward in heaven: for so persecuted they the prophets which were before you. (Matt. 5: 12; Luke 6:23, 35)

General Overview

The Gospel of Discipling Nations (Good Works) is many times mentioned alongside the Gospel of Salvation in the scripture and could also be called the Gospel of Peace. In Rom. 10:15, the full text of Is. 52:7, cited by Apostle Paul is:

> How beautiful upon the mountains are the feet of him that bringeth good tidings, that publisheth peace; that bringeth good tidings of good, that publisheth Salvation; that saith unto Zion, Thy God reigneth!

This passage obviously refers to Jesus Christ. Although the passage may be thought to be an example of Hebrew's synthetic parallelism, it may not be. In the NIV, the word "publisheth" is replaced with "proclaim"; Paul replaces it in Rom 10:15 with "preach the Gospel of". So, in Is. 52:7, there are likely two different Gospels mentioned. Also, in Heb. 12:14,

> Follow peace with all men, and holiness, without which no man shall see the Lord – Hebrew 12:14

Peace with men is the Gospel of Good Works; holiness is the Gospel of Salvation, see the Lord is in the Kingdom of God.

Some clergies and Christian organizations already teach the Gospel of Peace. I believe it is about this generation we are. We can understand more about this Gospel of Discipling Nations if we go back to the scriptures with the guidance of the Holy Spirit (for reflection: Ps. 119:33-40; Prov. 30:5; Is. 28:9-11; 1Cor. 2:6-14; 2Tim. 3:16-17; Heb. 1:1-2, 4:12; 2Pet. 1:20-21). Landa Cope, for example, provides biblical references to each of the spheres of influence.

MISSIONAL REFORMATION

Cardinal Principles

Theology of good works should cover how to:
1. make disciples (evangelizing) (Matt 28:19);
2. make peace (Heb. 12:14);
3. give (Luke 11:41; Acts 20:35);
4. be good stewards (Gen. 2:15; Matt 21:43);
5. enlighten the world (Matt 5:14-16; Rom 12:2);

These are the five cardinal principles of good works revealed to me. Each of these principles could be a sub-Gospel of their own; they all teach us how to portray the image of Christ to minister to others. In a nutshell, the assembly of the following sub-Gospels makes the Gospel of Good Works:
1. Gospel of Discipling;
2. Gospel of Peace;
3. Gospel of Giving;
4. Gospel of Stewardship;
5. Gospel of Light.

Two of the principles (discipling and enlightening) require one to receive salvation first. So, a regenerate provides a more effective good works. The Church Planting and Cell models alone (discussed in Chapter 3) do not have enough scriptural bases to implement the cardinal principles of Gospel of good works which is more than growing the church. Churchshift (Chapter 8 forward) has provided a package of ideologies that implements the Gospel of good works, at least to a great extent.

GRACE

GRACE AND GOOD WORKS

For over 1500 years now, the Church has been debating over the issue of grace and good works. All adopted and adapted doctrines (Calvinism, Augustianism, or Arminianism) agree that Salvation is possible only by God's grace, which cannot be merited. Paul echoes this in Eph. 2:8-10. But James seems to be saying something different, so arguments developed on which comes first, grace or good works.

> It is not as if a good life of some sort came first, and that thereupon God showed his love and esteem for it from on high, saying: "Let us come to the aid of these men and assist them quickly because they are living a good life". No, our life was displeasing to him. (Augustine)
>
> Good works come as a result of receiving grace through faith. The order cannot be changed, and this is an essential point of Christianity. No man can do anything to earn God's favor or approval. (www.acts17-11.com)

Arguments expanded to include other terms and into the order of grace, faith, Salvation, and good works, resulting in different permutations. After the Protestant Reformation, here is, for example, a writer comparing the Catholics' view with some other, each providing a rationale for the chosen order (justforcatholics.org):

MISSIONAL REFORMATION

> The works which merit eternal life originate in the grace of God: grace → good works → Salvation
>
> Good works are not the cause, but the fruit and result of Salvation: grace → Salvation → good works

The confusion in interpreting some of Paul's writings adds to the prolongation of the debate. The grace under debate here is later known to be one of two categories of grace from God. For so long the Church focused on arguing on grace and good works leaving God out of the equation. Firstly, good works do not add to anyone's Salvation, it is only special grace. Secondly, good works and Salvation are separate and both are required for the Kingdom of God; one does not lead to the other.

The issue of justification became one of the strong contentions in the Protestant Reformation (Chapter 2):
<u>Catholics say</u>: justification is by faith and good works;
<u>Luther says</u>: No, justification is by faith alone.

For this, the book of James is a pain in the neck for Reformed theologians; James writes *"shew me thy faith without thy works"* (James 2:18); this seems to contradict Paul. But in reality there is no contradiction (see *Grace Theology* (Olowe 2009)). Interestingly, Luther corrected the Catholics in error. Paul did not write the word "alone" in Rom 3:28; Martin Luther was the one who added it. The Catholics were partially right.

For the Catholics, a combination of faith and good works does not result in Salvation (that is where they were wrong), but in securing the Kingdom of God. The Catholics are correct if they say that justification for Eternal Kingdom is by faith (Salvation) and good works. The Church has made this error of thinking that good works is part of fulfilling Salvation or that Salvation and the Kingdom are the same. No, good works Gospel is the other slab God gave to Moses in Exodus 34:1 and which has not been sufficiently preached. At the foundation of the Church, the Apostles were preoccupied with the doctrine of Salvation trying to justify Christianity. Combating false teachings took much of their time.

For the Reformers, if one uses "grace" instead of "faith", it could be agued that because one also needs a grace (the universal grace) to implement good works, then it is right to say that "justification is by grace only"; in that case, grace means both special grace and universal grace. The two will be discussed in the next section. However, the Catholics seriously question (newadvent.org), and correctly too, the addition of the word "alone" after faith by Luther. They argue that Paul never says anywhere that justification is by faith alone. Judaism finds a way to harmonize faith and works by interpreting faith as "belief and action".

> When dealing with the texts of the "New Testament," the English language word "faith" must be interpreted in the Hebrew context it was originally conceived in by the author. As such, the word "trust" may be a better one to use, as it conveys a combination of belief and action. (Yashanet.com)

So, to the Hebrew, "justification by faith" means "justification by belief and action". The action is, of course, good works. The issue of justification is well covered in *"Grace Theology"* (Olowe 2009).

The grace-works debate is still alive today. Commenting on Michael Horton's argument in his book, *Christless Christianity*, that a semi-Pelagian understanding of the Gospel most endangers the American church, a blogger (churchplantingnovice.wordpress.com) on Dec. 19, 2008, wrote:

> Semi-Pelagianism, what I'll call a 50/50 understanding of the Gospel - we are saved by fifty percent grace and fifty percent works - God's assistance in our choosing. This Gospel unabashedly undermines the doctrine of original sin and total depravity.

Equating Salvation to grace and works was the same error of the Catholic Church as read above. Both Salvation and works need grace of God. The study of the works of Augustine, who had to deal with both the Pelagians and the semi-Pelagians (Chapter 2), should help us to understand how the issues started. The fact that they were dealt with 1500 years ago, and are still causing debate, shows that no amount of intellectual exercise can match the revelation from God Himself. The era of philosophical arguments is over, God is giving us the answer; He gave a hint to Landa Cope, and now He has advanced it with the hint of the Great Commandments. And coming to look at it, it is a simple equation, *Kingdom = Salvation + good works*

I listened to an Islamic cleric preaching on the Internet (faithoflife.com) that "Mercy of Allah and our action will take us to Paradise". So, Islam, as well, believes in the Gospel of "Allah" in two parts, mercy and action. So other Abrahamic faiths have this same belief. It is not surprising that there are close to 2 million charity organizations in the USA to fulfill the good works part of the Gospel. However, the Eternal Kingdom of God ("Paradise") is not guaranteed without Salvation through Jesus Christ.

UNIVERSAL GRACE AND SPECIAL GRACE

Kuyper explains universal (common) grace as follows:

> God arrested sin in its course in order to prevent the complete annihilation of His divine handiwork, which naturally would have followed. He has interfered in the life of the individual, in the life of mankind as a whole, and in the life of nature itself by His common grace. This grace, however, does not kill the core of sin, nor does it save unto life eternal, but it arrests the complete effectuation of sin, just as human insight arrests the fury of wild beasts.

As we have just discussed in the previous section, the debate on Salvation and good works would have been clearer if we understood that the Gospel of the Kingdom is in two parts, Salvation and good works. Similarly, the doctrine of grace would have been clearer if we understood that the grace of God is in two parts, universal grace and special grace. Augustine used the term "free grace" in his debate to refer to "special grace"; it was thought to be the same and only grace. Both graces are free. The grace discussed in the previous section is the "special grace".

In Chapter 3, we discussed about Kuyper's doctrine of common grace. Kuyper postulates two types of grace:

> There is a particular grace which works Salvation, and also a common grace by which God, maintaining the life of the world, relaxes the curse which rests upon it, arrests its process of corruption, and thus allows the untrammeled development of our life in which to glorify Himself as Creator.

> For not only did God create all men, not only is He all for all men, but His grace also extends itself, not only as a special grace, to the elect, but also as a common grace (gratia communis) to all mankind

So, the two kinds of grace we receive from God are:
- Common (or universal) Grace for life preservation, work, and to facilitate Salvation;
- Special Grace for Salvation and good works;

Both of them are available to all mankind.

The term "universal" is more appropriate than "common" in the sense that the Earth and its riches constitute part of this grace. On the doubt that two forms of grace could exist, Kuyper noted that without common grace, special grace cannot function because humans would not have been allowed to exist in such a sinful state. As we have read previously in this Chapter that the purpose of good works is to glorify God, both common grace and special grace are united in purpose for this reason. Universal grace assists man to be able to choose good from evil, but man is still not able not to sin. The doctrine of universal grace is solid and gives a clearer picture of God's grace and His Kingdom. It is deeply covered in *Grace Theology* (Olowe 2009).

Proof of Universal Grace

The most convincing passages "common grace" theologians use to defend its existence is found in Matthew 5:

> Love your enemies, bless them that curse you, do good to them that hate you, and pray for them which despitefully use you, and persecute you; That ye may be the children of your Father which is in heaven: for he maketh his sun to rise on the evil and on the good, and sendeth rain on the just and on the unjust. Matt. 5: 44-45

God, by His grace, sends rain to the just and the unjust and He is asking us to love everyone. Besides these passages, the passages below justify that God does not want the destruction of mankind; hence His universal grace is available to all.

> God saw all that He had made, and, behold, it was very good (Gen. 1:31); And I will establish my Covenant with you; neither shall all flesh be cut off any more by the waters of a flood; neither shall there any more be flood to destroy the earth (Gen. 9:11);
> For God so loved the world (John 3:16)

Without the universal or common grace, humans would not have continued to exist because of the total depravity. If there is no universal grace, how do we explain the many philanthropists that are non-believers? Why does the unbelieving world excel in many things? How do we explain God's gift of talents to all mankind? How do we explain divine favor to the unregenerate? How do we explain *conscience*? Wikipedia defines conscience as *the ability that distinguishes whether one's actions are right or wrong; it is an inner sense of what is wrong morally; it leads to feelings of remorse when one does things that go against his/her moral values.* Every man has conscience through the universal grace of God. Universal grace works us to receive the special grace.

> It is common grace which makes special grace possible, prepares the way for it, and later supports it; and special grace, in its turn, leads common grace up to its own level and puts it into its service. (Herman Bavinck)

John Cassian and Semi-Pelagians called special grace "cooperating grace" that enables a person to complete the process of becoming a Christian; they mixed up universal grace with special grace. John Wesley also called God's work in us, a "Prevenient grace", which undoes the effects of sin sufficiently that we may then freely choose to believe. Augustine almost also said it in this statement:

> It makes clear that though grace must come before any good works that are truly pleasing to God, grace necessarily leads to good works which are really God's works in and through us. – From Augustine's sermon

As can be seen above, good works can be interpreted as of two kinds: God's work in us and our outer manifestation of good works. Although Augustine thought it to be the same and only grace, "God's work in us" is actually the universal grace. Every mankind benefits from universal grace. It is the good works of God in us that serves two purposes: to work us to Salvation and for our own good works.

Manifestation of Universal Grace

Universal grace generally manifests in three forms: material, divine, and spiritual grace. The gifts or grace could be *intrinsic* (or innate), before man's birth, or *extrinsic* (or obtained), after birth. Divine grace manifests in two broad categories: divine restraint and divine favor; they are all extrinsic. Divine restraint communicates fear of God to prevent man from following the desires of his heart. There are cases in the Bible where the Lord showed favor to the unregenerate. Other universal gifts include gifts of the earth, destiny and virtues. God gives each man gifts of talent to succeed. Every man has a purpose of creation and an assignment to carry out. Universal gifts are well covered in *"Grace Theology"* (Olowe 2009). There are millions of them.

Man does not have the power to resist any grace because it is unmerited in the first place, but he may not respond to it. Universal grace assists man in making the right choices, but man does not have control over sin. Man is expected to use the universal grace for his benefits and to profit others. When utilized with special grace, universal grace produces good works to the glory of God.

POINTS IN CHAPTER 4

Revelations show that the Gospel of God is the two Great Commandments. God gave Moses the Ten Commandments in two slabs of stone representing the Gospel of God in two parts.

The Gospel of the Kingdom of God, or simply the Gospel of God, comes in two parts: Salvation and good works (or discipling).

Full Gospel means Gospel of the Kingdom. A Missional Church is a Full Gospel Church.

Gospel of Salvation connects us to God while good works connects us to each other. Neither Salvation alone nor good works alone can guarantee that one reaches the Kingdom of God.

Good work is using the God given universal grace to serve and profit others.

Special grace of God relates to Salvation while universal grace from God relates to good works.

Spiritual gifts are rewards received on Earth in proportion of Faith; Reward in the Kingdom is received in proportion of good works.

5. THEOLOGY OF GOOD WORKS

THE base theology of the Gospel of Discipling Nations (good works) is the theology of special and universal grace. This has been partially covered in the last section of Chapter 4. In this Chapter, we will develop theology specific to the five cardinal principles (sub Gospels) mentioned in Chapter 4, which are: discipling, peace, giving, stewardship, and light. The Gospel of discipling nations (good works) in essence is to mould us to be Christ-like, to do and teach what Christ taught and demonstrated. Jesus gave this commission before His ascension.

MISSIONAL REFORMATION

> And Jesus came and spake unto them, saying, All power is given unto me in heaven and in earth.
> Go ye therefore, and teach all nations, baptizing them in the name of the Father, and of the Son, and of the Holy Ghost: Teaching them to observe all things whatsoever I have commanded you: and, lo, I am with you always, even unto the end of the world. Amen. (Matt 28: 18-20)

DISCIPLING

Of the five sub-Gospels of good works, Discipling and Light stand out as the ones that require Salvation before they can be implemented. The basis of Discipling Gospel is the Great Commission of Matthew 28. Key words in the Great Commission are in verse 19:

> Go ye therefore, teach all nations ...

GO YE

We need to step out of the boundary of the church and radiate the Light (Matt 5:13). This is a charge to all Christians and not just to Pastors alone. All Christians must bear fruit (John 15:5).

THEREFORE

The word "therefore" is a deduction from the statement in the previous verse:

> And Jesus came and spake unto them, saying, All power is given unto me in heaven and in earth. - Matt 28: 18

Jesus has provided the necessary tools to carry out the Great Commission. He knew it would not be easy, so He has acquired all Power for us to use.

TEACH

The commission says teach and not just win. In other Bible versions, the phrase "make disciples" is used in place of "teach". Many believers are content with winning souls to Christ, but the Commission doesn't end there. Making disciples is not just winning souls, the souls should remain.

> Ye have not chosen me, but I have chosen you, and ordained you, that ye should go and bring forth fruit, and that your fruit should remain: that whatsoever ye shall ask of the Father in my name, He may give it to you. – John 15:16

We need to make use of our gifts to help others grow. The Great Commission therefore includes stewardship. Different views have emerged in the interpretation of the phrase "disciple all nations" as discussed in Chapters 3 and 4.

ALL NATIONS

We need to reiterate that the Church understood the importance of the Great Commission for centuries. It is the interpretation or understanding of the phrase "All nations" that

MISSIONAL REFORMATION

has evolved. For centuries, missionaries have taken the Gospel to countries to fulfill the Great Commission. This means that geography has been the sole basis of defining a nation. In the dictionary, the following words have been used as synonyms to describe the word "nation": country, land, people, population, realm, sphere, dominion, Kingdom, territory, terrain, area, region, etc. All the synonyms suggest that a nation can best be defined in three ways:

1. Geography (country, land, territory, terrain, area, region)
2. People (population, Kingdom, people, race, gender)
3. Influence (sphere, realm, dominion, domain, jurisdiction)

Note that tens of other ways of defining a nation, such as by education, religion, culture, and so on, have been packaged under "Influence" as sub categories. In his own understanding of "all nations", Apostle Paul used "people"; he divided people into Jews and Gentiles.

> For I speak to you Gentiles, inasmuch as I am the apostle of the Gentiles, I magnify mine office (Rom 11: 13)

Many have wondered why the Church has not been really effective to impact the secular world.

> Every Sunday, millions of Christians attend church services, and yet our surrounding communities and our society remains relatively unaffected. Many have asked the question "Is my church irrelevant?" (church-reform.com)

1. Missionaries have used geography (countries) for centuries to fulfill the Great Commission. Once they take the Gospel to a country, the impact and spread in that country be-

comes relatively slow. With diversity of cultures, there are many nations in any country; so, geography alone is not sufficient to disciple nations. In modern dispensation, the use of the third category, that is, area of influence, to define a nation is becoming predominant and adaptable to any country. "All Nations" is represented here by "all spheres" of the society. Once the Gospel is taken to a country through a missionary, it is more effective to spread the Gospel in that country through Missional Churches, with local missionaries working in specific spheres. Mission is more effective when the missionary works in his area of gifting. One of the aims of writing the *Missional Church* book edited by Guder is to sensitize North American Christians on the European cultural transfer through the contemporary missionary work.

> It has become increasing clear that Western mission had been very much a European-church-centered enterprise... The Gospel to which we testified around the world had been passed along in the cultural shape of the Western church...
> North America is a mission field – the idea sounds strange to North American Christians who associate 'mission' and 'missions' with something that happens in other parts of the world. (John Mulder in *Missional Church*)

One other advantage of spreading the Gospel through Missional Churches locally working in specific spheres is that it is a template that will work in every country of the world and will make worldwide inter-spherical cooperation easier. A missional reformation in the sports sphere in India may likely be adaptable in Ireland, and one that works in the arts sphere in France may also likely work in USA.

2. For so long, the Church has focused on the Gospel of Salvation alone, which is just half of the package of the Gospel of the Kingdom of God. Mission work has been considered as an option; but it is not. When Landa Cope asked God what has gone wrong in Africa that the nations remain poor in spite of vigorous evangelism. The Lord told her: *"The devastation you see is the fruit of preaching Salvation alone, without the rest of the biblical message."*

STEWARDSHIP

Good works, as used in the scriptures, is all about stewardship. Many parables of Jesus are about stewardship. Other cardinal principles of good works, discipling nations, giving, peace, and light could actually be covered under stewardship. However, they are covered separately for specificity and focus. The theology of stewardship here will be restricted to the basic definition and not the all-encompassing definition provided by the mainstream churches. Stewardship will be defined as:

> The management of resources God has given to us.

In order to do good work, God knows that we need resources, and He provides them to us by grace.

Scripture reading: Parable of the talents (Matt 25:14-30).

The resources (potentials) that God provides for mankind can be categorized as follows:
1. General material resources (time, Earth and its riches)
2. Personal resources
   a. Material resources (monetary, goods)
   b. Non-material resources
      i. Special gifts (Salvation, spiritual gifts)
      ii. Universal gifts (talent, virtues, etc)

All these resources are needed for stewardship with the exception of 2(a) (personal material resources) which is treated under "giving". The popular slogan of the stewardship movements is "Time, Talent, and Treasure"; the material resources are the "Treasures" while the non material resources are "Time and Talent (Gifts)".

GENERAL MATERIAL RESOURCES

The general material resources are universal material gifts (treasures and time) that are available to all mankind and that are not specific to any individual. The treasures are the Earth and all of its riches, including, but not limited to, plants, animals, minerals, air, and sea. God the creator is the owner of the Earth and all its resources (Gen. 1:1; Ps. 24:1, 50:10, 89:11, 104:24; Hag. 2:8; Acts 17:25; 1 Chr. 29:11), but He graciously allows us to use them (Deut. 8:18). Man's duty is to manage the resources for Him (Gen. 2:15; Ps 8:6).

PERSONAL NON-MATERIAL RESOURCES

The personal non material resources are made available to individuals by God for stewardship according to His purpose. They are obtained through the universal grace and the special grace as follows:
Universal grace: spiritual universal gifts;
Special grace: Salvation and spiritual special gifts;

All mankind are given the universal spiritual gifts but only believers receive the special spiritual gifts.

Universal Gifts

There are millions of universal gifts (virtues and talent) that are given to mankind. That is why no two persons have the same exact characteristics. One of these universal gifts is talent. Through universal grace, God endows individuals with the gift of talent within a particular sphere (see Chapter 6), according to His purpose for us; for example, in Exodus, Bazeleel received his in Arts and Science spheres.

> And I have filled him with the spirit of God, in wisdom, and in understanding, and in knowledge, and in all manner of workmanship, to devise cunning works, to work in gold, and in silver, and in brass, and in cutting of stones, to set them, and in carving of timber, to work in all manner of workmanship. (Exo. 31: 3-5)

Your talent is God's gift to take you to your promised land, your destiny, for your prosperity and fulfillment, if used according to His purpose. There are several other gifts given by the Creator to all mankind, to help the individual accomplish his purpose in life; this is covered extensively in *"Grace Theology"* (Olowe 2009). Augustine, a Church Father, said the very beginning of faith, even the thinking and willingness to believe, are gifts of God. Augustine's example is of universal grace.

Special Gifts

Special gifts are given to believers only. The first gift a believer receives is Salvation, and afterwards, the spiritual special gifts follow. Special gifts are needed for discipling.

Gift of Salvation

Salvation is received through special grace.

> For by grace are ye saved through faith; and not of yourselves: it is the gift of God: not of works, lest any man should boast. Eph. 2:8-9

Spiritual Special gifts

Spiritual special gifts are given to empower believers according to the proportion of faith (Rom. 12:3) and for the building of the Church. There are four lists of spiritual gifts distributed to believers in the epistles of Paul (Rom. 12:3-8; 1 Cor. 12:8-10; 1 Cor. 12:28; Eph. 4:10-11). In addition, Jesus has given us all Power on Earth and in heaven to carry out

MISSIONAL REFORMATION

His Commission (in gift of working miracles). The gifts are given to enable man to manage His affairs on Earth;

> As every man hath received the gift, even so minister the same one to another, as good stewards of the manifold grace of God. (1 Pet. 4:10)
>
> For we are His workmanship, created in Christ Jesus unto good works, which God hath before ordained that we should walk in them. Eph. 2:10

Out of gratitude for the free gifts, we should help and serve others. God gives us talent for the benefit of others. The gifts are needed to run all the sub-Gospels of stewardship, discipling nations, giving, peace, and light.

PROMISED LAND

The promised land is the ultimate goal of a believer; it should be a Churchshift ministry (Chapter 9) in one of the seven spheres that will be fully discussed in Chapter 6. The promised land is where God has purposed every man to be productive and fulfilled. Productivity and fulfilling God's purpose is the reason for the material and personal resources we receive from God.

> Not because I desire a gift: but I desire fruit that may abound to your account. – Philippians 4:17
>
> That ye might walk worthy of the Lord unto all pleasing, being fruitful in every good work, and increasing in the knowledge of God; Colossians 1:10

5. THEOLOGY OF GOOD WORKS

And let ours also learn to maintain good works for necessary uses, that they be not unfruitful. – Titus 3:14

Reason to be productive or fulfilled:

Herein is my Father glorified, that ye bear much fruit, so shall ye be my disciples. – John 15:8

Here are some quotes on potential, purpose, and fulfillment:

Whatsoever thy hand findeth to do, do it with thy might; for there is no work, no device, nor knowledge, nor wisdom, in the grave, whither thou goest. Eccl. 9:10

All Christians are called to develop God-given talents, to make the most of their lives, to develop to the fullest their God-given powers and capacities. (Oswald Sanders)

Nothing is worse on earth than death of a dream. The wealthiest spot on earth is the cemetery; there is filled with books that were never written, ministries that never started, music that was never played, poetry that was never read – that wealth is called potential (Myles Munroe)

Potential is what you can do and that you have never done (Myles Munroe)

You are the only person on earth who can use your abilities (Rick Warren)

Make your goal to be a Kingdom builder rather than just a wealth builder (Rick Warren)

The more you till your promised land, the more treasures you discover (Sunday Adelaja)

MISSIONAL REFORMATION

GIVING

Giving is the stewardship of our personal material resources. It is a very important principle of good works and it has to be treated separately; it can redeem a believer from the sins he commits after receiving Salvation. Giving cuts across both the Gospel of Salvation and of good works. The Bible requests us to give to God and to men; anything relating to God is the Gospel of Salvation and anything relating to men is the Gospel of good works. While giving to God is mandatory, giving to man is charity and is counted for us as righteousness (Luke 11:41) and can redeem us from our personal sins (Matt. 5:7) to justify us of works.

FORMS OF GIVING

There are three principal ways to give to God or to man. These three are also the popular slogan of the stewardship movements: Time, Treasure, and Talent. However, in their consideration of Treasure, they only speak of finances. Treasure is both monetary and goods; both are acceptable forms of giving one's treasure. To execute the work of God in Exodus 30, 2 Kings 12, 2 Chronicles 24, and Nehemiah 10, we see that the people contributed time, talent, money, and goods. So, all four are acceptable ways of giving to God or to man. It is even a practice in the Old Testament to pay tithes of goods (Gen. 14:20-21).

GIVING TO GOD

Giving to God should be regarded as part of a believer's duty to maintain Salvation. It is applicable to *Gospel of Salvation*; it is included here to drive in some points. As an acknowledgment that all things came from Him, the Lord directed that a portion of His resources should be returned to Him to sustain His worship. We need to give to God in forms of Time, Treasure, and Talent. We can use our talent to work in the house of the Lord; we give our time to Him in fellowship, and our treasure in money and goods. We are going to examine only the financial aspect here because it is critical.

Financial Ways of Giving to God

The Church has inherited from the Old Testament the practice of financially giving to God through tithes and offerings. For what God has given to us, we have a financial obligation to Him. Tithing is giving a tenth of one's income. Offerings are given as determined by the individual's evaluation of what he is able (Luke 21:1-4). The more you give, the more you receive (2 Cor. 9:6-7, Luke 6:38). Tithing is a controversial issue among Christians. Some say it was the Old Testament tradition of the Hebrews to compensate the Levites (Num. 18:24). The tithing system did not even originate with the Hebrews. Before the nation of Israel was established, Abraham paid tithes to Melchizedek the priest (Gen. 14:20) and Jacob promised to pay tithes to God (Gen. 28:22). Tithing was legally instituted as the nation of Israel was about to be established (Lev. 27:30, Deut. 14:22) and it became one of the divinely ordained statutes. The New Testament teaches about giving to God but is silent about tithing. Jesus mentioned the tithe only twice, one in rebuke of the Pharisees (Matt. 23:23; Luke 11:42) and the other in a parable of two men praying (Luke 18:12). The only reference to tithing in the epistles is in Heb. 7:5-9, where the story of Abraham and Melchizedek is recounted. However, Jesus admired sacrificial giving (Mark 12:41-44; Luke 21:1-4), and preached about giving (Luke 6:38). Paul also preached about giving cheerfully from the heart (2 Cor. 9:7) as God has prospered us (1 Cor. 16:1-2). It is our duty to give to support the work of God. Grace Doctrine Church provides a balanced view about tithing in their doctrinal statement:

> Tithing was a system of income tax in the Old Testament. Thus, tithing was not a spiritual function but a civic obligation. In fact, being a part of the Mosaic Law, it was directed only to the nation of Israel. The people of Israel were to make two annual tithes; 10% for the maintenance of the Levitical Priesthood (Numb 18:21,24) and another 10% for the Levitical sacrifices (Deut 14:22-24). Since the priesthood and sacrifices are no longer valid, these tithes are not pertinent today. Every third year, Israel was required to collect a charity tithe of 10% for those who legitimately needed help (Deut 14:28-29; Mal 3:8-10). This is the only tithe pertinent today. As far as giving to the church is concerned, this should be based solely on your personal motivation and as God has prospered you. You may give whatever percentage you wish before the Lord. (gdcmedia.org)

Global Giving Trend

Worldwide statistics provided by Barrett and Johnson (2009) on Christian giving to the Church are as follows:

Personal income of church members	$18,520 billion
Giving to Christian causes	$410 billion (2.21%)
Churches' income	$160 billion (0.86%)

The percentages are on personal income. The Church receives less than 1% from members. Let us make a grotesque error of allocating all Christian contributions as tithes; the total percentage (3.07) is still less than 10. This means that the average Christian doesn't give enough to the church. There are three questions that can be raised from these statistics:

1. Are people sceptical to give to the church?
2. Is the church not teaching correctly about giving?
3. Are Christians diverting their finances to other causes (such as individual ministries) that are not tracked?

The greed and corruption of some ministers (or "false teachers") may have discouraged believers from giving to the Church; Peter warns about false teachers:

> And through covetousness shall they with feigned words make merchandise of you (2 Pet 2:3)

Here is Application Bible's comment on the verses:

> Teachers have a right to financial support (1 Cor 9:1-14; Gal6:6; Tim 5:17,18), but is money the teacher's or group's prime motivation? Before you send money to any cause, evaluate it carefully. Is the teacher or preacher

clearly serving God or merely promoting his/her own interests? Will the person or organization use the money to promote valid ministry, or will it merely finance further promotions or extravagant lifestyles?

Nevertheless, God wants us to give generously back to Him. Many Christians attend church services in expectation to be blessed by God; we are blessed in return when we bless God. Paul's exhortation to the Ephesians elders recalls the words of Jesus Christ: *"It is more blessed to give than to receive"* (Acts 20:35).

Why Give to God

1. To acknowledge that all things came from Him (Lev. 27:30, 1 Chr. 29:14);
2. It is God's command (Deut. 14:22-25);
3. He is responsible for your wealth (Deut. 8:18);
4. To honor Him (Prov. 3:9);
5. Your treasure is in Heaven (Matt. 6:19-21);
6. To finance the work of God (Exo. 30:12-16; 2 Kings 12:4, 5; 2 Chr. 24:4-13; Neh. 10:32, 33);
7. To be blessed (Mal. 3:10; Luke 6:38; 2 Cor. 9:6).

GIVING TO MAN

Giving to men is part of good works. The scripture commands us to take care of the widows, the fatherless, and the needy. The scripture also tells us that our generosity to the needy is counted for us as righteousness.

> But rather give alms of such things as ye have; and, behold, all things are clean unto you. Luke 11:41

According to the scripture, there are always poor people in the society and God commands us to be generous to them.

> For the poor shall never cease out of the land: therefore I command thee, saying, Thou shalt open thine hand wide unto thy brother, to thy poor, and to thy needy, in thy land. Deut. 15:11

Materially giving to man is termed "almsgiving" in the Bible. It is an act of helping the poor and needy; almsgiving is an expression of compassion, empathy, and love for the poor and needy. Giving can be done directly to the needy or through charitable organizations. In the USA, there are about 1.8 million registered non-profit organizations.

Forms of Giving to Man

There are three ways to give to man (as also unto God): Time, Talent, and Treasure. All three have values; you can give one way or another.

> A busy traveling salesman may not have the time to work hands-on with a charity group, but he can donate money or goods. A college student may not have extra cash or goods but can certainly contribute time. Everyone can give something (charitywatch.org)

Treasure

Treasure is giving materially (monetary or goods) to man. Money is obviously the simplest way to give, and usually it can be done quickly to charitable organizations through the Internet or by land mail. Goods, such as used clothes, books, furniture, and so on, may also be given to individuals or charitable organizations that have need of them.

> You may think that old, gently worn coat will never be worn again, but there are plenty of organizations who would be thrilled to give that coat to someone who needs it. (charitywatch.org)

Time and Talent

Your time and talent are what God needs for you to develop your own *Missional* ministry (your promised land); it has been discussed under "Stewardship" and will be discussed further in Chapters 9 and 14 (Volume 2). You may make your time and talent available to individuals or charitable organizations that have need of them.

Why Give to Man

1. Almsgiving could be a form of redemption of personal sin and from calamity (Prov. 11:4, 16:6, 21:4);
2. It is God's command (Deut. 15:11; Luke 12:33);
3. To honor Him (Prov. 3:9)
4. Your reward is in heaven (Matt. 6:1-18; Luke 12:33-34)
5. To be blessed (Deut. 15:10; Prov. 28:27);
   > He that giveth unto the poor shall not lack: but he that hideth his eyes shall have many a curse. (Prov. 28:27)

PEACE

Christians should be concerned with two kinds of warfare, worldly and spiritual (Eph. 6:18). The Bible talks about two kinds of peace:
- Inner peace with God;
- Outer peace with ourselves.

Therefore, like giving (giving to God and giving to man), the Gospel of Peace also exists in both Salvation and good works. The Prince of Peace, Jesus Christ, has reconciled us to God so that we can have peace with God (Rom 5:1,10; Eph. 2:13-18; 2 Cor. 5:18-19). If we have inner peace with God, we are equipped for the spiritual warfare. This should be covered under the Gospel of Salvation. But Jesus is requesting us to reconcile men to Him, for inner peace, as He has done for us.

> And all things are of God, who hath reconciled us to Himself by Jesus Christ, and hath given us the ministry of reconciliation; to wit, that God was in Christ, reconciling the world unto Himself, no imputing their trespasses unto them; and hath committed unto us the word of reconciliation. (2 Cor. 5:18-19)

We can achieve that through making disciples. The Bible also requests us to have outer peace with ourselves:

> Therefore if thou bring thy gift to the altar, and there rememberest that thy brother hath ought against thee; Leave there thy gift before the altar, and go thy way; first

> be reconciled to thy brother, and then come and offer thy gift. Matt. 5:23-24
>
> Follow peace with all men, and holiness, without which no man shall see the Lord – Heb. 12:14

The ultimate goal of world peace is as described in Isaiah 2:1-4 for an ideal world when war instruments are turned into farming tools.

Jesus' main teaching on peace is found in Matt 5:38-44. I heard a preacher say peace on earth is Jesus' business and not ours. I guess he is saying that from a believers' interpretation of the book of Daniel and Revelations. We don't have to move ahead of time; Jesus did not say we should wait for him to make peace on earth. So, we don't have to wait till the second coming of Christ to have peace on earth. It has to start with us making peace with ourselves.

PURPOSE OF PEACE

1. To have peace with God and perfection (Matt. 5: 48);
2. To reconcile men to God;
3. To set mankind free from destructive cycle of violence at all levels of life;
4. To be the light of the world, proclaiming the Gospel of peace and reconciliation (2 Cor. 5:19) through Jesus Christ who is our peace (Eph. 2:14).
5. Love of all human beings, even the enemy (Matt. 5:44)

5. THEOLOGY OF GOOD WORKS

6. Community and solidarity; there is only one citizenship in Heaven (Phil. 3:20) for the Body of Christ (1 Cor. 12:27).

> When the peaceable way of Jesus becomes an inseparable part of the message and mission of the whole church, we should be seeing our buildings filled with disciples who know that they are truly being saved. Grounded in that faith, they will hold strong convictions on Kingdom values, including peace, justice and service. (J. R. Burkholder)

RESPONSIBILITY OF THE CHURCH

1. Addressing conflicts (reconciliation) (2 Cor. 5:18-19);

   > Peace service is needed wherever tensions are increasing or conflict has already broken out. The experiences we gather in learning to practice reconciliation in the daily life of a Christian community can help us tremendously in this kind of service to others (Von der Recke).

2. Becoming relevant in peace efforts at all levels;

   > The mission of Jesus Christ and his church is to serve all peoples regardless of their government, ideology, place of residence, or status...The church is called to look beyond human boundaries of nation, race, class, sex, political ideology, or economic theory and to proclaim the demands of social righteousness essential to peace.

3. The Church is to be a people whom no one should fear;

   > If Jesus Christ is our peace, then our message consists in just living as peace communities in which the word peace becomes incarnated. Peace will be lived out in prayer, in

worship, in sharing and working together (Von der Recke).

4. Peace and justice are the responsibilities of the Church;
   But with righteousness shall he judge the poor, and reprove with equity for the meek of the earth: and he shall smite the earth with the rod of his mouth, and with the breath of his lips shall he slay the wicked. Is. 11:4

   Peace convictions, grounded in adequate theology, should be as fundamental as talking about Jesus, the Gospel, the meaning of Salvation. Peacemaking is part of the essential work of the church; it must be upheld and modeled by all those in leadership (J. R. Burkholder).

HOW DO WE MAKE PEACE?

The following are the principles of peacemaking based on the teaching and life of Jesus. Some of them apply to both inner and outer peace. Burkholder in his sermon on the Gospel of Peace highlighted some of them.
- forgiving; Matt 18:27-35
- loving and blessing those who wrong us (Matt 5:44)
- being ready to suffer rather than to retaliate against violence (Matt 5:38, John 18:11)
- trusting God for our life, protection, and security;
- pursuing alternatives to violence;
- sacrifice (pride, injustice, etc.);

The doctrine of Forgiveness is important for believers to understand; it is an important weapon for individual Christians to retain a position in Heaven. This is more elaborated under "Justification" in "*Grace Theology*" (Olowe 2009).

LIGHT

This sub-Gospel can only be implemented by a believer after Salvation, and it is supposed to give a set of guidelines to demonstrate Kingdom principles and to help a believer not to fall from grace while interacting with the society. The guidelines may vary from sphere to sphere because of differences in worldview. It is important.

PRINCIPLES

Who we are
Salt and light
> Ye are the salt of the earth – Matt 5:13
> Yea are the light of the world – Matt 5:13

Source of Light
Jesus and the word of God are the sources of light
> Thy word is a lamp unto my feet, and a light unto my path. Ps. 119: 105

> For thou art my lamp, O Lord: and the Lord will lighten my darkness. 2 Sam. 22: 29

> The Lord is my light and my Salvation. Ps. 27: 1

> Then spake Jesus again unto them, saying, I am the light of the world: he that followeth me shall not walk in darkness, but shall have the light of life. John 8: 12

Our Responsibilities

Abide in Christ

> I am the vine, ye are the branches: He that abideth in me, the same bringeth forth much fruit: for without me ye can do nothing. – John 15:5

> The Lord is my light and my Salvation; whom shall I fear? the Lord is the strength of my life; of whom shall I be afraid? Ps. 27: 1

Be Christ-like

> As long as I am in the world, I am the light of the world. John 9: 5, 8: 12

> In Him was life; and the life was the light of men. The true Light, which lighteth every man. John 1: 4, 9

> This then is the message which we have heard of him, and declare unto you, that God is light, and in him is no darkness at all. I John 1: 5

Do not conform

> Be not conformed to this world, but be transformed by the renewing of your mind ... (Rom. 12:2)

Your action should reflect light

> Walk in the light of the Lord. Isa. 2: 5

> A city that is set on an hill cannot be hid (Matt 5:14); Let your light shine before men, that they may see your good works, and glorify your father which is in heaven (Matt

5:16); For ye were sometimes darkness, but now are ye light in the Lord: walk as children of light. (Eph. 5:8)

Impart Kingdom principles to the society

A light to lighten the Gentiles... Luke 2: 32

And the light shinneth in darkness; and the darkness comprehended it not. John 1: 5

Do ye not know that the saints shall judge the world? (1 Cor. 6:2)

That ye may be blameless and harmless, the sons of God, without rebuke, in the midst of a crooked and perverse nation, among whom ye shine as lights in the world; Philip. 2: 15

CONSEQUENCES

But if the salt have lost his savour, wherewith shall it be salted? It is thenceforth good for nothing, but to be cast out, and be trodden under foot of men – Matt 5:13

Every branch in me that beareth not fruit He taketh away: and every branch that beareth fruit, He purgeth it, that it may bring forth more fruit. – John 15:2

Christians are in fault, if the world is not enlightened, because they can have any degree of spiritual illumination which they need to carry forward and complete the enlightening of the world. (Charles Finney)

POINTS IN CHAPTER 5

The base theology of the Gospel of Good Works is the theology of universal (common) grace.

The five cardinal principles, making disciples, making peace, giving, being the light of the world, and stewardship, are sub-Gospels good works.

The Gospel of Good Works in essence is to mould us to be Christ-like, to do what Christ taught and demonstrated.

Spiritual special gifts are (a reward) received on Earth in proportion of Faith; Reward in the Kingdom is received in proportion of good works.

6. THE SEVEN SPHERES

EVERY Christian is a minister of the Gospel. A sphere is the area a minister of the Gospel exerts his/her influence. In Sunday Adelaja's words, it is his/her promised land.

THE CONCEPT OF SPHERES

In Chapter 5, we defined the term "all nations" as "all spheres" of the society; discipling all nations means discipling all spheres of the society. This concept enables a Missional Church to be effective in its community without having to go across countries. Abraham Kuyper, Prime Minister of the Netherlands 1901 to 1905, could be credited to be the first to use jurisdictions to define nations in theology.

In the Foreword to Landa Cope's *"An Introduction to the Old Testament Template: Rediscovering God's principles for discipling all nations"*, Loren Cunningham wrote (about spheres):

> This is not new, but a renewed revelation. In the 19th Century, Abraham Kuyper of Holland had a list of four 'jurisdictions' from God through His Word. William Carey, a London shoe cobbler who became a pioneer missionary in India, launched programs in all seven spheres of society. He published the first periodical in all of Asia, founded a lending bank for the poor, started schools, planted churches, and helped change laws to stop widow burning, to name a few...

SPHERE MODELS

WILLIAM CAREY MODEL

William Carey (1761–1834) dubbed "Father of Modern Missions" was a shoemaker in England before the Lord led him to co-found the Baptist Missionary Society in 1792 with eleven others. William Carey introduced Christians to missions on a grander scale than the Pietists who created Christian groups in tiny islands. It was when he went to India as a missionary that he used the seven spheres of influence to evangelize. For seven years Carey had daily preached Christ in Bengali without a convert. Then he started to influence the society through reforms in:

1. Family
2. Science
3. Economics and Commerce
4. Government
5. Education
6. Religion
7. Humanity

> In the social heirarchy of the Raj, religious specialists, such as missionaries and clergymen, occupied a rather humble position on the periphery of fashionable European society. Even among themselves, the missionaries were subdivided among several denominational subcastes with their own territorial sphere of influence. (csichurch.com)

ABRAHAM KUYPER MODEL

As covered in Chapter 3, Dutch reformer Abraham Kuyper was the first to provide theological backbone for imparting Christianity in different spheres of life through his doctrine of common grace. This doctrine has been covered in Chapter 4. He is considered the Father of Dutch Neo-Calvinism. Kuyper's active involvement in Dutch politics and church reforms helped in the development of his spiritual social reforms skills. While in Dutch parliament, he showed particular interest in education, especially on equal financing of public and religious schools. His writing of "Our Program" in 1876 laid the foundation for the Anti Revolutionary Party.

> The concept of sphere sovereignty was very important for Kuyper. He rejected the popular sovereignty of France in which all rights originated with the individual, and the state-sovereignty of Germany in which all rights derived from the state. Instead, he wanted to honour the "intermediate bodies" in society. – Wikipedia

His six lectures at Princeton University in 1898 under the auspices of The Stone Foundation, covered application of Calvinism in four areas of life (www.lgmarshall.org):

1. Religion
2. Politics (State)
3. Science
4. Art

Although he wrote about applying Calvinism in these four spheres, Kuyper actually recognizes that there are other spheres from this statement:

> In a Calvinistic sense we understand hereby, that the family, the business, science, art and so forth are all social spheres, which do not owe their existence to the state, and which do not derive the law of their life from the superiority of the state, but obey a high authority within their own bosom; an authority which rules, by the grace of God, just as the sovereignty of the State does.

CUNNINGHAM AND BRIGHT MODEL

In August of 1975, Loren Cunningham, founder (with wife) of the Youth With A Mission (YWAM), received in prayer from the Lord the seven spheres of the society. A day after he received this revelation, he and his wife Darlene, were invited to meet the founders of Campus Crusade for Christ, Bill and Vonette Bright, in Colorado. At the meeting, Bill announced that God had shown him the strategy for discipling a nation and showed a list that included the same areas Cunningham provided (David Saw 2008). This list, shown below, will be referred to as the Cunningham and Bright model (www.reclaim7mountains.com):

1. Family
2. Church
3. Education
4. Media (electronic and printed)
5. Celebration (arts, entertainment and sports)
6. Economy (research and development, production, sales and service)
7. Government (all branches)

Loren also founded the University of the Nations in 1978.

> These seven spheres of influence will help us shape societies for Christ. - Loren Cunningham (1988)

> As we disciple the nations by giving them godly economic systems, Bible-based forms of government, education anchored in God's Word, families with Jesus at the head, entertainment that portrays God in His variety and excitement, media that is based on communicating the

> truth in love, and churches that serve as sending stations for missionaries into all areas of society, we will see the fulfillment of the Great Commission and multiplied millions coming into the Kingdom of God. Jesus promises that as we do this, 'I am will you always, even to the end of the age' (Matthew 28:20). Loren Cunningham

The revised version of Cunningham and Bright Model (Parsley p. 29) has been widely used in the United States:

1. Arts, Entertainment, and Sports
2. Commerce (Business), Science and Technology
3. Church (and Religion)
4. Media
5. Education
6. Family (Home)
7. Government and Politics

The revised Cunningham and Bright Model is discussed fully at www.reclaim7mountains.com.

COALITION ON REVIVAL MODEL

In 1984, as many as 112 Christian leaders and theologians came together to form the Coalition on Revival (COR). According to its statement at the International Church Council Project website (www.churchcouncil.org/Reformation_net), COR's basic mission is *"to encourage and help the universal Church of Jesus Christ obey God's Cultural Mandate and the Great Commission"*. COR's founding director is Dr. Jay Grimstead. In 1986, COR published the 17 Worldview Documents; these emphasize fundamental biblical principles governing 17 spheres of human life. The 17 spheres of influence are:

1. Law
2. Government
3. Social / Political
4. Education
5. Discipleship
6. Medicine
7. Psychology / Counseling
8. Science / Technology
9. Art / Media
10. Economics
11. Business / Occupation
12. Evangelism
13. Christian Unity
14. Family
15. Poor / Hurting
16. Pastoral Renewal
17. Colleges / Universities

These 17 areas of influence are actually expanded version of the more popular 7-sphere models. As a matter of fact, if broken down further, the number of spheres is more than 17. Sports and Religion have not even been considered in the COR model. However, all areas of influence can be classified under the 7 major areas that are more popular. We can see that in the COR model above, Government, Political, and Law, can be grouped under one sphere. As defined in Chapter 1, the word "social" cannot be used as a sphere of influence, it represents the entire society.

MISSIONAL REFORMATION

LANDA COPE MODEL

Cope lived and worked in North Africa, the Pacific and Europe. She currently lives in South Africa. Cope has worked with Youth With A Mission (YWAM) since 1971, preparing young missionaries to communicate the Gospel and to disciple nations; she is the founding International Dean of the College of Communications for YWAM. In 2005, Cope founded The Template Institute committed to providing comprehensive Biblical approach to issues. On the Institute's website, Cope has listed eight domains of reference from the Bible, namely:

1. Arts and Entertainment
2. Church
3. Communication
4. Economics
5. Education
6. Family
7. Government
8. Science and Technology

Cope added:
> This is a list of suggested Scriptures for starting to study the Bible from the perspective of domains. The lists are not exhaustive and we ask that you take into consideration the overlap of domains in many of the text. However this will give you a "jump start" in the process.

Cope's model is the only one that has Science and Technology as the eighth sphere. However, she has omitted Sports and Religion.

SUNDAY ADELAJA MODEL

Sunday Adelaja developed seven spheres of the society suitable for use at the Embassy of God Church (Adelaja 2008):

1. Spiritual and Social
2. Government and Politics
3. Business and Economy
4. Education
5. Media
6. Culture and Entertainment
7. Sports

Adelaja's model has included Sports as a separate sphere and merged Religion with Family (called Social). However, the word "Social" has been reserved as qualifier for the society. Also, merging sports with entertainment (termed "celebration" by Cunningham) is acceptable.

STANDARD MODEL

Over the years, the Cunningham and Bright model has been restructured in other countries, most especially in Asia, so that the starting letters read ABCDEFG. In a sermon on October 14, 2007 (Annadorai 2007), and in a Foreword to a booklet *"See You at the Top"* (David Saw 2007), Pastor George Annadorai presented the seven spheres as:

1. Arts / Entertainment (Including Sports)
2. Business / Finance

3. Churches / Para – Churches
4. Distribution / Media (Including Technology)
5. Education / Schools
6. Family / Homes
7. Government / Law (Including Science)

In some models, "Design" is used instead of "Distribution". Design can still fit in the Arts sphere. This ABCDEFG model is here revised to include Science and Technology with Education, rather than with Law or Media. I must admit that it has been somehow hard to find the appropriate sphere to house Science and Technology which could not be isolated as a separate sphere. The Education sphere seems to be the most appropriate home. Cunningham regarded Science and Technology as a "Research and Development (R&D)" component of the Business sphere. R&D fits more appropriately in the Education sector. Also, "Religion" is an important sphere not to be excluded (as done in many models) from the standard model. The revised ABCDEFG model is:

1. Arts, Entertainment, and Sports
2. Business and Finance
3. Church and Religion
4. Distribution and Media
5. Education, Science and Technology
6. Family and Home
7. Government and Law

For completeness and ease, this revised ABCDEFG model will be adopted as the standard. Note that we stick to seven spheres rather than eight (appropriately defined by Cope) because many people, organizations, and movements such as Restore America Organization, International Coalition of Apostles, and Disciple Nations Alliance have all embraced the same number - seven - for the spheres of influence.

POINTS IN CHAPTER 6

Over the years (since the 16th century), the concept of spheres of the society has been developed; six major models have been studied.

The standard model proposed is the revised ABCDEFG model and it is adopted in this work.

The standard model is:
1. Arts, Entertainment, and Sports
2. Business and Finance
3. Church and Religion
4. Distribution and Media
5. Education, Science and Technology
6. Family and Home
7. Government and Law

7. ILLUSTRATION OF REFORMS

AS I ponder on how to understand further the four types of reforms defined in Chapter 1, especially the mixed ones involving both the Church culture and the Society culture, the Lord spoke to my heart *"Draw two closed curves and an arrow pointing in an appropriate direction"*. As I explored this graphical representation, it opened my heart to an amazing understanding of various issues concerning the Church and the secular world. It clearly teaches in a simplistic manner, the principles of the Kingdom. We can virtually determine if a reform supports the principle of the Kingdom by simply drawing two circles, one representing the Church and the other the element of the society involved in the reform, and then sticking an arrow in the appropriate direction. If the arrow does not point away from the Church, it does not support the principle of the Kingdom. This concept of illustration will help in understanding Churchshift, our model Reformation.

GRAPHICAL ILLUSTRATION

GUIDELINES

Here are the guidelines for understanding the graphical illustration of Figure 7.1:

A. The circle representing the Church is shaded in a bright (yellow) color because it is the source of salt and light to the world (Matt 5:14-16); Church (or spiritual) reforms are exposed to the church (closed boundary) only and could be itself open to several areas of the church (broken boundaries). A church reform can itself be reformed as shown by concentric circles within the church boundary in Figure 7.1A.
B. Like church reforms, social (or secular) reforms (Figure 7.1B) are represented by a solid boundary. The circle could be shaded with any color except the bright color of the church. Social reforms can also be open to any area of the society.

C. A socio-spiritual (Syncretic) reform is represented by two overlapping closed curves and an arrow pointing towards the church; this kind of reform is against the Kingdom principles (see definition in Chapter 8);
D. A spiritual social (Missional) reform is represented by two overlapping closed curves and an arrow pointing away from the church; this is the principle of the Kingdom, the Gospel of Discipling Nations, applied in Churchshift reformation

Only in cases C and D (mixed reforms) are the walls of the Church opened and can there be an arrow. Also, the degree of overlap in these cases depends on how strong or effective the reform is.

HYPOTHESES

According to the Great Commission (discussed in Chapter 5) and the fact that the believer or the Church is the light of the world, the following assumptions are valid for mixed reforms:

1. A Missional reform can only either have a positive impact (solid arrow) or no impact at all (transparent arrow) on the society if strictly implemented based on Kingdom principles. A positive impact (solid arrow) indicates an effective mission. A Missional reform can only be negative if it is not based on Kingdom principles; an example

is the support of slavery by the Catholic Church in the 15th century (Chapter 2).
2. A Syncretic reform can only either have a negative impact (solid arrow) or no impact at all (transparent arrow) on the Church. It can not have a positive spiritual impact on the Church; a solid arrow (negative impact) is against the principle of the Kingdom. A socio-spiritual reform is what is termed **Syncretism**.

THE MODEL

The four kinds of reforms are illustrated in Figure 7.1. In this model, the wall separating the church and the society is solid in pure reforms. There have been several pure reforms within the Church (e.g. Martin Luther) and in the Society (e.g. Martin Luther King Jnr.) but the Church is separated from the society in those cases. Note that many Church Reforms have themselves been reformed over the years; this is illustrated with the concentric circles within the walls of the Church.

For Syncretic and Missional reforms, the arrow can either be solid or transparent; both are represented in each case.

7. ILLUSTRATION OF REFORMS

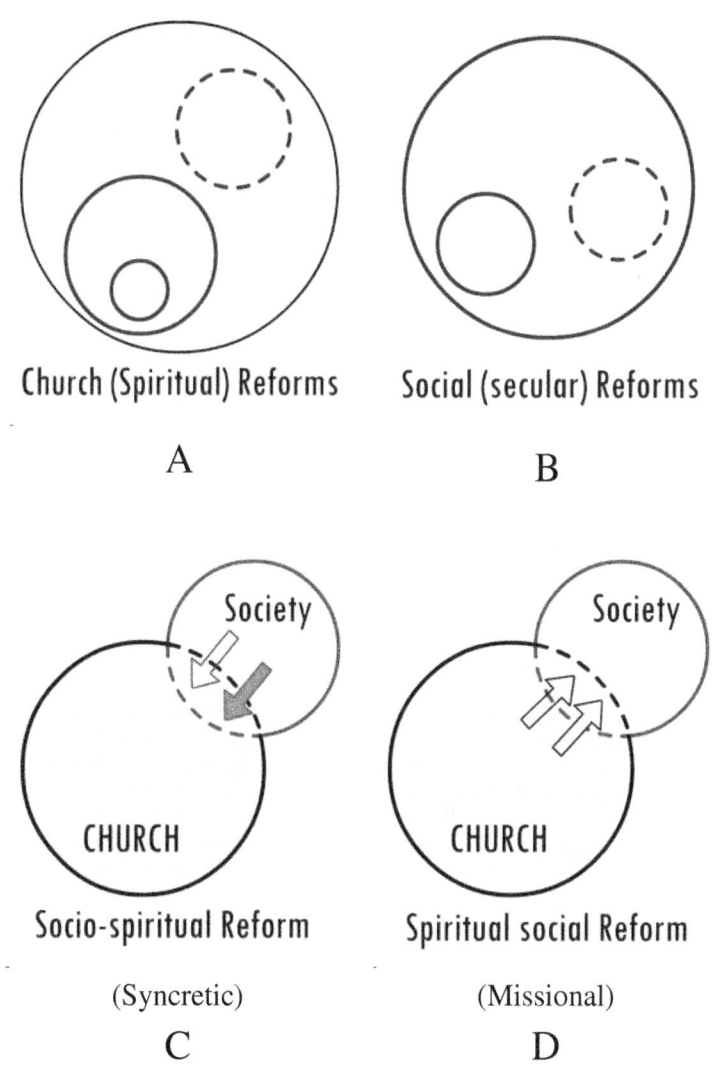

Figure 7.1: Graphical Illustration of Reforms

MISSIONAL REFORMATION

EXAMPLES OF MIXED REFORMS

As we have given quite a number of examples of pure social reforms and pure church reforms in Chapters 1 and 2, we will here provide examples of mixed reforms, that is, socio-spiritual reforms and spiritual social reforms.

SOCIO-SPIRITUAL (SYNCRETIC) REFORMS

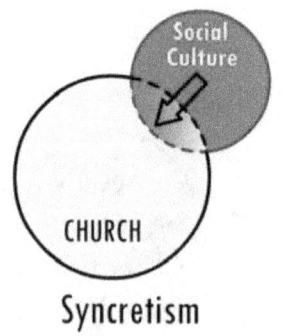

Syncretism

Syncretism is the allowance of secular cultural elements into the practice (or liturgy) of the church. Syncretism is the manifestation of all socio-spiritual reforms. Van Rheenen defines syncretism in the following terms: Syncretism is the reshaping of Christian beliefs and practices through cultural accommodation so that they consciously or unconsciously blend with those of the dominant culture. He continued:

> It is the blending of Christian beliefs and practices with those of the dominant culture so that Christianity looses it distinctive nature and speaks with a voice reflective of its culture.

As illustrated above, syncretism may not produce a uniform blend, but may produce spots of bright church characteristics, spots of secular cultural characteristics, and spots of blends. The degree of syncretism varies from 0, low (no) syncretism (a transparent arrow with no impact), to 1, strong syncretism (a solid arrow with negative impact). Syncretism can be expressed from all the seven spheres of the society.

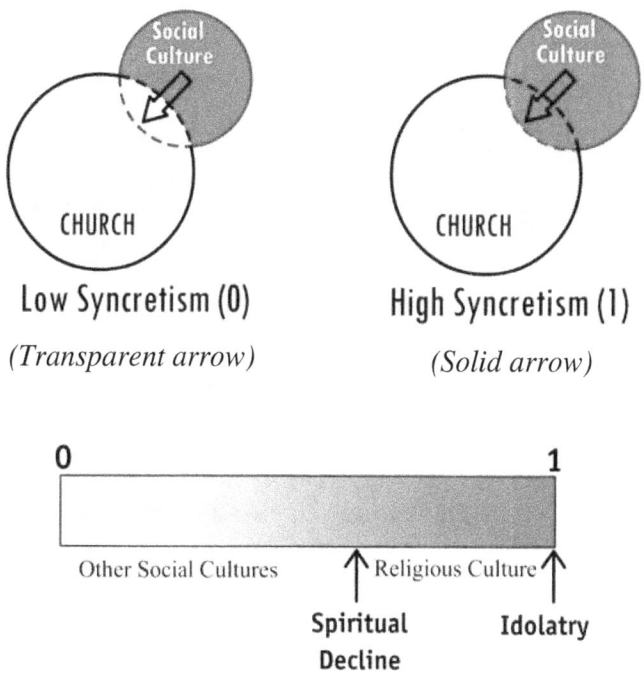

Figure 7.2: Scale of Syncretism

In the graphical illustration, strong (or total) syncretism is referred to as high syncretism. An example of low (or transparent) syncretism is when the cultural element is *language* (from the family sphere). It is universal that local churches use local languages in worship. This does not violate Kingdom principles; it is the handiwork of God Himself (Gen. 11:1-9). Syncretism becomes critical when religious elements are brought to the church; this results in spiritual decline. The extreme case of spiritual decline leads to idolatry. The religion-based reforms will be handled separately.

Kingdom principles allow only zero (transparent) syncretism because the light of the Church is preserved. In defense of the "blending", Philip Jenkins wrote:

> A people's tradition can not be swept away overnight

It is true, but the tradition has to eventually be absorbed totally into Christian principles for it to fulfill the Gospel of the Kingdom. Any syncretism greater than zero is harmful to Kingdom principles; it will dim the light by tarnishing the bright color of the Church, as is evident from the illustration.

Governmental Syncretism

The type of reform started by Emperor Constantine in 313 AD (detailed in Chapter 2) is Socio-Spiritual with the government imparting reforms on the Church (as indicated by the arrows in the figure); Constantine had good intentions and even struggled to keep the Church as one, but this is against the principle of the Kingdom. As the light of the world, the Church is supposed to reform the government (influencing government

policies and legislation) and not the other way round. The Great Commission is "Go ye" and not "Welcome ye". The Church systematically got swallowed by the state and resulted in elitism and corruption. The Church had to be rescued from the government by separation. Elitism and corruption brought to the Church still exists till present day. Kuyper was a strong advocate of separation of state and church; he wrote in *Calvinism and Politics*:

> The sovereignty of the State and the sovereignty of the Church exist side by side, and they mutually limit each other.

History usually ends up repeating itself if we don't learn from it. The patriarch of Kiev Orthodox, Father Boris Zabrodsky in an interview with Anna Verbitska in 1997, lamented bitterly over the influx of Protestant churches in Ukraine; he added:

> And the government is doing nothing to support the Orthodox Church

Father Boris is inviting and waiting on the government to lord it on the Church again (which is against Kingdom principles) instead of trying to influence government policies.

MISSIONAL REFORMATION

SPIRITUAL SOCIAL (MISSIONAL) REFORMS

Missional reform is a term that is being used to represent spiritual social reforms. Missional reforms are expected to be positive, or at the minimum, not make impact to the society. As stated in Chapter 1, the underlining guideline that determines whether a mission is effective or not is found in Rom. 12:2. The scripture tells us not to be conformed to the society. This leads to defining the term "cultural conformity".

Cultural Conformity

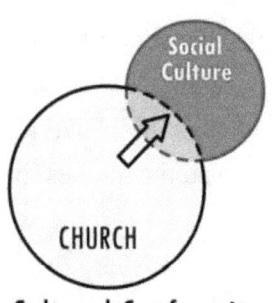

Cultural Conformity

It is important that we understand cultural assimilation or conformity as it applies to effective mission. Cultural conformity is a measure of the impact the Church makes in applying Kingdom principles to the society. When the Church fails to make an impact, its bright color blends with the color of the society as illustrated. It is an indication that cultural conformity can not produce a negative impact to the society but may dim the light of the Church.

> Interestingly, the stumbling block for the Church is not its theology but its failure to apply what it believes in compelling ways. The downfall of the Church has not been the content of its message but its failure to practice those truths. (George Barna)

The degree of cultural conformity (like syncretism) varies from 0 (not conformed; a solid arrow with positive impact) to 1 (fully conformed; a transparent arrow with no impact). In the illustration of Figure 7.3, zero assimilation, represented by low conformity, is the goal of a missional reform; strong assimilation is referred to as high conformity.

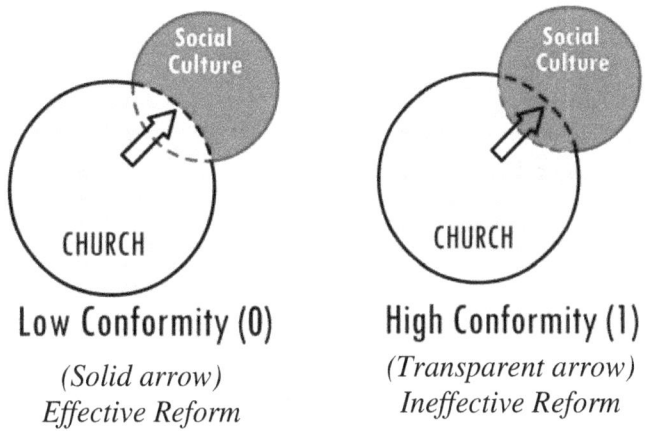

Low Conformity (0)
(Solid arrow)
Effective Reform

High Conformity (1)
(Transparent arrow)
Ineffective Reform

Figure 7.3: Scale of Cultural Conformity

Over the years many believers have compromised morally to the world. The Church can be morally separated from the world and still be connected to it by influencing the society through Kingdom principles (see Chapter 8).

You cannot run away from the nation (Adelaja 2008)

Cultural conformity (assimilation) is opposite to syncretism and both must be at zero level to satisfy Kingdom principles.

MISSIONAL REFORMATION

In syncretism, the culture is brought to the church. In cultural conformity, the church goes to the society and conforms to its culture. Rod Parsley, in his book titled *"Culturally Incorrect"*, puts it right. Chapter 1 of the book excellently provides an insight into issues of cultural conformity (he termed "why the Doctor is sick") in America. He was able to identify four issues:

1. Assimilation syndrome

    In America, those who claim to have the distinction of having faith in God have been assimilated into the broader culture (Parsley)

2. Me and my comfort syndrome

    Pastoral imperative stopped being "Feed My Sheep" and became "Entertain My Sheep". We have traded Gospel preaching motivated by a heavenly desire for redemptive change for worldly diversions motivated by a sensual desire for temporal pleasure.

    ...We now have vast segments of the church that are self-oriented instead of others-oriented. They are inward-looking and comfort-seeking. They are therefore ill-equipped to challenge the dominant secular culture or lead through servanthood. (Parsley)

3. Withdrawal and isolation

    The failure of the church to actively, vigorously, and positively engage the culture has led to defeatism and isolation.... We have forfeited leadership in each of the seven spheres of society. (Parsley)

    "The effect of Christian principles is decreasing in public life" (Cited from Nancy Pearcey, Total Truth: Liberating

Christianity from its Cultural Captivity, Crossway books, Wheaton, 2004)

Christians are at the forefront of the cultural debate but they are not generally at the forefront of the battle. (Parsley)

4. Worldview confusion

RELIGION BASED REFORMS

Mixed reforms in the religion sphere, as in any other sphere, can either be syncretic or missional.

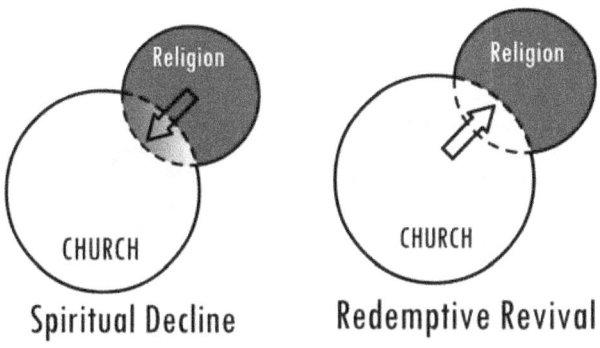

Figure 7.4: Religion-based Mixed Reforms

Syncretic (Spiritual Decline)

During the fourth to sixth century when the emperors took over the church, pagan customs and other religious beliefs came into Christianity with the masses of "converts" that came in. Even before then, Mani, born around 216 AD in Persia, was the founder of Manichaeism. He fused Persian, Christian, and Buddhist elements into a major heresy. Many, even Christians, subscribed to this religion. It became a major controversy in the middle ages. Even Augustine subscribed to the religion before he was fully converted in 386 into Christianity. Fusing religion into Christianity will produce an example of spiritual decline. Spiritual decline at the extreme could lead to idolatry as demonstrated in Figure 7.2.

Missional (Revival)

Reversing the arrow in the Spiritual Decline model would produce a revival (Figure 7.4). There are two types of revival, redemptive and spiritual (Olowe 2007). If the religious sector of society that the Church is imparting upon is the Church, that kind of revival is spiritual; however, if the religious sector is another religion, then that kind of revival is redemptive:

Church → Church (Christian believers) = spiritual revival
Church → Religion (or non believers) = redemptive revival

A great redemptive revival has been defined as an event that results in bringing people *en masse* to worship the true God after a period of persistent idolatry and sin (Olowe 2007).

> Carey was not the man to wish or to expect that Government should step out of its sphere in order to enforce

> Christianity upon the natives. "Do you not think, Dr. Carey," asked a Governor-General, "that it would be wrong to force the Hindus to be Christians?" "My Lord," was the reply, "the thing is impossible; we may, indeed, force men to be hypocrites, but no power on earth can force men to become Christians." - W. Pakenham Walsh

A great revival (redemptive or spiritual) cannot be engineered by humans; it is God-driven (Olowe 2007). In his last book on prayer schedule during Lent period (Babalola 1959), Apostle Joseph Ayo Babalola wrote:

> May the Lord bring up a great prophet among the Muslims that will proclaim the Gospel of Jesus Christ.

POINTS IN CHAPTER 7

The four types of church-society reforms are: *Spiritual* (within the church only), *Secular* (within the society only), *Syncretic* (from society to church), and *Missional* (from church to society).

A Missional reform is represented by a church circle overlapped by a closed curve of the sector of the society, and an arrow pointing *away from* the church circle.

A Syncretic reform is represented by a church circle overlapped by a closed curve of the sector of the society, and an arrow pointing *towards* the church circle.

Syncretic factor measures, on a scale of zero to one, the impact of a Syncretic reform; the extreme case of syncretism is idolatry.

Syncretic reforms do not advance Kingdom principles; only syncretic factor of zero is tolerated by Kingdom principles.

Conformity factor measures, on a scale of zero to one, the absorption of social culture by a missional reformer; a missional reformer needs to maintain a conformity factor of zero.

Missional religious reforms may lead to great revivals (spiritual or redemptive).

8. PRINCIPLES OF CHURCHSHIFT

WE HAVE examined more closely the Gospel of the Kingdom of God in Chapter 4. Summarily, the Gospel of the Kingdom is an intertwined two-fold process, which includes Salvation and good works.

OVERVIEW OF CHURCHSHIFT

THE CONCEPT

Churchshift has been defined in Chapter 3 as *"discipling all nations by stewardship"*. The concept and practice of Chur-

MISSIONAL REFORMATION

chshift is a package of Missional Reformation that has been practically well executed in all spheres of the society by a church. Churchshift revelation was given to Sunday Adelaja at the Embassy of God Church in the Ukraine in the year 2000. The entire reformation package came gradually bit by bit to him through visions, his personal relationship with the Lord, and studying. By the year 2008, the revelations had matured and were packaged as "Churchshift" He published the book with the same name that year. Unless otherwise stated, all references to Sunday Adelaja in this Chapter and the next are from the *Churchshift* book.

The base theology of Churchshift is that of good works (Chapter 5), which primarily, is based on the second Great Commandment and the Great Commission:

> Thou shalt love thy neighbour as thyself. (Lev 19:18; Matt 22:39)
>
> Go ye therefore, and teach all nations,... (Matt. 28: 19)

DEFINITIONS

The following terms are frequently used in Churchshift:

Kingdom Resource

A Kingdom resource is an individual Christian with his gifts.

Kingdom Principle

A Kingdom principle is a principle that does not violate the two Great Commandments; that is, the principles of Salvation and the principles of good works.

Promised Land

Promised Land is the sphere (or ministry) that a Kingdom resource is destined to influence the society; it is in this area God has destined the individual to prosper and be fulfilled.

> Promised Land - The place where you are to exercise Kingdom influence. (Adelaja, p. 29)

RATIONALE FOR CHURCHSHIFT

Responsibility of the believer

All believers are commissioned to execute the Great Commission. Also, Paul describes the Church's responsibility in 2 Corinthians 5:18-19:

> And all things are God who hath reconciled us to himself by Jesus Christ, and hath given us the ministry of reconciliation; to wit, that God was in Christ, reconciling the world unto himself, not imputing their trespasses unto them; and hath committed unto us the word of reconciliation.

God's ultimate goal is to reconcile all mankind unto Himself, and it is the Church's responsibility to teach and ensure this.

MISSIONAL REFORMATION

> The church fulfills its mandate when it changes society, not when it is confined to its sanctuary and Sunday school classrooms... The isolation of the church from the world has led to ineffectiveness and failure to carry the Great Commission (Adelaja, p.7)
>
> If there is any nation that is suffering under a godless culture, it's because Christians have not subdued it with Kingdom principles. (Adelaja, p.9)

Salvation-Focused Churches

For almost 2000 years, the Church has focused on the Gospel of Salvation alone; this has created a false sense of security of the believer into the Kingdom. The Gospel of Salvation is just a part of the Gospel of the Kingdom of God.

Church-Focused Churches

Many churches have been church-focused, closing their walls to the society, and building their churches.

> Too many Christians and Christian leaders spend their energy, creativity, and precious time promoting churches instead of the Kingdom. They believe that by building churches and ministries they are building the Kingdom. (Adelaja, p. 7)
>
> The Great Commission is not what many of us have understood it to be. We have understood it to be evangelism – bringing people from the world into our church buildings. But the Great Commission mandate is to go out and disciple nations. (Adelaja, p. 8)

Isolation from Society

Many churches do not have programs to alleviate the problems in the society; many Christians isolate themselves from the "sinful" world in order not to conform.

> The isolation of the church from the world has led to ineffectiveness and failure to carry out the Great Commission. (Adelaja, p. 7)

> As a church we are called out from the evil principles of this world, but we are still required to live here. We are not built for monasteries. Our calling is to operate from a different and superior set of principles. (Adelaja, p. 11)

Not of This World

> Some people object to this teaching and quote John 18:36, where Jesus said "My Kingdom is not of this world… my Kingdom is from another place." Christians have been using this phrase out of context for decades to forfeit this realm to Satan and neglect their calling to the nations. (Adelaja, p. 19)

Hoarding Kingdom Resources

In many churches, Kingdom resources are not fulfilling their purpose in life because the church is serving as a jail house.

> When Christians change the goal of the church and make it a place of conservation and escape rather than equipping and sending, we are working against the Great Commission. We are conserving crowds, not sending them out. We are hoarding Kingdom resources, namely, people and their gifts. In many churches, God's workers

are in captivity. They are like prisoners and the pastors are the wardens. (Adelaja, p. 10)

The Embassy of God Church is known for not imprisoning Kingdom resources. An observer writes:

> Unlike many Pastors who are keepers of the aquarium, Pastor Sunday after building a strong local church consistently takes his best leaders and releases them to help his young Pastors succeed in planting new churches. (Paul Davis)

Kingdom resources are underutilized, says another observer:

> The 'unemployment' of the laity is a very serious issue that is facing the church today. The typical teaching and preaching ministry on Sunday morning does not involve enough lay people. Only very 'gifted' and 'highly educated' people are allowed to use their gifts. The Western church has in many ways contributed to the widening gap between lay people and clergy. (Comiskey)

Insufficient Training

> Pastors need to train and teach their members to stop being pew warmers and to become a people called out of the world's life style to subdue every sphere of their lives to God and Kingdom principles. (Adelaja, p. 46)

Egocentricity

When church leaders and members are egocentric, the Kingdom becomes a secondary issue.

Egocentric Leaders

Egocentric leaders are difficult to reach:

Many famous non believers are easier to approach than some pastors... (Adelaja p.54)

Egocentric leaders are possessive:

One of the biggest symptoms of egocentric leadership is the ownership mentality. When a pastor refers to "my church" and "my people", he often betrays his true feelings. He sees the church as his flock, even his bride – and the measure of his career success. (Adelaja p.54)

Too many church leaders talk about "my ministry" and "my church". I have heard men weep and plead with God, "O Lord! Do this or that in my church". They are trying to bribe God with their tears. They would make God a mere means to fulfill their own dreams. They are church minded, not Kingdom minded. (Adelaja p.56)

We are simply God's co-workers... We are not the owners but the laborers. (Adelaja p.56)

Egocentric Churches

Egocentric churches compare themselves in terms of numeric strength.

It's OK to talk about numbers and to rejoice in God's blessing of numerical growth, but it's childish to revel in it and compare ourselves with others. (Adelaja p.57)

Egocentric Followers

Egocentric followers see the church as a place to meet their needs.

Egocentric leaders produce egocentric followers. When a pastor is using the church to meet his own needs, the motivation trickles down to people in the pew who begin to see the church as existing to meet their personal needs. (Adelaja p.57)

KINGDOM PRINCIPLES

The principles discussed here are based on specific teachings of Sunday Adelaja on Churchshift. It should supplement the theology of good works discussed in Chapter 5.

FOR THE CHURCH

Kingdom Mandate

> The church fulfils its mandate when it changes society, not when it is confined in the sanctuary and Sunday school classrooms (Adelaja, p. 7)

> God holds the church responsible for the societies, because through it, and only it, the Kingdom can come. (Adelaja, p. 11)

Teaching

Kingdom-driven church teaches the Gospel of Good Works

> The Gospel should not only focus on the man, but also on imparting the society. (Adelaja)

> When you teach a half-truth you destroy the truth. (Adelaja, p.60)

> Our enemies attack us because we preach half the Gospel. (Adelaja, p.61)

National Influence

Kingdom-driven church influences the nation

> The promise of God is "Ask of Me, and I will make the nations your inheritance" (Ps. 2:8) (Adelaja, p. 9)

> The destiny of our countries is in the hands of the church. (Adelaja, p. 27)

> God eagerly awaits the redemption of the nations; God wants preeminence in all things in every nation. (Adelaja p. 18)

Kingdom-driven church obeys government

> As Kingdom people, we are not allowed to ignore governments, because they are established by God and are part of His plan for the earth (Adelaja p. 18)

Training

Kingdom-driven church equips Kingdom resources. The church is to be a training ground for people who will impact the society.

> First Timothy 3:15 calls the church the pillar and foundation of the truth. It upholds the Kingdom by being the school, the equipping place, and the place of support for world changers. But our focus must remain outside, not inside. We are to go from the "school" into the world and bring the powerful Kingdom principles to bear on its problems. (Adelaja)

MISSIONAL REFORMATION

FOR THE LEADER

Kingdom Minded

Kingdom leaders are not egocentric

> Kingdom leaders try to elevate people by encouraging them and building them up into the people God wants them to be. But ungodly leaders rule by control. (Adelaja, p. 124)

> Today, I could leave my church and become an ordinary member of its congregation or get involved in something quite different without the slightest regret, sorrow, or inner pain. (Adelaja p.56)

> Kingdom leaders use their authority to make others successful... But a worldly leader sees people as tools for his own success. (Adelaja, p. 125)

Kingdom leaders are deliverers and do not isolate themselves from their nation.

> To be a deliverer you must first identify with your nation. You need to believe that God cares for your nation as a whole. (Adelaja, p. 117)

Kingdom leaders must leave the comfort zone

> Moses was willing to give up comforts of Pharaoh's palace, where he was raised. (Adelaja, p. 119)

Boldness

A Kingdom leader boldly speaks for God

> Moses spoke for God. You must speak for God in your place of influence. (Adelaja, p. 120)
>
> Sometimes speaking for God means confronting powerful rulers as Moses did. (Adelaja, p. 121)

Persecution

A Kingdom leader must persevere

> God speaks to you in times of persecution; in persecution you learn new skills; persecution may be the fastest way to be Kingdom minded. (Adelaja, p. 82,86,88)

Battles

A Kingdom leader must learn to fight the battle

> Some Christians fail the test of battle because they are timid. They claim they are being humble, but they are actually afraid to fight battles because they are not dead to their own ego (Adelaja, p. 121)

FOR THE BELIEVER

Kingdom Mandate

> God created this earth for mankind to rule. – Gen 1:26 (Adelaja, p.20)

Promised Land

Discover your promised land from your hobby, passion, or frustration.

Your promised land is where your love and pain intersect; it will always involve meeting other people's need. (Adelaja, p.31-33)

Destruction and boredom are signs that you are missing your promised land. (Adelaja, p.33)

Gifts and Talents

Your gifts are to benefit others
> By definition, your talents can only be useful when they bless others. (Adelaja, p.33)

Your gift is useful for effective evangelism
> Evangelism is only truly effective when you are operating in your area of gifting. (Adelaja, p.29)

Hard Work

Work is necessary
> If a man does not work, he gives nothing of value to the world. He is a thief... (Adelaja p. 77)

Put gifts to work

> You will not fulfill your potential in God's Kingdom without hard work. Failure in life never means a person lacks gifts; but it may mean he failed to put the gifts to work (Adelaja p. 77)

> Some Christians have amazing talents but experience little success because they have not learned to work. Others are nothing but dreamers. They sit and wait for a breakthrough to come. (Adelaja p. 77)

Hard work produces results

> It gives us money to pay for basic needs... It reveals our gifts... It is the means by which dreams, ideas, and goals become reality...It makes us a blessing to other people...It keeps us mentally healthy by focusing our minds on something productive. (Adelaja p. 78)

POINTS IN CHAPTER 8

Churchshift is defined as *discipling nations by stewardship.*

A Kingdom resource is an individual Christian with his gifts.

A Kingdom principle is a principle that does not violate the principles of Salvation and the principles of good works.

Promised Land is the sphere (or ministry) that a Kingdom resource is destined to influence the society.

Kingdom principles apply to the Church, Church leaders, and individual Christians.

God holds the Church responsible for the societies, because through it, and only it, the Kingdom can come.

A Kingdom leader uses his authority to make others successful.

Evangelism is only truly effective when you are operating in your area of gifting.

9. COMPONENTS OF CHURCHSHIFT

IN this Chapter we will examine the necessary components that make Churchshift Reformation work. The graphical illustration discussed in Chapter 7 will be useful to achieve this goal.

GRAPHICAL MODEL

The graphical illustration of Churchshift Reformation is shown below. The model includes The Church, the spheres, and the arrows. The spheres represent the society divided into seven areas and each overlapping with the church. In this

MISSIONAL REFORMATION

model, the wall of the church is broken and becomes dynamic. Very importantly, reformations emanate from within the church towards the society; the church wall expands and makes more souls to be connected into the Kingdom. This is Churchshift Reformation. It is a collection of Missional reformations that involve all spheres of the society. The color illustration of Figure 9.1 can be seen at the back cover of this book or at www.missionalreformation.com

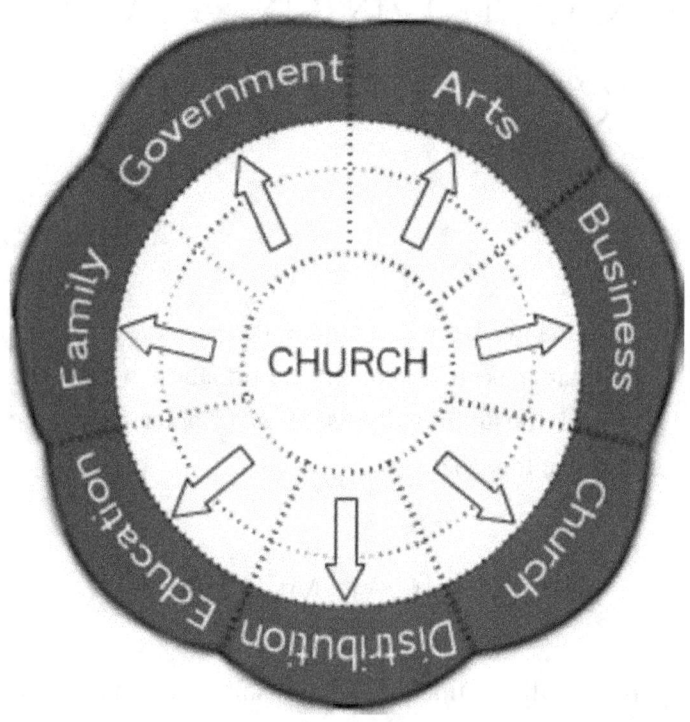

Figure 9.1: Churchshift Reformation Model
Go ye therefore teach all nations (Matt 28:19)

THE CHURCH

ROLE OF THE CHURCH

Besides its role in the Gospel of Discipling Nations as a missional center that will be the focus here, the Church also has the primary role of implementing the Gospel of Salvation. It helps to maintain connection to God through Jesus Christ. Prayers, worship, sacraments, and sermons are conducted in Church to implement the Gospel of Salvation.

In Churchshift Reformation where the Great Commission is implemented, the Church is an important tool.

> Church has never been the focus of the Great Commission, but it has always been the most important tool for carrying out the great Commission. The church is the primary vehicle God uses to train people so they know how to find their promised land and rule in their nation. Church is the headquarters, but the battles are not fought at the headquarters. They are fought in the field.
> Sunday Adelaja, *Churchshift* p. 10

From Figures 9.1 and 9.2, it can be seen that the Church is at the center of the Churchshift Reformation. The church has three major layers (the school, the ministries, and the expansion) represented by the three dashed concentric circles.

1. At the core of the Church is the Leadership Ladder School (Salvation and Churchshift School) which includes the pool of new members who receive training from beginner to min-

isterial leadership. Attendees receive instructions in the Gospel of Salvation and in the Gospel of Good Works (discipling nations).

2. The second layer, the Churchshift Ministries, represents members in active application of Churchshift reformation. Members of this layer are drawn from members in steps 3 to 5 in the Leadership Ladder School discussed below.

3. The third layer represents the expansion of church wall due to the application of Churchshift.

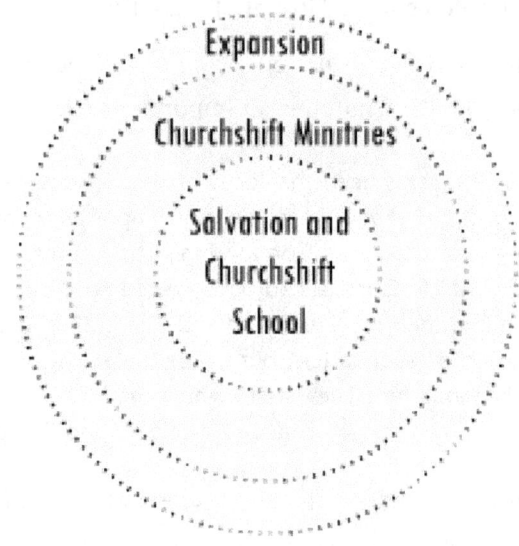

Figure 9.2: The Church

The following sections will discuss each of these three layers.

LAYER 1: LEADERSHIP LADDER SCHOOL

Any Missional Church needs to have a program or structure where leaders are trained for executing the Great Commission. In Churchshift, a Leadership Ladder School provides leadership training. The Church serves as a Leadership Training Center. The Leadership Ladder School is at the core of Churchshift Reformation and it is the foundation of the reformation, without which the entire structure will collapse. The ladder as implemented by the Embassy of God Church is ideal for Churchshift. We should remember from Chapter 3 that the G12 movement also has a ladder school. Although the Embassy of God Church also implements a system of twelve, the implementation of its ladder school is different from that of the G12 movement. The Embassy of God Church's cell groups are tasks oriented (see Chapter 10) and as such the ladder school is designed to support Churchshift. This school is provided free of charge to members at the Embassy of God Church. It consists of five classes (or five steps) a member must complete before he or she can effectively start a ministry. One can categorically say that the Gospel of SALVATION is taught in the first two steps and Gospel of GOOD WORKS (discipling nations or Churchshift) is taught in the last three steps. This school (of five steps) is aside the regular church sermons which focus on both Gospel of Salvation and Discipling Nations.

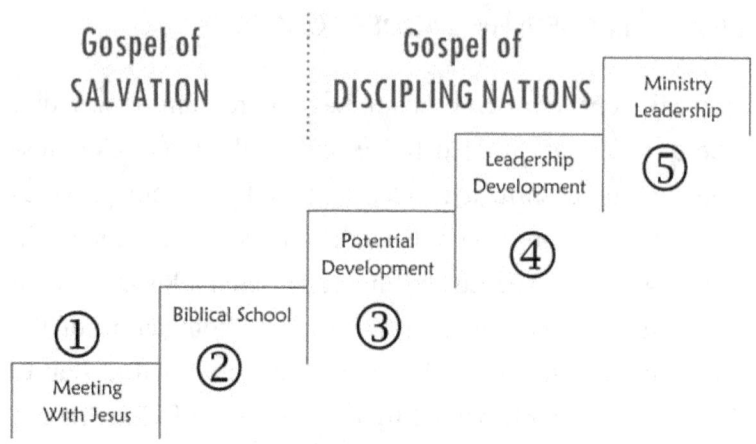

Figure 9.3: Leadership Ladder School

Step 1: Meeting with Jesus

In the first step, new members go through two lessons, the first one being on the day of repentance. New members are taught about Jesus, why He died for us, about sin, and resurrection. A short movie about Jesus is shown.

Step 2: ABC Bible School

The second step, called the ABC school, consists of seven sessions of Bible lessons, once a week. Once a member has become a leader, he/she can teach this class. Topics taught include how to communicate with God, how to read the Bible, and how to pray.

Step 3: Potential Development

The third step, Potential Development, also consists of seven sessions. Here is where the Myles Monroe effect (see Chapter 10) is put into practice. The church has developed a comprehensive curriculum where members are taught the concept of spheres, potential, purpose, and destiny. By the time a member completes the lessons of this step, he/she would have identified his/her sphere of influence and can serve in an existing ministry to apply Churchshift reformation.

I have always considered understanding one's calling or purpose (or promised land) and Potential Development as the most important step (after Salvation) in the life and development of a Christian. The teaching of this important piece in the development of a Christian is what is missing in most churches. I have attended several denominational churches and this is not taught. Some churches do, once in a while, invite speakers gifted in this area to minister to them; however, I have noticed that it doesn't last. Once the preacher leaves town, the initial enthusiasm starts to diminish until no one remembers what the preacher had taught. The problem is that, when an important topic like this is treated just as a sermon, it will not have the correct effect. It is a good thing that the Embassy of God Church identified this and immediately incorporated it in their curriculum. It is one of the reasons for the success of the church.

According to a Barna Group survey of American born-again Christians, less than half of the Christians polled claimed to possess a biblical spiritual gift. 46 percent were either not aware of spiritual gifts, had not identified one, or even believed that they did not have one! And it is certain that many of those who do claim to possess a biblical gift do not put it to regular use.

> Imagine what might happen if nearly half of all believers had a clear and firm conviction that God has given them a supernatural ability to serve Him in a specific manner. If more believers understood the nature and potential of that special empowerment, the global impact of the Christian body would be multiplied substantially. One of the functions of the local church is to help believers understand who they are in Christ, and how to live the Christian life more fully. Focusing on spiritual gifts - what they are, who has them, how to discover one's giftedness, and how to use gifts most appropriately - could ignite a movement of service and influence unlike anything we have experienced during our lifetime. (George Barna)

1 Corinthians 12:7 tells us, "*But the manifestation of the Spirit is given to every man to profit withal*". This is saying that every believer in Christ Jesus has been given a spiritual gift in order to build up the Church.

> From whom the whole body, being fitted and held together by what every joint supplies, according to the proper working of each individual part, causes the growth of the body for the building up of itself in love (Eph 4:16).

Potential development grows the individual and the church as a whole. In Chapter 3 of *Churchshift*, Sunday Adelaja writes in detail how one can reach the promised land.

Step 4: Leadership Development

In step 4, members are trained to be leaders. After this training, a member is deemed fit to lead a cell group.

Step 5: Ministry Leadership Development

Churchshift ministries (see next section and Chapter 14 of Volume 2) are more or less parachurches. To effectively manage a Churchshift ministry, the member is expected to complete the training in this step. At the Embassy of God Church, besides the training received in this step, many ministry leaders still enroll in colleges or universities for further education in their sphere of influence.

LAYER 2: CHURCHSHIFT MINISTRIES

Once a member has gone through Steps 1 to 3 in Figure 6.3, he or she can join a ministry of his or her calling. The ministries are separated into the seven spheres by dashed lines in Figure 9.1. The dashed lines indicate that members can cross from one ministry sphere into another. To lead or start a ministry, the member must have completed Step 5 of the Leadership Ladder School. The ministries apply Churchshift reformation (or the Gospel of Discipling Nations). This is the general picture of the reformation. In a more complex view, the reformation and strategies in each sphere are different, and additionally, may be different from country to country. I agree with Parsley (2007) that we have to understand the worldviews of each sphere in order to make an impact.

> The Great Commission does not offer us the luxury of simply abandoning the culture to the despair and self-destructiveness inherent in its false worldviews. Our mandate to be the salt and light doesn't give us the option of writing people off. (Parsley)

The Churchshift Ministries at the Embassy of God Church are discussed in more detail in Chapter 14 of Volume 2.

LAYER 3: EXPANSION OF CHURCH WALL

The application of Churchshift Reformation results in the expansion of Church walls. The wall, including the new pool of scholars (Leadership Ladder School), may increase or decrease depending on the net outflow from the school into the ministries. Consider the following analysis at a particular instance:

x_0 = initial number of members in school;

x = total number of members in school after Churchshift;

x_N = total number of new members;

y = number of members who join a ministry (expansion);

Then,

$$y = x_0 + x_N - x$$

An example of the Arts sphere is illustrated in Figure 9.4.

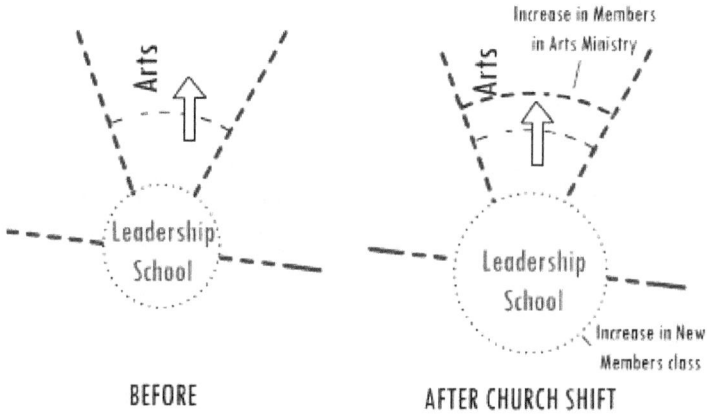

Figure 9.4: Effect of Churchshift on Arts Sphere

THE SPHERES

There cannot be a general reformation. Even in each sphere, we cannot generalize as it depends on the country or subcultures. That is why at the Embassy of God Church, individuals starting ministries are left to establish their own strategies or reformations. The standard spheres discussed in Chapter 6 are:
1. Arts, Entertainment, and Sports
2. Business and Finance
3. Church and Religion

4. Distribution and Media
5. Education, Science and Technology
6. Family and Home
7. Government and Law

In order to satisfy Kingdom principles in discipling nations in any particular sphere, the conformity factor must be zero (see Chapter 7). Also, one must stay connected to Christ as He said: "He is the vine, ye are the branches, without Him, ye can do nothing". Let us examine some challenges in discipling in some of the spheres.

BUSINESS AND FINANCE

Of all the seven spheres, the one that is most challenging to pass the cultural conformity test (see Chapter 7) is Business and Finance. Money has the power to corrupt one's integrity and distract one from what he/she is called to do. Greed is a money sickness, a spiritual problem caused by money-centricity. The Parable of the rich fool (Luke 12:13-34) and the example of the rich young ruler (Luke 18:18-30) teach us several principles concerning the money disease.

> Then said Jesus unto his disciples, Verily I say unto you, That a rich man shall hardly enter into the Kingdom of heaven. (Matt. 19: 23)
>
> And the disciples were astonished at his words. But Jesus answereth again, and saith unto them, Children, how

hard is it for them that trust in riches to enter into the Kingdom of God! (Mark 10: 24)

What Jesus is saying in the two verses above is that love of money can be an easy way to violate Kingdom principles if care is not taken.

> Money has a rightful place in creation; Genesis teaches that we were created both to make and to own things. But money also has the power to corrupt our integrity, magnify our self-absorption, and distract us from what we are called to do as Christians. This is because we look to money, instead of to God, for our significance and security. (Tim Keller, 2004)

So, when we work in this sphere we need to stay focused on Christ and maintain our Salvation.

GOVERNMENT

Next to the Finance sector is the Government sector in the order of likelihood of conforming. As money corrupts, so also does power. But what is pertinent to know is that government (or power) is ordained of God and the scripture tells us to abide by the authority.

> By me kings reign, and princes decree justice. Prov. 8: 15

> Let every soul be subject unto the higher powers. For there is no power but of God: the powers that be are ordained of God. Rom. 13: 1

Discipling in the government sphere entails influencing government policies without usurping power. Abraham Kuyper is a good example of influencing government through Kingdom principles. He was a theologian as well as politician. His political views and acts influenced Dutch politics. He was Prime Minister of Holland between 1901 and 1905. Kuyper wrote several theological and political books. He is the author of the doctrine of common grace which is the backbone of good works.

> God's Word must rule, but in the sphere of the State only through the conscience of the persons invested with authority. The first thing of course is, and remains, that all nations shall be governed in a Christian way; that is to say, in accordance with the principle which, for all statecraft, flows from the Christ. But this can never be realized except through the subjective convictions of those in authority, according to their personal views of the demands of that Christian principle as regards the public service. (Kuyper)

FAMILY

The family sphere is the widest. Most Non-Government Organizations (NGOs) and parachurches operate in this sphere. It involves humanity, issues with well being of parents and children. According to Kuyper, it is the primordial sphere of the society.

> For the vast majority of our race, marriage remains the foundation of human society and the family retains its position as the primordial sphere in sociology. (Kuyper)

Some other churches also have programs in this sphere as a church program. For example, Elim Welfare Town in Korea was founded by Pastor Cho in order to provide for the homeless elderly and the troubled youth. At the Embassy of God Church, such programs are designed and managed by individual members of the church. Jesus said we must each bear fruit, not collective few members of a church, but all individuals.

CHURCH AND RELIGION

As illustrated in Chapter 7, religion-based missional reformations are expected to lead to revivals. If a great revival is to come, it will come through this sphere. Reaching out to other Christians in this sphere (that is, Church to Church) can only lead to spiritual revival at best; this does not have much numerical effect on Kingdom population. The real challenge in this sphere is to penetrate other religions towards redemptive revivals (Olowe 2007). As mentioned earlier, this can not be engineered by humans; it requires the move of God Himself through a great revivalist.

POINTS IN CHAPTER 9

The Church has the primary role of implementing the Gospel of Salvation. It helps to maintain connection to God through Jesus Christ.

The Church is also the central tool of implementing the Gospel of good works through leadership development.

In implementing Churchshift, the Church has three layers: training, ministries, and expansion.

When we evangelize in any sphere, particularly in the Business sphere or Government sphere, we need to stay focused on Christ to maintain our Salvation.

The Family sphere is the primordial sphere of the society.

VOLUME 2

PRACTICAL APPLICATION

INTRODUCTION TO VOLUME 2

IN this Volume, the practical aspect of discipling nations by stewardship, concept of spheres, cultural engagement, missional home groups, monospherical churches, and all theological background of a Missional Church discussed in Volume 1 will be elaborated, using the Embassy of God Church in Ukraine as the model Missional Church. The term "model" suggests the employment of certain methods, techniques, procedures, etc., that has been shown to make possible the achievement of specified results.

In Volume 1, it is shown that between the Church and the Society, there are four types of reforms: Church (Spiritual), Social (Secular), Socio-spiritual (Syncretic), and Spiritual Social (Missional). It is also stated that everyone is gifted in at least one of the seven spheres of influence. An effective mission is carried out in the area of gifting of the missionary. The central aim of a Missional Church is *cultural engagement and transformation* in the seven spheres. The major revelation in Volume 1 is about the Gospel of the Kingdom of God. The two slabs of stone on which God wrote the Ten Commandments that were given to Moses represent the Gospel of God in two parts. The Gospel of the Kingdom of God is two Gospels in one, salvation and good works. Both special grace and universal grace are needed for effective good works. A full Gospel church implements the Gospel of the Kingdom of God. A Missional Church is a Full Gospel Church.

Some major differences between a Classical Church and a Missional Church are summarized in the Table below:

Classical Church	**Missional Church**
Focus is on Gospel of Salvation	Focus is on Gospel of the Kingdom (salvation and good works)
Missionary work is church's responsibility	Missional work is individual's responsibility
Few members are missionaries	All members are missionaries
Me and my God	Me, my God and my people
Focus on personal miracles	Focus on societal transformation
Focus on church growth	Focus on Kingdom growth

In this Volume, we will clearly recognize the difference between a Classical Church and a Missional Church and also the difference between a church ministry and a missional ministry. These are elaborated in Chapters 13 and 14.

10. THE MODEL CHURCH

THE Embassy of God Church in Kiev, Ukraine is the first truly Full Gospel church in the history of Christianity; and that is why it is our model church. It was founded and is led by a Nigerian immigrant, Pastor Sunday Adelaja. The church has developed and mastered the Gospel of discipling nations. This is not to say that the Embassy of God Church is a perfect church, but it is close to a perfect model of a Missional Church in the execution of the Great Commission as will be seen in the next six chapters.

HISTORY OF THE EMBASSY OF GOD

In April 1993, Sunday Adelaja was offered a job by the 7th Channel of Ukrainian TV and he moved from Belarus to Kiev in Ukraine. Through a television program, he invited people for Bible studies. Seven people, mostly alcohol and drug addicts, turned up. Natalia Potopayeva, who later became a major instrument to the growth of the church, was one of the seven. Others include Aleksandr Boldesko, Yury Mischenko, Valentina Chabannaya, and Sergey Komovsky. Adelaja was discouraged by the turn out and the kind of people that came. He had his plans; God too. Today, there are over 2,260 leaders region at the Embassy of God Church in Kiev region.

When the church was formally being opened in February 1994 as "Word of Faith Church", John David, a preacher

10. THE MODEL CHURCH

from the USA, was invited. There were 49 people in the first service. Energized Natalia Potopayeva, soon after the church was opened, told Sunday Adelaja that the Lord had shown her a vision of a hall filled to capacity. They prayed intensely and walked around the city every day evangelizing and inviting people to their services. By the end of 1994 there were already about 700 people in attendance.

Since many of the converts were drug and alcohol addicts, the church developed the vision to rehabilitate people. Before the end of 1994, the Love Rehabilitation Center was established with Natalia Potopayeva as the leader, and with four people at the first meeting. From 1994 to 2003 over 2,500 people had been rehabilitated from alcohol and drug addiction through the center. Several other ministries to take care of destitute, handicapped, and elderly people, started to spring up. For example, between 1994 and 2003, the Mercy Ministry visited about 1,540 shut-ins, delivered about 1600 food packages, ministered to 9,000 people in hospitals, assisted about 500 people with buying medicine, and so on.

Through television programs where people from Kiev testified about changes in their lives, the church became known in the city. By the end of 1995, the church had grown to 2000 capacity. In that year, Pastor Sunday and the church came under the spiritual covering of Apostle Ulysees Tuff. Also in that year, Pastor Sunday

wrote his first book *"Victory over Thoughts and Feelings"* and the Joshua Bible Institute was opened.

Services were initially held in a cinema house and thousands of people from Kiev were coming there. The church continued to grow in spite of mounting persecutions coming from atheists and the Orthodox Church. Gradually Adelaja began to implement visions as they were coming from God, teaching through books and tapes and spreading to other former Soviet Union territories. The first Missional Church planted in Gomel, Belarus was pastored by Sergey Komovsky, one of the seven foundation members. More Churchshift ministries continued to emerge during this time.

In 1997, the church was renamed from "Word of Faith" to "The Embassy of God". Daughter churches started in 5 districts in Kiev that year. The media was exceptionally hard on the church in 1997, attacking the church, Pastor Sunday Adelaja, and Leonid Chernovetskyi, the mayor of Kiev as of 2007 and a prominent member of the church. Most of the attacks were racially and politically motivated. Several false allegations and racial slurs were directed towards Adelaja. Several lawsuits were filed against the church. The church faced opposition from local Eastern Orthodox, Catholic Church, government authorities, and political groups that oppose Westernization of the Ukraine. They believed the

Embassy of God was planted by the USA for that purpose. But the pressure and persecution seemed to have strengthened the church spiritually and numerically. The church continued to grow and more daughter churches were opened.

The year 1999 was a turning point in the history of the church. Myles Munroe delivered a sermon about personal calling, purpose, and destiny that had a great impact on the church; it helped Adelaja to develop his teaching.

> Many church members positively received this teaching and began to make new steps in their callings as they started businesses and found their place in life. In spite of the continuing lawsuits and negative publications about our church in the press, many church members became successful and the church rose to a new level. (Adelaja)

In the year 2000, the church won a long-standing lawsuit and introduced "The System of Twelve." By the end of the year, the church grew from 8,000 to 15,000 people. In the

MISSIONAL REFORMATION

same year, the church opened her first branch in the USA in Sacramento, California, pastored by Vasily Biletsky.

The church now has about 25,000 members in Kiev alone and over 400 daughter churches in Ukraine. Furthermore, it has more than 700 daughter churches in 35 countries, including Belarus, USA, UAE, Israel, India, Czech Republic, and South Africa.  The church has members from all the spheres of the society, including well-known businessmen, politicians, lawyers, scientists, athletes and pop stars; these people take upon themselves to minister through stewardship in all spheres of the society. The resident Pastor of the Central Church in Kiev is Bose Adelaja, wife of the Senior Pastor.

LITURGY

The Embassy of God is a truly full Gospel charismatic church. It believes in doctrine of tongues (glossolalia). In liturgy, we will study how the church practices the Christian faith. Opinion polls usually find praise and worship, prayer strength, and sermon as the three most important factors in worship service and in retention of a prospective member.

Who wants to step back in time a few hundred years in order to attend a church service? Who wants to listen to a bunch of cheesy songs and then yawn as a guy speaks from a podium for a straight hour? Why have we so needlessly made Christianity so tedious and unattractive? (church-reform.com)

PRAISE AND WORSHIP

Defending the old liturgy of "Sit, Stand, Kneel, Bow, Turn, Cross, Walk" of the Anglican Church, Bosco Peters wrote:

> There are Anglicans (also called Episcopalians) essentially doing the same all around the world. And we've been effectively doing this (along with Roman Catholics, Eastern Orthodox, and others) for a hundred thousand Sundays.

Bosco needs to visit some other countries, especially Nigeria. The young generation, especially of the tropical regions, is finding such old mode of worship boring. One Anglican member in Nigeria told me "If you don't introduce charismatic praise and worship into your liturgy, people won't come to your church anymore". Most of the Anglican churches in Nigeria are charismatic. The quotation below is from an American youngster.

> The Church continues to be out-of-touch with most people, particularly the younger generations, and seems to be insensitive when it comes to understanding the outsider's perspective. These are the facts: the vast majority of people under the age of 50 find traditional church ser-

vices boring, and very few are willing to accept traditional Christian culture in order to become Christian. And as long as Christianity can be labeled cheesy, boring or archaic, it will itself stand as an unnecessary offense to believers and non-believers alike. (church-reform.com)

A Missional Church should seriously consider the comments made above. At the Embassy of God Church, one can never be bored. It is highly charismatic. The church has multiple praise and worship teams that rotate on a weekly basis. Some of the songs are composed by the church, and sometimes I have identified English (especially American) praise songs that have been translated into Russian. The church is very lively and one always wants to be there. It is difficult for an unbeliever to step into that church and leave without repenting; the atmosphere during praise and worship and preaching is always Holy Ghost charged.

Also noticeable at the Embassy of God Church is the waiving of colorful flags during praise and worship. I was initially uncomfortable with the idea, thinking it was distractive and a form of syncretism. Some Christians, for example,

Rev. Emmanuel McCarthy, have written articles against keeping flags in church; it is regarded as symbolizing syncretism. I followed in this line of thought until I met with the leader of the banner ministry who explained the biblical im-

plications. McCarthy is right about the symbolism. Flags at the Embassy of God symbolize *banners*

and they are not specific to any country. The case that most American Christians write against is when it is politically motivated; in such cases, a specific flag is kept in church as a symbol of loyalty. For example, typically, an African American considers the Confederate flag a symbol of terror, oppression, and racism. The praise and worship and banner ministries will be discussed further in Chapter 13.

PRAYER

At the Embassy of God, prayer is given a high priority and

many members spend a generous portion of each day and the week in prayer. I believe that is what keeps the church strong spiritually. At any

time of the day and of the week, there are always people (home groups) praying together in the church, at the lobby, in remote corners, and everywhere. The church says loud prayers and often in tongues. One of the members told me that when they pray, they emphasize on the word of God according to Eph. 6:17; they quote the scriptures to remind God of His promise on that particular prayer subject. The scripture has passages for any situation in life. This means that the members study the Bible scrupulously. Also, when the members of a home group are praying together, they always pray for the lost souls. They understand that glorifying God and reaching the lost brings greater satisfaction than any other activity. During a regular Sunday worship service, prayers are said at the beginning for quite an ample amount of time and they are being led by several Pastors, each taking a turn.

Special Prayers

In 1996, one of the church leaders, Pastor Yury Mischenko received a revelation from God to organize a night prayer for the Senior Pastor, Sunday Adelaja, and the needs of the church. Prayer was held every night. Over 300 people attended the Night Prayer each month. The church won a long-standing lawsuit against her in 2000.

Night Prayer

Different groups from the church meet every night from 11pm till 6 am, which is seven good hours of prayer and worship. All church members come for a general night prayer every Friday, also from 11pm till 6 am. It is amazing to see the turnout and how prayerful the church is. Every week, one finds different groups from different daughter churches gathering at the senior pastor's residence for a round the clock 24-hour prayer session. There are at least four of such sessions in a month.

Fasting

Twice a year (in August and in December) the church organizes a fasting program (ranging from 3 to 12 days) at a location near Kiev; the program started in 1997. It was initially designed for Pastors but later was extended to members. People gather at this location and remain there till the end of the fasting program. Forty people participated in the first Pastors' Fast. In 2003, the fast became international, with more than 1,000 believers from different countries of the world in attendance.

THE WORD OF GOD

The Word is preached to members of the church through various media: at the pulpit, through audio and video cassettes, through books, and through Bible schools. The Senior Pastor, Sunday Adelaja, has written over 50 books and so also are some other Pastors and members of the Church in specific spheres they minister. In regular church sermon, many of the messages are focused on the Gospel of Salvation. The Leadership Ladder School (of five classes), as discussed in Chapter 9 of Volume 1, is used to develop individual mem-

MISSIONAL REFORMATION

bers in Gospel of salvation and of discipling nations. So, both Gospels are taught at the school. At the Embassy of God, the members are well equipped with the word of God. Also, they all have deep knowledge of the concept of "spheres". Any member that has gone through the Leadership Ladder School, and desiring to be an ordained minister of God, has the opportunity to do so through the Joshua Bible Institute.

SACRAMENT

The only sacraments practiced at the Embassy of God are water baptism and Holy Communion. These are also the only

two recognized by most Christians; they are the two most important ordinances or sacraments because they are the only ones established by Christ Himself. Baptism is the visible beginning of the Christian life; the Lord's Supper continues and nourishes that life. At the Embassy of God, baptism is conducted by immersion at a lake by the church. Holy Communion is taken once a month.

ACTIVITIES

CHURCH ANNIVERSARY

In 2002, the Embassy of God celebrated her 8th anniversary at the Palace of Sports. The celebration was attended by thousands of people from Kiev, from other Ukrainian cities, and from the world over in the largest hall in Ukraine's capital city. Aleksandr Omelchenko, the mayor of Kiev then, came to congratulate the church. Since then, the church holds this event yearly at the Palace of Sport around April. It is a single event that unites all daughter churches and home groups worldwide.

At the event, different Churchshift ministries make presentations and reports of their activities for the past year. The celebration lasts for 12 hours each day of the 4 consecutive days with intermittent breaks. It is usually a busy period for the guest department, planning the schedules for individual guests. Guests from all over the world attend this anniversary to learn about the activities of the Embassy of God Church. Several seminars and tours are organized.

MARCH OF LIFE

In May of 2001, the Embassy of God in Kiev held the March of Life in support of those who have AIDS or are addicted to drugs or alcohol. About 20,000 people, from different denominations, walked down the main street of Ukraine's capital to proclaim that there is a future for Ukraine, and with the Lord God this future is wonderful. This March of Life was in support of the International AIDS Remembrance Day. This March of Life has since then become a yearly activity. In 2002, over 30,000 people participated including the Mayor of Kiev shown in the picture, and in 2003 there were about 35,000 people, including about 4,000 people from other countries. A consulting office for HIV-infected people has been established by the church for anonymous assistance.

The church also participated in a political March termed the "Orange Revolution". This will be discussed in Chapter 14 under government sphere.

CHURCH GROWTH

The rate of growth of church membership at the Embassy of God in Kiev region is shown in the chart of Figure 10.1. The factors that contribute to the growth will be discussed.

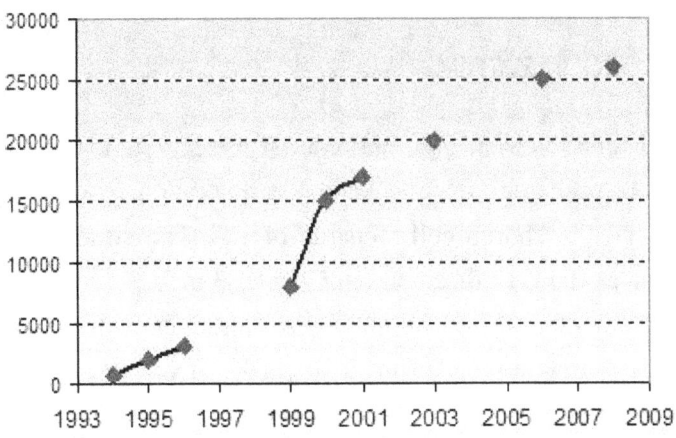

Figure 10.1: Church membership in Kiev region by year

MYLES MUNROE EFFECT

In September 1999, Myles Munroe visited the church and his sermon gave Pastor Sunday a new boost in the development of his teaching about personal calling and purpose. The

church rose to a new level. Many church members positively received this teaching and began to make new steps in their callings as they started businesses and found their place in life. Many long-time members I spoke with mentioned Myles Munroe's visit and preaching as having a boost to their growth.

HOME GROUP SYSTEM

Myles Munroe's visit gave the church a jump start, but the real shoot up came after the Senior Pastor, Sunday Adelaja, introduced the church cell "System of 12". The structure is the same as the G12 discussed in Chapter 3 of Volume 1, but the implementation is different. After introducing the "System of 12" (as they call it to distinguish it from the known G12) in 2000, the church grew exponentially from 8,000 to 15,000 people by the end of the year. Pastor Sunday explains the primary motive for establishing the System of 12:

> A key problem in a large, growing church is the lack of personal pastoral care, support and friendship. It is very easy for someone to get lost and slip through the cracks of a large organization unless specific steps are taken to guard against it. When the Embassy of God had grown to

several thousand people, it was impossible for Pastor Sunday to personally greet, fellowship and council with each person. Many people were coming to the church, finding Jesus, but then not coming back to church. There had to be a way to encourage these people to stay in fellowship and to give everyone the attention needed.

According to the Pastor, he sought for God's solution to the problem and found the answer similar to the G12 system. The current members then formed a tree of groups of twelve, starting with Sunday Adelaja.

Microscopic Characteristic

The Embassy of God has a comprehensive stewardship system. The church, through the members, has ministries in the seven spheres of influence; the ministries are categorized as such. Members serve in their area of gifting (see Chapter 5 of Volume 1) which must be in one of the seven spheres; some members serve in more than one ministry. Because of the stewardship nature of the church, most cell groups are more or less task-oriented. This means that most cell groups are *Meta* or *Missional* described in Chapter 3 of Volume 1. The *Meta* cells are for cell groups from church ministries such as choir, ushers, security, and so on. These ministries are covered in Chapter 13. The *Missional* cells are composed of members of a Churchshift ministry (Chapter 14) working in the same sphere. In both the *Meta* and *Missional* models, the cell groups are not necessarily for church growth, although that is desired. *Missional* cells often result in church growth, but they are designed for winning souls in specific spheres and then growing them spiritually.

Macroscopic Characteristic

Macroscopically, the church cell system at the Embassy of God is the *Tree Model* described in Chapter 3 of Volume 1. Pastor Sunday began by choosing 12 people to assist him and be taught by him; this first home group at the Embassy of God is called "The Apostolic Council". Each member of the Apostolic Council selected 12 people and each of those people selected 12 people and each of those 12 people selected 12 people, and on and on until everyone was in a group. With the system, each church member attends two home group meetings; one organized by his/her leader and the one that the member leads. When someone comes to the church for the first time and is born again, he is directed to home groups in his region, enabling him to become involved and anchored into the church. The leadership structure and training motivate those at the extreme end of the tree to form their own group and, as such, recruit members in order for them to become leaders. This is quite creative. Membership at the Embassy of God ballooned after the entire initial members have each been absorbed into a home group. This system is used in marketing, but it also works well for church growth, both spiritually and numerically.

Pastor Sunday had his first group in the beginning. He poured himself into these people so that they could then reach others. Many of his original 12 have left Ukraine and are pastoring in other countries. Yet, others are still in Ukraine heading ministries and expanding in their spheres.

Values

Some of the values of the church cells at the Embassy of God are expressed on the church's website:

> The main reason for these groups is discipleship. Every new believer or church member is in a group. Here, they will learn the foundational principles of the Bible, be encouraged to stay in church, receive teaching on prayer and healing, learn how to overcome trials and not fall into temptation, and discover how to live a Christian life. As the new believers grow, they begin their own groups and help teach others. The object is not for the leaders to dictate the lives of the group, but to teach them the Word and prepare them to be able to make the right decisions. A strong bond is formed between leaders and the group members. Birthdays are celebrated, weddings and anniversaries are a time of joy for the entire group, and holidays are times for group fellowship and parties. The fellowship and friendship is not just spiritual, but extends into every other area of life, including having fun. Relationships are strengthened and cemented over a game of soccer and a picnic lunch. Fun and prayer go hand in hand and everyone has a good time. (godembassy.org)

Also, the home group is a potential source for leadership growth and training. As a member matures, he/she may be asked to lead the group if the leader is absent or to teach or lead a segment of the group. Each person is encouraged to participate in the meetings and to offer his/her thoughts or opinions. In this way, the entire group can learn from the experiences of others and avoid making the same mistakes.

Meeting Locations

Since they become part of a family, many home groups meet at members' homes and sometimes at the church premises.

On any given evening at the Central Church, there are always at least five home groups meeting in different corners of the building. In the spring and summer, the surrounding terrains of the complex are filled with small groups singing, praying and sharing the Word. This is truly one of the elements that played a large part in the success of the church. Everyone in the mega church is able to be a part of a small, family-like unit and feel special.

Challenges in Starting a Home Group

Valeriya Mashchenko, came to the Embassy of God with her mother in 2002 but repented a year after. She went through

the Leadership school and was absorbed in one of the home groups in 2004; however, this group was suspended because the leader gained admission into a college to further her education. Valeriya joined another home group in 2006; she found joy in this group because she felt at home and believed that God led her to the group. Although she had been taught that she could be a leader, she never imagined herself being one. The home group system is practical. The leader motivated them; she found herself aspiring to be a leader. In three months after she joined this home group, she became a leader and started her own home group; she discovered her calling in the family ministry, so, she also became a family leader.

She recruited her first home group member from a new member at the English church service and always looked out for new members to recruit. She now has 10 members but some of them are unstable because they are not devoted. She recruited two of the members from the orphanage home. One of the difficult tasks of the leader is to hold the new converts and not to let them fall back to the world; this is Valeriya's main challenge. Starting a home group has developed her leadership skills. She works one-on-one with her members besides the regular meetings. She has managed to stabilize her group now.

POINTS IN CHAPTER 10

The Embassy of God Church, led by Pastor Sunday Adelaja, was formally opened in February 1994 as "Word of Faith Church".

It is a lively church with members full of zeal and passion. The church witnessed an accelerated growth in 2000 after introducing the system of 12.

Microscopically, most home groups at the church are missional.

The church now has about 25,000 members in Kiev alone and over 400 daughter churches in Ukraine. Furthermore, it has more than 700 daughter churches in 35 countries.

11. STRUCTURES

THE structure of any particular church organization can be broken down into two: the spiritual leadership structure and the administrative structure. When the Embassy of God Church started in 1994, there were no structures in place; the current structure developed gradually. In the early years, Sunday Adelaja was the only Spiritual leader and Iurii Ivanovich Mishchenko became the only administrator. Iurii was responsible for many things; he was responsible for getting the church registered, assisting Pastor Sunday, and managing the church's finance. Iurii gives a testimony of the development of the church structure. Iurii Ivanovich Mishchenko is an artist of sculpture and painting. He started to drink alcohol in 1956 at the age of 12 until it got out of hand; he became addicted and not submitted to God. He tried to stop several times but to no avail. Somehow, he became a single parent to his daughter, but he was not able to provide proper upbringing because of his addiction. In 1990, he got fed up and he locked himself up for three days and cried to God for help. After that, the Lord spoke to him at a park saying that he would start a new life. Truly, he stopped getting drunk. He later got baptized at an orthodox church. He sought vigorously to learn the Bible and consulted the Orthodox priest who gave him a cold response; *"Go and read your Bible"* he said. He did not get much out of church until 1994 when he met Pastor Sunday through one of the foundation members of the church. He totally became a new person. Ivanovich was active in the church and he became the head of administration during the early months of joining the church. The church was poor and Pastor Sunday was on a low salary. At a point, the church raised money to give to Pastor Sunday, but he refused it and the money was given to someone who really needed it. Pastor Sunday said God told him not to touch the money. Anatoy Belonozhko (now Bishop) took over the administration from Iurii. In 1999, Pastor Sunday requested Iurii to start a prayer ministry; which he did. In the first assignment of the prayer ministry, they prayed 6 hours a day from the beginning of the year 2000 till the end of March. That was when the home group system, which accounted for the membership explosion, was introduced to the church. Iurii Ivanovich Mishchenko was ordained as a Pastor in March 2000 after going through the pastoral training.

In 2000, the Spiritual leadership structure and the general administrative structure became more defined.

SPIRITUAL GOVERNANCE

The Spiritual structure started to take shape in the year 2000 after introducing the "System of twelve".

APOSTOLIC COUNCIL

The Apostolic council is the highest ruling and decision making body at the Embassy of God Church. The council started as the Home Group of Pastor Sunday when the system of twelve was introduced. Therefore, there were initially, 13 members. However, some of the members of the council, such as Visily Biletsky, Natalia Potopayeva, and Tope Omotoye, left Ukraine as missionaries to other countries. Currently, the membership of the council has increased to 16 and will soon reach 24. The Apostolic council meets once a year during a 7-day fasting and praying period before the anniversary. Major decisions on policies and directions for all the Embassy of God Churches and Churchshift ministries are discussed. Decisions of the council are passed to the National Spiritual Council.

SPIRITUAL COUNCIL

The spiritual council oversees the day to day running of the church. There are three levels of the council.

National Spiritual Council

The national council, also called the extended council is composed of all assembly pastors in the Ukraine. They usually meet once a month. Bishop Anatoy Belonozhko is the head of the National Council. He makes sure that every vision and decisions of the Apostolic Council, of which he is a member, are implemented by all the churches.

Regional Spiritual Council

The Regional Spiritual Council is composed of all leaders of assembly spiritual council in a particular region. Bishop Anatoy Belonozhko heads the Kiev Regional Council.

Assembly Spiritual Council

Each local assembly has its own council. It is made up of the church leaders. The assembly Pastor heads the council. For example, Pastor Bose Adelaja heads the Spiritual Council of the Central Church and of the English Assembly. The Assembly Spiritual Council meets once a week.

ADMINISTRATION

The administration started as one unit in the early years. However, as the church grew, administrative responsibilities became overwhelming. Although, Bishop Anatoy Belonozhko is the overall administrative head at the Embassy of God, the church has three administrative units that work independently; they are Management, Missions, and Finance. The Bishop heads one of them.

MANAGEMENT

As stated earlier, the first head of administration (now called senior manager or administrator) was Iurii Ivanovich Mishchenko. He was succeeded in the following order: Anatoy Belonozhko (now Bishop), Alex Boldesko, Alex Sichenko, Henry Okoi, Vasiliy Bileski, Andrei Kuksenko, and Marina Pirskaya (the current senior manager). Andrei Kuksenko became the administrator in 2001 during the peak growth of the church. Andrei created a complex system of administration using volunteers. He developed his strategy from a sermon by Pastor Sunday on spirituality and administration, referencing Reinhardt Bonnke. Andrei created several departments including Missions, Accounting, Mailing, Information, Computer, Maintenance, and Security. He hired drivers, secretaries, and office managers. Andrei relocated to the USA in 2006 to establish a daughter church. He left a void

that was difficult to fill. The current senior manager, Marina Pirskaya, rose up to the task. She has been able to stabilize the administration by hiring paid managers to oversee some of the departments. They all report to her. Marina also heads the organization of festivals, exhibitions, concerts, and the church anniversaries. Some of the departments the senior manager oversees are: Maintenance, Security, Mail, Transportation, and Guest.

Mail Department

The Ministry of Mailing was established in 2000 primarily to distribute invitations and newsletters in Ukraine. Every month 150,000 copies of the Embassy of God newspaper are distributed.

Guest Department

Svetlana Kutsenko started the guest department as a ministry. Svetlana joined the Embassy of God Church from an Orthodox Church on June 30, 1996. She believes her true repentance was at the Embassy of God. Svetlana attended the leadership classes and joined the praise and worship team in September 1996. She left the worship team when she gained admission into a Uni-

versity. She studied International Economics and management between 1997 and 2003. She learnt German as a foreign language and took some classes in English. After her graduation, Svetlana went to Sweden in June 2003 and came back to Kiev in November. She started the guest department in December 2003 when the church started to have many foreign guests, the management of which became clumsy. Andrei Kuksenko was the senior manager then and the church's anniversary was three months away. The church received over 500 foreign visitors at the 2004 anniversary. In January 2004, Svetlana started to train volunteers on how to handle the guests. The training includes planning, welcoming, visa arrangements, transportation, and site seeing. She selected 50 of those who attended the training to work for the anniversary. Ludmila Kalitenko joined the guest department on February 1, 2005 and shared the planning of the 2005 anniversary with Svetlana. The headship of the guest department was transferred to Ludmila in May of that year after the anniversary as Svetlana had to return to the University for a Ph.D. program. Ludmila inherited about 100 volunteers.

Transportation Department

This department works closely with the guest department by providing transportation to guests. They pick guests up from the airport, drop them at the airport and provide services within the city. The drivers are volunteers who provide their services as a ministry; they do not charge for what they do;

some even refuse gratuity being offered to them. Sometimes they have to hire cars from rental services to provide transportation to guests. Depending on the circumstances, sometimes they rent the cars and cover all expenses; sometimes the guest department rents the cars and pays all expenses. In any case, the guest department usually pays for the fuel.

MISSIONS

The Embassy of God Church is about missions (planting churches and establishing missional (Churchshift) ministries), and that is why the Bishop heads the Missions Department. Anatoy Belonozhko gave his life to Christ on May 22, 1994 at the Embassy of God Church (known as Word of Faith then). He was a smoker and light drinker. His wife brought the entire family (with two children) to the church. A woman had told her that there is a living God at the Embassy of God with a black Pastor. Anatoy graduated from all of the Embassy of God schools. He soon became the general administrator of the church, taking over from Iurii Ivanovich. The general administrator also serves as the Personal Assistant of the Spiritual leader, Pastor Sunday Adelaja. Alex Boldesko took over the general administration position from him and Anatoy joined a daughter church to become the praise and worship leader. After his ordination, he became the Pastor of the church. In

2003, Anatoy was ordained as the first Bishop of the Embassy of God Church. His ordination changed the administrative structure of the Embassy of God Church. The general administrator remains as the Personal Assistant of Pastor Sunday and the head of some of the church ministries of the Central Church providing direct services to the church. Bishop Anatoy Belonozhko became the Head of Missions. This means that he is the administrative head of all the Embassy of God daughter churches (Chapter 12) and Churchshift ministries (Chapter 14). The Missions Department also trains potential Pastors and missionaries.

The responsibilities of the Bishop include primarily fulfilling the global vision of the church and pastoral counseling. The visions come from the Apostolic Council of which he is a member.

Missionary Center

The Missionary Center is responsible for the administration of the church's network of daughter churches. The Center coordinates and gathers information about all the daughter churches. The Center also provides guidance to Missionaries who want to establish daughter churches in and outside Ukraine. The Center has a vision of planting 1,000 daughter churches worldwide in two years. At the Embassy of God, pastors have the freedom to develop their missions so that they can make the necessary impact to the society.

Mission Schools

In order to equip missionaries in church planting and establishing Churchshift ministries, the church runs three schools: Joshua Bible Institute (JBI), Pastoral School, and Missionary School. JBI is run as a church ministry and will be discussed in Chapter 13.

Pastoral School

At the Pastoral School, students are taught how to run a church, planning and registration of churches, creating projects, social directions (spheres), how to influence the society, and other church and Churchshift related matters. The pastoral school is intended for those who want to become a Pastor or Churchshift minister. Here are the prerequisites to attend the pastoral school. The candidate must:

o have graduated from the Joshua Bible Institute;
o lead a cell group with 12 disciples;
o sign an affidavit to run a church within one year.

Missionary School

The Missionary School is a 4 to 8 weeks' program that teaches how to carry out missionary work. It teaches how to study the spiritual atmosphere of a city and how to create Churchshift ministries.

Churchshift Ministries

The administration of the Churchshift ministries came under the Missions Department in 2008 when the need became obvious. Churchshift ministries are also (wrongly) called social ministries at the Embassy of God. Formerly, Pastor Ludmila Gannoha coordinated all social activities with Pastor Tatiana Galusko who was the Head then. They are both Social Pastors. Ludmila was an Engineer by profession before the collapse of the former Soviet Union. She later went to Business School to study Accounting Economics. She was not a believer until 1997 when she joined the Embassy of God Church. Her 19 year old son then, her only child, was a drug user. He used all kinds of narcotics including marijuana, cocaine, and heroine; he graduated from one drug to the other. She was barren for 5 years before she could have the child; she was afraid of losing him. She didn't know where to get help; the hospitals couldn't help. They tried a seer who the husband found in a newspaper to no avail. Her son came home one day with his Jewish girlfriend; Ludmila had sympathy for the girl friend and so she advised her to leave him; she was surprised when she told her not to worry that God can help. The girl friend talked about Natalia Potopayeva and the Love Rehabilitation Center. Ludmila came to see Natalia in August 1997 and her son came for rehabilitation in September of that year; the Center always wants par-

MISSIONAL REFORMATION

ents to come first when it is a family problem. This pushed Ludmila to enroll at the University to study sociology, in a quest to know more about the problem. She joined the rehabilitation center before the end of 1997 as a volunteer. Ludmila's son left the rehabilitation center after two weeks, without completing the program, and ended up in jail; God touched him there and he began to preach in prison. When he got out of jail, he went to the University to study Theology and later Psychology. He is now a director of a rehabilitation center, working closely with the mayor of Kiev. He owns a good business and pastors a daughter church of the Embassy of God. Ludmila herself became the director of Love Rehabilitation Center in 1999. By the time Natalia Potopayeva moved to Germany, Ludmila had become the director of all rehabilitation centers established by Natalia. She was ordained as a Social Pastor in 2004. She was appointed in 2008 to administer the activities of Churchshift ministries while Tatiana Galusko enrolled for a Ph.D. program.

FINANCE

The Finance Department reports directly to the Apostolic Council and the Spiritual Council of the Central Church. Vera Melnik, a factory worker, was one of the first 49 members of the church. She had eye disease and was becoming blind but

God healed her of the disease at a leadership meeting of the Embassy of God Church. The finance (accounts) department started when there was a need to count offerings and need for proper accounting for the church. Vera volunteered to be taking and counting the offerings; there was almost nothing to count initially. The responsibility of all monetary issues fell on the shoulders of Vera. She now prepares the budget and payroll. Pastor Sunday started to receive a salary in 1995 with a stipend of about $20 (USD) per month. As the church grew, Sunday's salary increased to about $80 a month. Because of the poor financial situation, that was what the church could afford. Pastor Sunday started to publish books and audio tapes; so he stopped getting salary from the church. He now even supports the church from his income. Because of the increased responsibilities, Vera now works with 10 volunteers and she remains the only paid worker in the finance department. She took interne courses in accounting in order to become more efficient. In 1999, she left the factory job and became a full time church worker, heading the finance department. None of the volunteers has ever betrayed her. Every month the department gives a report to the senior Pastor.

MISSIONAL REFORMATION

POINTS IN CHAPTER 11

The Apostolic Council is the highest Spiritual governance body of the Embassy of God Church. The Council passes its decision to the National Spiritual Council.

The Spiritual Council exists at three levels: National, Regional, and Assembly Councils.

The Head of Administration at the Embassy of God is Bishop Anatoy Belonozhko. The Missions Department is directly under his Administration.

The administration has three units: Management, Missions, and Finance. The church has several Departments that keep it functioning.

12. DAUGHTER CHURCHES

BISHOP Anatoy Belonozhko is the head administrator of all daughter churches. By 2008, the Embassy of God Church had 31 daughter churches in Kiev region and over 400 in the Ukraine. In addition, there is an estimate of over 700 daughter churches worldwide. This is an underestimation because during the 2009 anniversary, the Malawian mission reported over 100 affiliations which were not counted in the estimates. Each daughter church is allowed to have her own vision and mission in response to her environment. When Pastor Sunday announced his revelation to start missionary work around the world, many key leaders of the church rose to the task; it is a tough decision for any church to release such key people, but Pastor Sunday obeyed God and released them. He says the church belongs to God. Pastor Sunday does not encourage his Pastors to draw members from other existing churches. Anyone planting a church must recruit fresh members. There is no specific church planting model, but the one most frequently used is the parachute drop (see Chapter 3 of Volume 1). Some of the churches are *monospherical*, also described in Chapter 3. This is so because of the stewardship nature of church members in specific spheres. It becomes easier for the planter to get members in his/her sphere of influence. We will now discuss a few of the daughter churches, randomly selected.

KIEV REGION

SERGEY PYSHNNY

Sergey Pyshnny was on drugs for 5 years, stealing to survive. In the year 2000, he went to a rehabilitation center managed by the Embassy of God Church. When he was released, he had no money and by God's design, a man walked to him and offered him an apartment. He served at the rehabilitation center. In 2002, Sergey joined a daughter church of the Embassy of God founded by Pastor Alexander. This daughter church went through a lot of persecution and had difficulties finding a place of worship. In May 2007, Sergey was ordained as a Pastor after completing his training and took over the church founded by Pastor Alexander. He started by having street crusades. Pastor Pyshnny has found his life back to normalcy; he currently works for the Mayor of his city and he is regarded as a major candidate to be the next mayor of that city. Eventually, he got a building and his church has a worship location now. His membership has increased from about 30 when he started to about 150 now.

BOSE ADELAJA

Bose Adelaja, an engineer by training and wife of the Senior Pastor, Sunday, has a lot of responsibilities at the Embassy of God. Before she got married, she wanted to live a "normal" life; she would have preferred her husband not to be a pastor. But now, Bose has grown to be a force at the church. A strong worship leader, she is the resident Pastor of the Central Church as well as the Pastor of the English church. On a typical Sunday, she would rush to the Central Church to pastor the second service after concluding the English service. Pastor Bose Adelaja is one

> The role of a wife is to stand by her husband and to be a blessing and relief to him. - Bose

MISSIONAL REFORMATION

of the top three leaders of the Embassy of God Church. She is soft spoken off altar but very vibrant, energetic, and on fire when on altar. For being the resident Pastor of the Central Church, the management and the finance department report to the Senior Pastor as well as to her. She also heads the spiritual council of the Central Church. There are 10 to 12 Pastors at the Central Church; she counsels them. Each of these Pastors is in charge of at least a church ministry (Chapter 13).

Because her original home group grew to well over 12 members, Bose now leads three home groups, each with an average of 20 members. Her home groups are basically the *Meta* type (see definition in Chapter 3 of Volume 1), filled with ministers or church ministry leaders. The Central Church spiritual council is counted as a home group for her. She meets with each of two groups every other Tuesday at 6:30 pm and the third group on Fridays at 7:30 pm. She allows transparency in her home groups; people share their experiences openly and learn from each other. They also have Bible study and pray together. She does one-on-one counseling only on extremely confidential issues.

Pastor Bose started the English church in 2003 primarily to cater for new foreigners in Kiev. Most of the members are students who come and leave after completing their studies. The church always counts between 80 and 100 attendees at a particular service. Dr. Ovie Oso-

Osoroh, a Nigerian by birth, is the assistant Pastor of the English church. Pastor Osoroh studied in the Ukraine and decided to go and practice his profession in Nigeria as a medical doctor; however, he was called into full time ministry and had to abandon his plans. There are about seven other English churches from other denominations in Kiev region.

Pastor Bose also has responsibilities of leading some church ministries, such as Pastors wives ministry and women ministry. She has however handed over the leadership of the Pastors wives ministry to Bishop Anatoy's wife. She took over the leadership of women ministry from Sophia Zhukatanskaya. Bose has written three books and co-authored two books with Pastor Sunday. Regarding the persecution of the church and the Senior Pastor, Bose says *"there is a purpose for tribulations; God always vindicates His servants"*.

VLADIMIR DZUBA

Vladimir Dzuba came to the Lord in another charismatic evangelical church in 1993. He owned a business. He received a prophecy that God would use him to raise missionaries. God brought him to the Embassy of God for this purpose through the Holy Spirit guidance. He is one of the first fifty members of the Embassy of God. God ministered to him that his ministry is in Asia. In 1997, he

MISSIONAL REFORMATION

started the "Power of Faith" Ministry, a daughter church of the Embassy of God with about 120 attendees. By 2008, the attendance grew to about 900 with about 120 home group leaders. Pastor Dzuba has also planted 11 churches, 1 in Kiev and 10 in other Ukranian cities. His churches also have several social programs. In 2005, he started a Bible College in China with 40 students. He was to start a church in Czech Republic in October 2008.

> God has brought meaning into my life. I understand that I am not here on this earth by accident, but to accomplish God's purpose.
> - Vladimir

TATIANA MAKSIMENKO

Tatiana Maksimenko is the current Pastor at the Embassy of God "on the right bank" with a regular service attendance of about 700 people. This church served as the Central Church before relocating. When the Central Church was relocated in February 1999, the church was left as its first branch and was pastored by Natalia Potopayeva. Tatiana gave her life to Christ at a Pentecostal church in 1993 before she joined the Embassy of God in 1996. A member had invited her to the Friday night prayer; she liked the meeting and she started to attend the prayer meeting regularly. She knew she belonged there rather than in the Pentecostal church where she was a member. She was a home group leader in her former church. When she decided to formally join the Embassy of God, her husband was surprised and initially resisted. All the members of her home group joined the Embassy of God with her. When Pastor Sunday moved in 1999 to a new location of the Central Church, some members stayed behind at the first branch; Tatiana was one of them. She became the assistant to Pastor Natalia Potopayeva and a member of the Spiritual Council. Before she joined the Embassy of God, Tatiana was timid and had low self esteem. She could never see herself on the pulpit. The Lord changed her; Natalia told her she would be a pastor but she doubted that in her mind. One day, Natalia walked to her and said "tomorrow you are going to lead the ABC Bible Class". Tatiana was astonished, more so that she was able to handle the class of 150 people. She did not know that she had this ability. Another day, Natalia walked to her and said "tomorrow you will preach". And that was how her career in the ministry started. Tatiana enrolled in the Joshua Bible Institute and graduated in the year 2000. Between 1995 and 2000, Tatiana worked in the Accounts Department of the Ukrainian Ministry of Education. In 2004, after Natalia left on a mission trip to Germany, Tatiana became the resident pastor of the church.

GALINA KOROBKA

Galina Korobka joined the Embassy of God Church in April 1994 at the very beginning. She came after watching a TV

MISSIONAL REFORMATION

program of Natalia Potopayeva; she immediately gave her life to Christ. Before then, she was divorced, jobless, an alcoholic, and futureless; alcohol was her joy. She dressed shabbily with a puffy bluish face. She knew that she was sinking deeper and deeper. After joining the church, she went for rehabilitation and fasted for 21 days. Her then ex-husband was surprised to see her stop smoking and drinking; she was completely transformed. By 1995, she had become a home group leader, and in January 1996, she was a coordinator of home groups; this was before the System of 12 was introduced. In that same year (1996), her ex-husband re-married her after keeping a sceptical eye-watch for two years. She calls him "my second first husband". In January 1997, Galina became the Assistant of Pastor Tope Omotoye while attending the Joshua Bible Institute. Galina was ordained as a Pastor in October 1997 and she planted a Family daughter church in Moskovsky district in Kiev region with 36 members. The church grew to 500 members with an attendance of 300 at any regular service. Pastor Galina Korobka has planted another church in another district in Kiev. The church works with social organizations, schools, hospitals, prisons, family,

> Looking at this lively and happy woman full of energy and humor, nobody would think that just a few years ago she was dying from alcohol. - Fares

and the handicapped. In 2008, Pastor Korobka was a college student of Philosophy and Religion. She is known by thousands of people in the Ukraine and in the North of Russia; she has shown many people the way to true life, being a follower of Jesus Christ.

UKRAINE

The Embassy of God Church has over 400 daughter churches in cities and villages of Ukraine. We will look at only one of the daughter churches in the Ukraine, outside of Kiev region.

IGOR TOMCHENKO

After the fall of the Soviet Union in the early 90s, iterant Missionaries came to Kozhanka town in the northern part of Ukraine; in particular, Ed Dickinson from Canada built a Christian Camp in the town and also, a lady from the Embassy of God Church in Kiev came to Kozhanka to open an orphanage home, and she invited Igor to the Central Church at Kiev in 1999. Igor lived in Kozhanka most of his life. He was kicked out of school in the 9th grade for having low grades. In 1994 to 1996, he attended a technical school in the town to learn welding. He served in the Ukrainian military from 1996 to

1998 at the Poland border. After serving, he came back to Kozhanka and resumed his alcoholic addiction without a job. In January 1999, one Lydia started an Embassy of God daughter church with 22 members at Fastov, a nearby town.

After Igor accepted Christ at the Central Church in Kiev, he stopped drinking alcohol and joined and grew with the church in Fastov in the middle of the year. He immediately joined theatre ministry and joined a home group. In 2000, Igor attended the Joshua Bible Institute

> I was only 24 at the time I became the pastor of the church and was only a believer for four years! But age doesn't matter with God. - Igor

and by 2003 he was ordained as a pastor. All glory to God, Igor is now in full time ministry owning four solid business ventures. Lydia moved to another town and Pastor Igor Tomchenko assumed as the pastor of the church. The church grew rapidly to 150 memberships, the largest in Fastov. Igor has received God's blessings abundantly that he owns a lot of properties in Fastov and Kozhanka. He is planting more churches and a Bible school in the area.

UNITED STATES OF AMERICA

VASILY BILETSKY

Vasily Biletsky, son of a Pastor, was an unbeliever until the age of 26. He had a good career during the communist regime; he was a leader of an organization in the former Soviet Union and was also a director of an apartment complex. By 1981, he had three children and was divorced. Vasily accepted Christ in 1982 at a Baptist Church. He was ordained as Pastor in 1985. In 1995, Vasily joined the Embassy of God Church. After 15 years of separation, he re-united with his wife. Pastor Sunday blessed the marriage. Vasily was re-ordained as a Pastor at the Embassy of God Church in 1997. He became

> God found people who were willing to sacrifice their time, finances, and skills, doing everything possible for the church to have its own building.
> - Vasily

the administrator after Henry Okoi, and also became the first resident Pastor of the Central church. Without speaking much English, Pastor Vasily responded to the call for missionaries and moved to Sacramento, California with his wife in 2001. They prayed fervently and were able to establish the first Embassy of God daughter church in Sacramento. Within a few weeks, the church had grown to over 120 members. In less than a year the church was able to raise 250 thousand dollars required by the bank to purchase their church building; members sacrificed their equity loans. Pastor Bilesky coordinates all mission activities in the USA. He plans to plant the Embassy of God daughter churches in 50 States within 10 years. Already, he has sent out leaders to several States including Georgia, Minnesota, New York, Illinois, Florida, Washington, and Pennsylvania. By 2008, there were 14 active daughter churches in the USA. The USA Mission follows a similar vision of the Central Church in Kiev. They have home groups (6 in Canada), hold a 3-day fast twice a year and establish Churchshift ministries.

YURI BINDER

Yuri got saved in 1993 at Odessa Calvary Chapel, a Baptist Church of 15 members which was almost closed down six months after he joined. The church was able to grow to 20 members after 9 years of existence. Many missionaries came to Ukraine in 1992-93. Yuri studied English and traveled to Moscow in 1994 with missionaries as an interpreter. In 1995, he came back to

Ukraine to attend a Bible School to be more equipped for ministry, after which he continued to travel with missionaries. Yuri left the interpreting job and came back to Odessa to join a small-sized Gospel church. He became the assistant Pastor and the Dean of the Bible School. The church grew from 12 members in 1998 to 450 members in 2001. Through the leading of the Holy Spirit, Yuri left Odessa to join the Embassy of God Church in Kiev in 2001. His former church in Odessa was enjoying growth, and the senior Pastor was very unhappy with him for leaving. After one year, the Pastor eventually took the church under the umbrella of the Embassy of God as a daughter church in Odessa. By 2007, the Embassy of God had 5 daughter churches in Odessa: 3 existing ones which came under its umbrella and 2 new ones which were newly established.

When Yuri joined the Embassy of God, the first thing he noticed was that Pastor Sunday was a unique preacher. He heard him preach messages he had never heard from any other preacher. Yuri also had the

> I saw Pastor Sunday in another dimension. He never fights with the devil, he has dominion. - Yuri

opportunity to work with Pastor Sunday as an interpreter for 3 years. He and his wife were ordained during the church's anniversary in 2003. He moved to New York in 2004 as a missionary of the Embassy of God. Pastor Yuri Binder started a rehabilitation center in New York in April 2008.

ANDREI KUKSENKO

Andrei joined the army at the early age of 14. He was in his third year at the military college when his sister, who had joined the Embassy of God Church a month earlier, invited him to the church as an English-Russian interpreter. On June 19, 1995, Andrei came to the church and gave his life to Christ. On the following day, he joined the ushers group, and after 9 months, he joined Pastor Sunday's security team. He became the leader of the team after 1 year. In 1996, Andrei started a home group. Yuriy Kravchenko, now a Pastor and a sports minister (see Chapter 14) was a member of this home group. Yuriy brought a lot of his workers to the group; the group had to split 18 times to multiply. Andrei graduated from the military college in 1997. He became the Embassy of God's administrator in 2001 when the incumbent administrator relocated to Sacramento, USA, on a missionary work. In 2006, Andrei himself moved to Tacoma, Washington State, USA to plant a church.

> It is a pity to say, but mostly in USA - church is a goal and business. And to go to church already became a cultural thing - Andrei

The Tacoma church started in September 2006 with 10 people. By early 2009, the church had grown to 100 regular members. A member of the church runs a rehabilitation center. On his experience as a Pastor in Tacoma, Andrei says:

> I think we need to return trust to ministers of God. But first of all, the minister needs to preach the Truth and confront any temptations just to build a church, instead of changing people's lives and spreading the Kingdom. Church is not a goal, but a tool. It is a pity to say, but mostly in the USA - church is a goal and business. And it already became a cultural thing - to go to church. And also, to be a pastor in USA, you need to be serious about your own relationship with God and self-discipline in studying and prayer.

GERMANY

NATALIA POTOPAYEVA

She is featured on the cover page of this book - the Embassy of God woman of two decades. People, they say, are unpredictable; but this one is going no where. It is like Ruth and Naomi; "where ever you go, I go, your God shall be my God, and your people, my people". Natalia and Sunday are bonded in

MISSIONAL REFORMATION

Christ. They are two compassionate beings and that is why their bond is strong. One of the Pastors at the Embassy of God remarks: "Pastor Sunday is like a father to Natalia even though she could be his mother". When Sunday Adelaja gave an invitation on his TV program in 1993 for those who want to learn about the Bible to meet him at a certain place, Natalia, a then alcoholic, was one of the seven that turned up. She introduced herself to Sunday as "Natalia alcoholic", and then Sunday asked if her last name was "alcoholic". Her father was also an alcoholic and died a terrible death. Depressed, not knowing where her life was leading her, she responded to the invitation out of curiosity, like the

> I tried every remedy for alcoholism there was; I tried poisoning myself with Teturam, I tried psychotherapy, I went through a Shishko treatment course, but all to no avail. - Natalia

six others, to listen to what the Black chap had to say. She doubted that a Black man could be a Christian; she thought that Christianity stopped with the White people. She was surprised when Sunday smiled and said there are millions of Christians in Africa. Natalia had tried to read the Bible before, but she didn't understand where to start from. After listening to Sunday, she became zealous and thirsty for God. The Bible courses became her daily bread. Then the potential that God had deposited in her began to manifest. One important factor one should note is that, Sunday was able to communicate effectively the Truth through the guidance of the

Holy Spirit. This is what most of the foundation members of the church say. Natalia was filled with joy, she became transformed and decided to help others too. She went to look for where the drug and alcohol addicts usually gathered and she found them. Revived Natalia took to the streets of Kiev with Sunday to win the souls of the addicts; Natalia would testify of her transformation and Sunday would preach and pray. This was not yielding much as the addicts were really not responding to their efforts. Natalia fasted and prayed for the first time and shared with Sunday the idea of speaking to the families of the addicts. Sunday arranged a TV program for Natalia where she testified and addressed the families of the addicts; it worked. Many responded to her call. She started the first the Embassy of God rehabilitation center at her home. Natalia had visited rehabilitation centers before, and she was able to create a Christian rehabilitation program with 10 steps on how to be rehabilitated. The center, named "Love", was formally opened on April 26, 1994; this center is now named after Natalia. The Love Rehabilitation Center is discussed further in Chapter 14.

Natalia was ordained as a Pastor in 1999. In that year, the Central church moved to a new location and Natalia remained at the old location (Right Bank) to become the first Pastor of the first branch of the Embassy of God. The Right Bank (Pravoberezhnaya) Church grew to about 3,000 members. Natalia was the only female Pastor in Europe with such a large church. In 2004, Natalia tried to establish a mission

MISSIONAL REFORMATION

work in Israel where her mother lives, but she was denied entry into the country. After having established several daughter churches in Kiev region, and after having transformed thousands of lives in Kiev, Pastor Natalia Potopayeva moved to Germany in 2005 as a missionary of the Embassy of God with a vision of changing the Spiritual climate of Western Europe. She is in popular demand as a preacher in many countries. By 2008, she had planted up to 15 daughter churches in Western Europe. The church has also established several Churchshift ministries. One of the ministries is the VIGAN medical massage saloons which have similar operations as the NUGA Best in Ukraine (see Business sphere in Chapter 14). Natalia says about Sunday Adelaja, *"such people are not ordinary. He is a reformer and he is making history. He is not about building churches but building new country in a country, a society in a society."*

RUSSIA

ALEKSANDR DZUBA

Alex (and his brother Vladimir) repented at a Pentecostal church in Vatutino in 1993 before coming to Kiev. They joined the Embassy of God Church in 1994. They were told of an African pastoring a church where

12. DAUGHTER CHURCHES

people jumped on the chairs while worshipping God. Out of curiosity, they visited the church but could not find people jumping on chairs. There were about 15 people when they came. Alex was touched by the preaching of Pastor Sunday and he and his brother decided to join the church. Alex started a youth movement focusing on marriage seminars in 1995. In 1996, he graduated from the Bible school and was ordained as a pastor that same year. Towards the end of that year, Alex started a daughter church in Borispol area with 20 people. Within 1 year, the church grew to about 500 attendees. By 2001, the church had 1,500 regular members. In 2001, the Lord instructed Alex to release the church to his assistant, Pastor Oleg, and move to Russia. Alex went to Russia with 3 people and $1,000 (USD) to sustain them. Once in Russia, Alex started a Home Group and within one month, the membership rose to 40. It was the Lord's doing because the $1,000 they had could only pay for 3 months' hall rent and the registration of the church. Later a former drug addict who was a director of a cinema house surrendered the premises of the cinema to be used by the congregation. By that time, the congregation had risen to 100. Due to police harassment, they moved from one location to another. Alex was arrested once during the year because he was preaching without a permit. By the end of 2001, the congregation rose to 500. In 2002, a pastoral school was opened in Moscow and about 150 enrolled for the first time. The congregation continued to grow and became financially stable.

MISSIONAL REFORMATION

Many elites joined the church and made substantial contributions. One of them even donated a house in a secluded area in Moscow for Pastor Alex Dzuba to live in. Alex returned to Ukraine permanently in 2006 but planned to attend the monthly anointing service in Moscow. At the second service, he was denied entrance to Russia. By then, several churches had been planted in Moscow and in seven other cities in Russia. Fifty existing churches in Russia came under the umbrella of the Embassy of God Church. When Alex returned to Ukraine, Yevgeniy Peresvetov took over the leadership of the Russian mission. More Bible schools and several social ministries have been opened since that time.

MALAWI

YEVGENIY PERESVETOV

Yevgeniy Peresvetov took over the leadership of the Russian Mission from Pastor Alex Dzuba. Yevgeniy was one of the three foundation members of the Russian mission that accompanied Alex from Borispol to Russia. Yevgeniy's father was a drug addict. Alex Dzuba found Yevgeniy homeless in a basement of an apartment complex at the age of 17. He is now an ordained Pastor of the Embassy of God and has extended the Russian mission to Malawi in Africa. Several churches have been planted and several Churchshift ministries, mostly in the family sphere (see Chapter 14), have been opened. Yevgeniy sent missionaries to Malawi and also grooms local Malawian ministers. The Malawi mission has also built several schools there. Many churches have been planted and many existing churches came under the umbrella of the Embassy of God Church. The Malawi mission is counting over 100 daughter churches. The mission has also trained over 400 pastors.

POINTS IN CHAPTER 12

As of April 2009, the Embassy of God Church has 31 daughter churches in Kiev region alone and over 400 daughter churches in Ukraine. Furthermore, it has more than 700 daughter churches in 35 countries.

Pastor Bose Adelaja, wife of the Senior Pastor, is the resident Pastor of the Central Church as well as the Pastor of the English church, which is one of the daughter churches.

Some of the churches are *monospherical*; these churches have a homogeneous composition of the members mostly from a specific sphere.

13. CHURCH MINISTRIES

THERE are two types of ministries: church ministry and missional ministry. Missional ministry at the Embassy of God is the Churchshift ministry mentioned in Chapter 9 of Volume 1. According to Sunday Adelaja, Senior Pastor of the Embassy of God Church, traditional church ministries are mere "housekeeping" ministries. Most ministries in a classical church are church ministries. A missional (or Churchshift) ministry goes outside the boundaries of the church.

> Some people believe that if they work in the nursery or sing in the choir, they are fulfilling their area of ministry. But this is not really ministry. It is merely housekeeping.

MISSIONAL REFORMATION

> Your work as a choir member, nursery volunteer, or usher is what we all must do to keep the church functioning, but it is not necessarily fulfilling the Great Commission. The Great Commission happens outside the church. - Sunday Adelaja, *Churchshift*, p.10

Home groups based on members in church ministries are of the *Meta* type while those based on members in Churchshift ministries are of the *Missional* type. Church ministries provide either direct or indirect services to the church.

DIRECT SERVICE

Some of the church ministries that provide direct services at the Embassy of God are Ushers and Security, Choir, Praise and Worship, Banners, Prayer, Hospitality, and Beginners.

PRAISE AND WORSHIP

Each church assembly of the Embassy of God has a praise and worship department coordinated by a leader. Natasha Dickson leads the praise and worship department of the Central Church. She also leads the mass choir when there is a joint service of the Embassy of God Churches, such as during the church anniversaries. Natasha also leads the praise and worship team for the monthly anointing service of all the daughter churches in Kiev region. Natasha Dickson, a graduate of musical education, was a member of the choir at a Pentecostal church before joining the Embassy of God Church in 1999. She was influenced after watching a television program of Sunday Adelaja. She attended the Joshua Bible Institute in the year 2000. By December 1999, she had become a background vocalist of the praise and worship team. The leadership of the praise and worship team fell on Natasha when the outgoing leader was going on a mission work in 2006. Every one in the team was surprised when Bose Adelaja, the resident Pastor of the Central church selected her. No one really saw her leadership qualities, but Pastor Bose did. The praise and worship team consists of four groups: banner ministry, choir, sound, and musical. Each group meets individually every week and the four groups meet together once a month for spiritual upliftment. The church has two teams of a combination of the musical group and the choir. Each of the two teams practice together twice a week. Natasha is responsible for scheduling which team ministers at a particular service. The team that is not ministering is always ready as a back up. Songs for the Sunday service are selected during the week through prayers and meditation. Four songs and an exaltation word are se-

> Everyone has the opportunity to use his or her potential at Embassy of God. The church trains you to be a leader even if you don't think you are one. – Natasha

MISSIONAL REFORMATION

lected for the Sunday worship service; the songs are in the following order: welcome or introductory, praise, exaltation, and worship. Before each service, the team fellowships together and the leader shares the exaltation word which should form theme of the worship that day. The praise and worship teams have released up to 15 music CDs.

BANNER MINISTRY

Tatiana Kornilova came to Christ and joined the Embassy of God Church in September 1995. She was invited to the church by one of her friends who had alcohol and smoking problems. Tatiana received the revelation for the banner ministry in 2000 while attending the Joshua Bible Institute. She started to develop the ministry in 2001 when her son had an accident and was amputated; that motivated her more. She started by making signs on handkerchiefs and distributing them to people to waive during praise and worship. A movement soon developed and the banner ministry was formally established in 2003. About 500 different flags were hand made including flags from different nations and many other banners with different color combinations. The ministry currently has 7 leaders. Members are trained on the significance of banners and choice of colors for any particular banner made. Much spirituality is attached to the ministry.

Below is what the ministry teaches as the significance of choice of colors.

Red	fire, love, blood, cross, battle;
Green	fruit, fertility, tree, new life, grace, growth, hope, God's Word;
Blue	water, Holy Spirit, Heavens;
Yellow	glory, joy, worship, sun, warmth
Gold, silver	noble, clean, God's presence, authority, glory, deliverance, King's dominion;
White	purity, holiness, Jesus, glory, light, justice, perfection;
Black	grief, justice, complaint, death, trouble;
Copper	confession of guilt, humility;
Violet	helpfulness, intercession, ministry of priest;
Orange	fire, joy, fearlessness

The banner ministry not only carries and waves flags during worship services, they also pray over the flags of nations of the world (Is. 13:2-3). The team prays together before any worship service; they believe that the carriers of the banners must be spiritually strong. The motto of the banner ministry is Jehovah-Nissi (Exodus 17:15), Lord our banner.

Banners are large flags with symbols to proclaim that Jesus is our Banner (Isaiah 11:10-12). Banners are significant in the following areas:
o worshipping God without words;
o as tools for glorification, intercession, declaration;
o as a signal (message is transferred);
o as means of spiritual communication;
o intensifying worship, prayer;
o opening new ways, new freedom;
o leading during battles;
o conquering the enemy's territory (Joshua 1:3)

Tatiana says *"There is connection and interaction between worship, prayer, dance, and banners. (Joshua 6). Banners represent victory (Exo 17:15). Each of the 12 tribes of Israel had its banner with the symbol of the tribe (Num 1:51-54)"*.

The banner ministry provides guidance for individuals who carry the banner.
o Pray in your heart (or aloud) while carrying the banner;
o Be aware that you are the armor bearer;
o Do not put your ministry and banners in your heart higher than God; they are only tools;

- Find out that your church approves using banners;
- Be humble; support worshipping; be united with a worship team;

Further reading: Ps. 20:5, 60:4; Sol. 2:4, 6:10; Is. 13: 2

PRAYER MINISTRY

Pastor Valentina Chabannaya is the leader of the prayer ministry; she is also the leader of the senior citizens ministry. Valentina is a vivid example of someone healed from depression and the fear of death, naturally from the coming of old age. Before she joined the ministry, Valentina worked as a medical doctor with little children suffering from cerebral palsy; this made her to wonder if God really exists and she thirsted for this knowledge. She read poems, occult books, and other theories about God. This made her to be far away from God. Then she realized she was seeking the wrong places and started to call upon Him. She approached an Orthodox church and asked "Where can I meet God?" She was not satisfied with the response she received; so, she continued in her search. One day, the Holy Spirit led her to switch on her TV set and immediately she heard Pastor Sunday asking people to join him for Bible

> When you seek God just for the sake of it, when you don't have a firm foundation, you begin to look in all wrong places - Valentina

studies. Valentina was one of the seven who responded to Pastor Adelaja's invitation in November 1993. Although she felt joy in her spirit but her flesh struggled to yield. She noticed that the prayer was strong. She asked herself: why do we have to be taught by a foreigner, a very young one at that? But, when she realized he was telling the truth, she decided to stand by the "boy". God taught her how to pray and has changed Valentina a lot through various experiences since 1993. When Pastor Sunday asked her to lead the prayer ministry, she hesitated and told him "I am not that candidate you need". Pastor Sunday responded and said "You have a week to think about it; you have a choice; God may choose another person and He may not". She accepted the challenge. When the system of twelve was introduced, she started a prayer team with her home group. She is currently a college student in Practical Psychology.

BEGINNERS MINISTRY

The beginners' ministry takes care of new members who have just given their lives to Christ. The ministry walks them through the leadership school of five steps. These steps are fully described in Figure 9.3 (Chapter 9 of Volume 1). The five steps are:
1. Meeting with Jesus (teaches about Jesus and salvation);
2. ABC Bible school;
3. Potential development;

4. Leadership development;
5. Ministry leadership;

A member who completes the five steps can further attend two more schools in the Missions Department to become a Pastor or a missionary.

INDIRECT SERVICE

Most of the ministries with indirect services could actually be mistaken as Churchshift ministries because they have tendencies to extend their services beyond the church. In other words, they have the potential of growing into a Churchshift ministry. Like Churchshift ministries, their activities are not financed by the church, but unlike Churchshift ministries some of them are profit making organizations. Some of the ministries that provide indirect services to the Embassy of God Church are: Bright Star Publishing House, Fares Publishing House, Creative Assistance in Television and Radio Programs, the Press Center, and Joshua Bible Institute.

PUBLISHING HOUSES

Olena Dobrovolska and Dmytro Kyrychenko jointly founded the first publishing house to publish the first book of Pastor Sunday Adelaja. Dmytro first visited the Embassy of God Church in 1994 but was turned off by the celebration; "too much dancing", he said. He attended an Orthodox church instead. He ran into debts and came back to accept Christ and to join the Embassy of God Church in 1996. The publishing house split into two (Fares and Bright Star) in 1999 because of differences in strategies, with Olena leading Fares and Dmitro leading Bright Star. Fares and Bright Star publishing houses are responsible for publishing and distributing most of the books written by the church organs and church members. While Fares focuses on the Embassy of God authors only, Bright Star welcomes writers from other church denominations. Fares has published 62 books of Pastor Sunday Adelaja and Bright Star has published 40. Most of the books initially written by Pastor Sunday were published in Russian but later translated into English. The publishing houses also help to distribute God's Word through audio cassettes and videotapes with sermons of popular ministers. Fares and Bright Star have also translated into Russian and published books originally authored by others such as Myles Munroe, T.L. Osborn, and Peter Daniels.

Andrew Usok joined the Embassy of God in 1998; his wife insisted he goes there. He was jobless and could not quit smoking and drinking. He stopped smoking and drinking in the summer of 1998 after his baptism. Andrew joined Bright Star in 1999 and worked with Dymtro for sometime and later crossed over to Fares to head the company. Andrew founded another company "Books Line" in 2004 for distributing all books published by Fares in Russian speaking countries. In 2007, Olena shifted to other responsibilities and Andrew became the Director of Fares Publishing House.

JOSHUA BIBLE INSTITUTE

The Joshua Bible Institute was established in 1995 as "Joshua Missionary Bible Training School". It is the first step after leadership training, for someone who opts to become a Pastor or a minister at the Embassy of God and who does not have a degree in divinity or theology. The vision is to create in Ukraine a strong church which will send out missionaries to take the Gospel to the entire world. The candidates go through a nine-month program of 4 hours per day. Topics taught include calling, faith, prayer, God, church, purity, sanctification, and doctrines. The Institute is headed by a Dean; the current Dean is Pastor Ruslan Makmodov. The first graduation of the Institute was in 1996 with 70 students.

MISSIONAL REFORMATION

In five years, 2,228 people had graduated from the Joshua Bible Institute. The picture above shows the 2008 graduates with Pastor Sunday at the middle of the third row.

PRESS CENTER

Unlike some other ministries providing indirect services, the  Press Center is non profit. It is constantly undergoing renovations. Primarily, it is responsible for all public communications from the church, through various media, journals, newsletters, tapes, videos, and Internet. Pastor Pavel Federov is the Head of this Department. The Center promotes books written by the church and church members. The Center also publishes two magazines, "*For Yours*" and "*Family*". Besides public communications, the center has expanded to include training in different areas. Various training schools are being established, such as Internet school every 3 months, Hardware school, School of Journalism, and Television school. The Center has a number of future Churchshift ministries lined up; they include organizing a Christian social network on the Internet, production of TV and radio programs, and the creation of a Christian News Agency.

Svetlana Malyutina leads the Content Management team for all Internet publications. She works round the clock, 7 days a week to make sure the information on the website is as current as possible. She edits and publishes 2 to 3 articles  per day. Through the website, the team evangelizes, promotes Pastor Sunday's teachings and books, and exposes the life and development of the Embassy of God. Svetlana, from Russia, repented in 1997 when Swedish evangelism flourished. She joined an evangelical group in March 2002 that invited her to Holland. She met Pastor Sophia Zhukatanskaya of the Embassy of God during her visit to Holland and she invited her to study at Joshua Bible Institute in July 2002. From 2003 to 2004 Svetlana served in the Bible Institute (cleaning, preparing food, and so on); she felt comfortable and liked the church; she believes God is there. In 2004 (till 2006) she volunteered to serve in the Web Department for secretarial work and in 2006 she became an official worker of the Embassy of God Church.

POINTS IN CHAPTER 13

Church ministries are ministries that provide services to the church and its members. Services could be direct or indirect.

A Church ministry providing indirect services has tendencies to be a Churchshift ministry.

Home groups based on church ministries are of the Meta type.

14. MISSIONAL (CHURCHSHIFT) MINISTRIES

WHAT is regarded as a real Ministry at the Embassy of God is actually what has been defined as Churchshift Ministry in Chapter 9 of Volume 1. Churchshift Ministries are the specific "Missional Ministries" at the Embassy of God. Missional Ministry is defined in this book as Churchshift. It has also been defined as the "Promised Land" of individual believers. The Embassy of God Church is about Churchshift ministries, with thousands of parachurch organizations worldwide.

OVERVIEW

PARACHURCH ORGANIZATIONS

Churchshift ministries at the Embassy of God Church are run like Parachurch organizations rising up in the USA. By definition, a Parachurch organization is involved in mass evangelism, urban missions, Christian education, political activism, social welfare, legal aid, media, prison outreach, rehabilitation, Bible schools, and so on. All these activities can be distributed over the seven spheres. They are self governing but often cooperate with churches across denomination barriers. So in a way, Parachurch organizations implement Missional (Churchshift) reformation. However, since these organizations are autonomous and are not church-based, some Christians see them as usurping the scriptural prerogatives of the church. On January 6, 2006, a blogger (triablogue.blogspot.com) commented on the accusation that Parachurch organizations drain away resources:

> Parachurch ministries arise to fill a vacuum. If the church were already assuming these responsibilities, then there'd be no need for Parachurch ministry.

At the Embassy of God the Parachurch organizations directly affiliate with the church. There are over 1,000 worldwide of such organizations at the Embassy of God. All ministries are run by individual members of the church and are financially independent. The ministries are run as non profits and most services are provided free of charge to the public. The ministries can be divided into seven the seven spheres.

CHURCHSHIFT PASTOR

A Missional or Churchshift Pastor ministers in a specific sphere of the society and does so through a Churchshift ministry. Many pastors at the Embassy of God are ordained as social pastors. A social pastor does not need a church building to minister; "social pastor" simply means Churchshift pastor. The church is beginning to get specific to the sphere; for example Valentina Sergeychuk in the Business sphere was ordained as the first Business Pastor. It is unique and well thought out; Church Pastors are differentiated from Churchshift Pastors.

EQUIPPING FOR MINISTRY

Every member of the church is expected to join a ministry after going through the Churchshift training discussed in Chapter 9 of Volume 1. The first training is the Step 3 of the Leadership Ladder School which entails potential development. That stage is very important in the ministerial future of the member because it is at that stage the member is expected to discover his/her "promised land", the sphere he/she is called into ministry. Other leadership training is received from the home group leader of the member.

MISSIONAL REFORMATION

In Step 4 of the Leadership Ladder, the member receives training in leading a ministry. After that training the member can lead a ministry of his/her own. One thing I noticed at the Embassy of God, besides their zeal for God, is that they take the ministry work very seriously and this is the main reason why the church members are being blessed in every aspect of life, finance, miraculous healing, happiness, and so on. The Senior Pastor, Sunday Adelaja, summarizes the church:

> The Embassy of God is a place where those who wanted to end their lives yesterday are rejoicing today; those who couldn't cope with their difficulties in their lives are helping others solve the unsolvable problems; those who had nothing to eat yesterday are creating jobs for others today; those who had no future are taking key positions in economics, politics and social spheres; the faceless crowd of the destitute is turning into a society of healthy and prosperous people living full lives. (Sunday Adelaja in *Fares* magazine 2005)

Another important thing to note is that, the ministry leaders educate themselves in their areas of ministry to be effective. Success is a priority for them; they realize that Church education is not enough to interact with the society, so, they go to college, usually to obtain a degree in Sociology and/or any field relating to their ministry. For example, a Social Pastor, who had a Bachelors degree at the start of her ministry, ended up with a Ph.D. in Sociology. There are many ministry leaders with Ph.D. degrees. They go all the way to be equipped.

GENERAL METHOD OF SOUL WINNING

Discipleship is a gradual process at the Embassy of God. Discipleship starts by winning the soul. Winning souls are achieved through Churchshift ministries and home groups. All the spheres use these common principles:

> You've got to know your audience. Paul preached and never mentioned the Bible. Don't slam the Bible into their face. Remember to assume that you are talking to someone who has no knowledge about the Bible and most governments don't want it.

ADMINISTRATION

As described in Chapter 11, the administration of the Churchshift ministries is under the Missions Department headed by the Bishop. In order to be able to effectively coordinate the overwhelming activities of the Churchshift ministries, the Missions Department has decided to create sub-departments which include Statistics, Projects Development, Partnership, Workers Preparation, and Public Relations.

GENERAL STATISTICS

The statistics given below were those reported by Churchshift ministries that responded to the request. The administration is now creating a statistics department which will make future statistics more accurate. Many of the numbers provided below are understated because many Churchshift

MISSIONAL REFORMATION

ministries did not provide their data by the time this book was written. At the 2009 15th anniversary of the Embassy of God Church, the following statistics were provided for the activities of Churchshift ministries:

- 217 Rehabilitation centers with more than 5,000 people who went through rehabilitation;
- More than 550 social organizations;
- Established 105 Educational and Social organizations with more than 23,000 graduates;
- Thousands of phone calls to the Trust Hotline;
- Work with 20 educational establishments in Kiev - youth (influence on 167,366 people);
- Work with 108 children establishments - homeless (influence on 165,190 children);
- Work with 35 nursing homes (influence on 64,096 people);
- Work with 25 hospitals plus 2 hospices (31,245 people affected);
- Work with 30 prisons (10,100 people affected);

Although the seven spheres have been defined slightly differently by Pastor Sunday Adelaja, we will stick to the standard ABCDEFG model described in Chapter 6 of Volume 1:

1. Arts, Entertainment, and Sports
2. Business and Finance
3. Church and Religion
4. Distribution and Media

5. Education, Science and Technology
6. Family and Home
7. Government and Law

In this Chapter, we will study some of the ministries in each of the spheres. The Education Sphere is the most distributed; every sphere has at least one education ministry.

ARTS, ENTERTAINMENT, AND SPORTS

> The highest art-instincts are natural gifts, and hence belong to those excellent graces which, in spite of sin, by virtue of common grace, have continued to shine in human nature, it plainly follows that art can inspire both believers and unbelievers, and that God remains Sovereign to impart it, in His good pleasure, alike to Heathen and to Christian nations. (Kuyper: Calvinism and Arts)

The arts, entertainment, and sports sphere has also been referred to as the *celebration* sphere. It has been proven times without number that entertainment and sports break race barriers and can therefore be valuable in healing racism and also in rehabilitating. At the Embassy of God, the Sports ministries work separately from Arts and Entertainment ministries. Other ministries in this sphere include the Christian Photography Center, Living Gospel, and Designers Ministry.

MISSIONAL REFORMATION

ARTS AND ENTERTAINMENT MINISTRIES

The arts and entertainment ministries at the Embassy of God combine to establish 12 directions. Natalia Chernyavskaya, a

graduate of Music, is the pioneer of these ministries. She studied jazz piano and classical piano. She started to teach at the age of 15 giving piano lessons. She also holds a BA in Broadcasting. Natalia repented at a Protestant church in 1994; she was depressed. A lady who was attending the Pentecostal church with her came to an Embassy of God conference and then joined the church. This lady invited Natalia to the Embassy of God. Before Natalia came to the church, she had a son, and was then diagnosed of not being capable of having anymore children, which means that she was declared barren. At her first service at the Embassy of God in 1996, the senior Pastor said that someone was having a problem having children. Natalia, who had been barren for 5 years, went on stage turning away from the camera because of the Pentecostal church which she still attended. Natalia joined the Embassy of God Church that year. She had a miraculous pregnancy after her visit to the church which surprised doctors. She had a son on June 27, 1997 and another son in 2004. Natalia found at the Embassy of God what she had been looking for in a church. Natalia attended the pastoral school and was ordained a Pastor in 2002. She pastors a monospherical daughter church where most of the members are in the arts and entertainment ministries.

Natalia joined the praise and worship team in 1996. She noticed immediately how members of the team didn't know musical notes. She felt God gave her the strategy to start a school. When Pastor Sunday gave the permission, Natalia started the Davir Musical School. On the first day, 50 people enrolled and then, 100 came the second day. The school started to teach keyboard basics. With no equipment, Natalia approached Pastor Sunday for help and he told her "*God is your supplier; I didn't give you the ministry, God did*". Today, the school has an excess of equipment and the ministry has grown to 12 different directions, the musical school being only one of the directions. The 12 directions are:

1. Musical (Davir)
2. Theatrical (music, drama, and dancing)
3. Circus
4. Dancing
5. Cinematography
6. Art (feature, painting, sculpture, photography)
7. Literature
8. Show Business
9. Broadcasting (television and radio)
10. Beauty saloon
11. Décor (florist, decorations)
12. Museum and Exhibition (galleries, collections)

We will briefly describe the activities of the first four directions that are currently running.

Musical

The musical direction started with Davir Musical School, which actually, was the first direction of the arts and entertainment sphere. Davir Music School was conceived as a project in 1997 but was formally established in 1999 purposely to teach the praise and worship team the elementary theory of music, to play various musical instruments, vocal coaching and how to lead praise and worship in church. It was originally intended to serve the Embassy of God Church members but the school opened its doors to other churches and the society in 2000 to become a Churchshift ministry. From 1999 till 2008, about 3,000 students have graduated from the center. The school started with 9 teachers in 1999 and now has 300 qualified teachers, 20 of which are fulltime. The school offers a 2-year program with opportunity to learn up to 40 various musical instruments. Natalia Chernyavskaya was the first director of Davir Musical School; the director in 2009 is Svetlana Kyzub. Svetlana was depressed when she joined the Embassy of God Church in 1999. In addition, she had a low self-esteem and was reserved. Her husband was an alcohol addict. She was a popular artiste, a composer, and a violin player. She became the director of the center in 2000. Svetlana graduated from the Academy of Executive Staff of Arts and Culture, and in 2009, she was already a Ph.D. student. Her husband has since given up alcohol and was rehabilitated.

Theatrical

Theatrical ministry works with over 20 theatres in Kiev region. Before the start of a show, the team gives a few motivational statements to the audience. They also give out invitations for people to come to their church services. Natalia's church is named "Symphony of the Kingdom of God". The church currently has 17 home groups and 20 leaders. They worship at the most popular theater in Ukraine where artists meet. One of the strong members of the church and of theatrical ministry is Elena Yeremenko, a popular artiste for 30 years; she has participated in 65 theatrical performances and in 45 movies and series. Elena says she has found God at the Embassy of God Church. Theatrical ministry distributes freely books and cards; they meet with various artistes. They also provide humanitarian help to veterans in the entertainment industry, including former entertainment stars of the Soviet Union.

Circus

The circus ministry started in 2007 and now has 20 members in their home group headed by a former drug addict. The director of the circus union is Valeria Gumenuk.

MISSIONAL REFORMATION

Dancing

The dancing ministry established a school of dancing art where native, classical, and ballet dancing is taught. One of the ballet dancers joined the ministry after calling Trust Hotline; she was depressed for losing her career due to age.

Popular Ukrainian dancer, Gregory Chapkis, now 79, is one of the teachers; he has been a professional choreographic dancer for 75 years.

DESIGN - LIVING GOSPEL MINISTRY

The Embassy of God is a militant passionate army for Christ. The church is always lively; there are always home groups meeting at different spots everyday. One could also notice several automobiles owned by individual members parked in front of the church with images and spiritual inscriptions boldly written in large characters on the vehicles.

The inscription on this car means *"I am healed, glory be to Jesus Christ"*

The inscription on this car translates to *"Jesus has taken away my pain and has given me back joy of life!"*

Living Gospel Ministry is a design ministry that started in

July 2008. A member from Germany had this idea and wrote something on his car. The church picked up this idea as an effective way to evangelize. In 9 months the ministry started, over 1,000

members in Ukraine have signs of images and texts on their automobiles. The ministry grew fast into other areas, using images and texts to evangelize on buildings (replacing graffiti), Tee-shirts, business cards, doors, exercise books distributed freely to students, and so on. The leader of the ministry is Pastor Alex Korman. This ministry has developed a website, www.god-agitation.com, to promote the idea.

The above design was on the van of the Senior Pastor, Sunday, with the text in Russian. The design has been reused by a guest from UK, Pastor Moses Alabi, who translated the text into English and used it on billboards and a van.

SPORTS MINISTRIES

Some of the sports ministries spread across various other ministries. They are designed as part of rehabilitation programs for addicts and also for physical development of homeless children. The children's sports program will be discussed under the family sphere. Boxing and football (soccer) are the common sports used in the sports ministries. State recognized competitions are organized by the ministries.

Yuriy Kravchenko

Yuriy Kravchenko used to be a light drinker, a smoker, and used easy drugs. He gave his life to Christ at the Embassy of God Central Church on April 27, 1997. He was a member of a gang in the streets of Kiev before then. After he gave his life to Christ, he decided to protect people. He was privy to know that many people wanted to assassinate Pastor Sunday Adelaja, including some people in government; there was an attempt with a bouquet of flowers. After he gave his life to Christ, he influenced other gangsters to join the church. Late in 1997, eight of the gangsters, including Yuriy, rallied and became Pastor Sunday's security men. Pastor Andrei, now in Tacoma in the USA, assembled the eight men. Some of the eight security men had once

MISSIONAL REFORMATION

served in the military. The persecutors, not happy with the security, published a slanderous article that Pastor Sunday was surrounded by gangsters. For four years he served in various other ministries. In 2001, he was invited to a boxing competition with Natalia Potopayeva who then advised him to use his talent to serve people. In that year, Yuriy started the sports ministry. In 2003, he organized people and started practicing in a gym to participate in future national boxing competitions; they prayed about sponsorship to pay for the gym. Yuriy approached the government's social organization that works with youth sportsmen and they were allowed to use some of the gyms. They trained physically and spiritually. They won trophies in a very short time and became famous in the city. Sports became the medium to evangelize. In 2007, the city asked Yuriy and his team to organize sports competition for non-believers which makes them to now have two boxing clubs. Yuriy registered a security company that employs most of the members of the club. Through personal relationships with the non-believer employees, they win them to Christ. Between 2003 and 2008, about 5,000 youth had passed through the clubs.

Yuriy graduated from Joshua Bible Institute in 1998. He was ordained as a Pastor in 2006. He got married at the Embassy of God and now pastors a sports monospherical daughter church of the Embassy of God.

Yuriy Verhman

Yuriy Verhman of Jewish origin was on drugs for 15 years; he was also the leader of a gang. He was jailed between 1994 and 1997 for fraud. When he got out of jail, he decided that he was going to have a new life and he got married; however, 50 gang members were waiting for him to get out. So, he returned to his former gangster business. At a point, Yuriy decided to move to Germany; but just before he left, he got into trouble, and his travel documents were seized. His family moved to Germany without him. Yuriy was at a crossroad. In 2004, he repented and joined the Embassy of God Church. God took all the bad habits away from him and he went through rehabilitation. Yuriy attended the leadership school and established a Churchshift ministry named "sports against drugs". He serves God through sport. The ministry works with children, teenagers, and other past criminals; they gather them from the streets and also work with parents.

> Sports rehabilitate and heal racism.
> - Yuriy

Sports rehabilitate and get them back their self esteem. The ministry also helps them to regularize their documents. They talk to them about Christian principles and about drugs. The church is at the soccer field; people usually don't want to come to a church building directly. People repent at the field and afterwards they go to the church. The ministry organizes competitions at different levels. They have 20 teams in Kiev region. Yuriy hopes to be a pastor.

BUSINESS AND FINANCE

Some of the ministries in the Business sphere at the Embassy of God Church are: Business Center, Finance Ministry, Land Ministry, Fitness Centers, and Club 1000.

CLUB 1000

Foundation

Club 1000, also known as "1000 Millionaires Club", was established in 2005 to encourage believers to gain financial control. The main objective then was to raise 1000 millionaires in the church. Only those, whose financial status is 50,000 dollars or more, are allowed to join the Club. More than 300 people joined Club 1000 during its first year. These foundation members found an atmosphere of friendship and financial development in the Club. They not only found solutions for their financial difficulties, but started to teach and help other people to become financially free. Since its inception, the Club has expanded its vision beyond a collection of wealthy Christians. At the opening of an affiliate of the Club in the USA, Pastor Sunday wrote:

> The opening of the "1000 Millionaires Club" (affiliate of the Club 1000 based in Ukraine), is not simply a meeting of wealthy people - it is a strategic step in history in these last days that holds the beginning of Christian economical freedom. We need to prove to the entire world that Christians can be financially influential; that they are

those who receive access to God's resources and treasures. The "1000 Millionaire Club" is a unique tool that creates a new revelation of Christian economy. It is an instrument that enables believers to understand and manage God's finances on earth. Now is the time that God wants to release huge cash flows to His people, but He will always ask one question first: "Who can I trust?" Thanks to this Club, we can show the entire world that money can be used for good and not evil. Money is the answer to needs, not only the needs of individual people, but the needs of entire nations. It only requires righteous people to manage it. Today, our hands are becoming the hands of God, that we might prove His love to the world. The problem with Christianity is that we have never united or concentrated all our resources on a specific goal. Right now, it is thought that the only people who come to God are those with problems, but, with the help of such financial tools such as the "1000 Millionaire Club" we can change the perception of Christianity. (Adelaja)

Vision and Mission

The vision of the Club has greatly developed since its first year of inception into what now seems to be a worldwide network of Christian businessmen. A delegate from Singapore came to Ukraine in September 2008 mainly for this purpose of networking. It is becoming a movement on its own. Christians worldwide are exchanging ideas and strategies about all kinds of businesses worldwide in network marketing, stock market, banking, and so on. In Kiev region alone, more than 200 people have officially become million-

aires by 2007 due to the Club's principles of work and well balanced teaching system of money management. Here are some of the important items in the vision of the Club:
- To influence the economy of nations while building upon Christian principles.
- To create a network of Christian business people in the world for furthering of projects of the Kingdom of God.
- To influence the decisions of judicial and legislative departments of world nations, bring alternatives to political corruption and illegal dealings.
- To create an example of holy and responsible ways of leading business.

Committees

The Club in Ukraine has created committees in order to effectively carry out its mission. Some of the committees are described as follows:
- *Regional Committee* is to be established in every affiliate country. The goal of the committee is to discover Christians in the business sphere.
- *Education Committee* is to organize systematic teaching for those who want to go into business.
- *Business Development Committee* is to research models of franchising. This committee trains entrepreneurs how to create and develop small and medium businesses based on Christian principles.

MISSIONAL REFORMATION

- *Bank Committee* teaches business people how to invest, plan, multiply, and work with banks.
- *Land Committee* teaches people how to own and develop land.
- *Research Committee* analyzes and evaluates business proposals.
- *Political Committee* prepares Christians to be politicians without conforming to the world.

Activities

Alexander Pozharizkiy is the current President of Club 1000. He used to be a member of the Orthodox Church in Odessa, Ukraine, but his life did not change. In 2001, he joined the Embassy of God Church. The President highlights some of the activities of the Club and their principles. The Club organizes trips for families. They strengthen families, promote harmony, and teach responsibilities of parents. One of the standing rules is that every member must pray in the morning and at night. The members do a lot of spiritual counseling. Their main focus is to influence the society and they are passionate about this because they know that they are doing it for the Kingdom of God. For example, they can buy a TV channel and replace the programs to support Kingdom principles. They are not lovers of money or wealth. Their spiritual state is of primary importance to them and they want to be fulfilled.

14. MISSIONAL (CHURCHSHIFT) MINISTRIES

The picture above shows members of Club 1000 at a get-together meeting.

FITNESS HEALTH MINISTRIES

The fitness ministry is one of the health ministries at the Embassy of God which should normally be classified under the family sphere. The ministries offer free services to the society but sell their products to individuals who so wish to purchase them; that is why they are classified under the business sphere. There are various types of these health saloons; they vary by products manufacturers and modes of operation. Some of these ministries are Fit Curves, The Island of Health, VIGAN, and NUGA Best.

Fit Curves

Gary and Diane Heavin started the Curves fitness club in the early 90s in the USA. They opened the first Curves gym in Harlingen, Texas, in 1992. These saloons are for women only; there are no male-oriented workout machines. They offer a simple 30-minute aerobic and hydraulic strength-training circuit. Curves also offers a weight management program to replace dieting. The Embassy of God members run Curves fitness franchise as a ministry. It is the only fitness saloon ministry that does not provide free services and does not sell any product. The members pay a monthly club fee to use the facilities. By 2008, there were about 500 members at 14 locations in Ukraine.

The Island of Health

This ministry deals with massage chairs, massage pillows in cars and so on. The products come from Germany. They do not have saloon centers of their own; they rather do demonstrations at shopping centers.

VIGAN

The VIGAN medical massage saloon started recently in Germany by Natalia Potopayeva. She designed the program to work for the body, spirit, and soul, as part of healing process and rehabilitation. Six saloons were opened by 2009.

NUGA Best

NUGA Best saloons are the most popular in Ukraine because they have the most developed strategies and programs. These strategies were developed by members of the Embassy of God Church. NUGA Best products are from Korea; a team from there came to Russia to introduce the fitness products.

Gleb Spivakov repented at a Pentecostal church in 1995 and joined the Embassy of God Church in 1998. He is the proprietor of the current location of the Central Church. Gleb at a point left business for sometime to be a missionary. He started a regular night prayer meeting from 12 am to 6 am. The vision for the saloon business came during one of these meetings. He also received a vision about the 2008 world economic crisis. God wants to change man's concept of doing business. Gleb sees that the crisis will relax in 2 years and there will be total restoration after 7 years of crisis. Businesses will be built on the principle to serve others not primarily to earn for money. They needed to do the saloon business differently from others. He developed two principles and he sees the new generation of businesses based on these two principles:

1. to reach out;
2. to create a network.

God gave Gleb a franchising model which he developed and started to implement on a spiritual level. He started the NUGA Best saloon ministry in 2003. He divided Ukraine into 4 regions, each having a regional director. Today, there are hundreds of saloons in Ukraine. Alexander Lutsenko, the North East director, has established 35 saloons and has expanded to the USA by starting a saloon in Philadelphia.

Viktor Kubishkin is the Kiev regional director; he repented at an underground Pentecostal church in 1996. He joined the

Embassy of God Church in 1999 during Myles Munroe's  visit to the church. He was planning to move to Canada then. Viktor opened the first NUGA Best saloon in February 2004. The saloon was empty because people didn't understand the new idea. The equipments were mainly used by Pastor Sunday and his team. Six months later, he held a Conference with 40 people. In June 2006, he formally started the saloon ministry. NUGA Best fitness ministry uses 6 types of products including thermal massage beds. The saloon is open to the public free of charge. Anyone can walk in at anytime to use the center as many times as he wishes with no obligation. The products are actually being sold to those who wish to have them at home instead of coming to the saloon; many rich people prefer that. Since the ministry officially started, thousands of people have come to the saloon to use the equipment. About 300 to 500 people visit a particular saloon everyday. The saloons were particularly flooded during the economic crisis; it seems people without health insurance are always afraid to fall sick. Many people gave testimonies of various healings of organs, nervous breakdown, rheumatism, and tumors by regular visits to the saloons. The saloon opens with worship service in the morning and prayers at night.

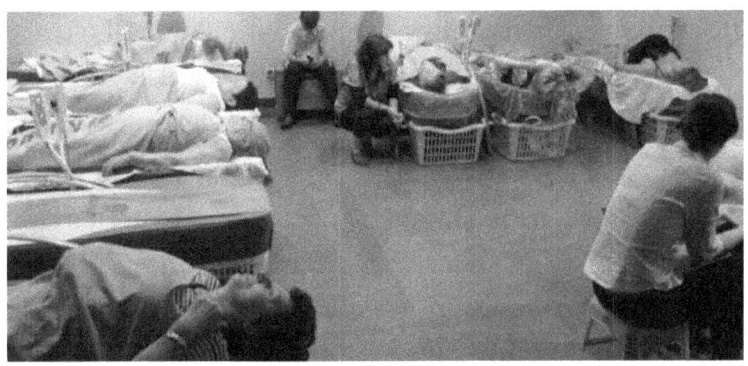

The Center also provides training and fitness education at several intervals everyday; all services are provided free of charge to the public. Churchshift ministries are always providing services to the public at no cost. Presentation is made on good health, emotional balance, anatomy and physiology of the body. NUGA Best centers are opened in several locations in Ukraine and in 16 countries. The attitude of people to serve, morning and night prayers, and relationships, create a kind of atmosphere that makes those who bought the equipment still come back to visit the saloon.

CHURCH AND RELIGION

There seems to be no specific ministries recorded in this sphere at the Embassy of God; however, the Senior Pastor, Sunday Adelaja, has been personally carrying out obligations in this sphere. He has been ministering outside the walls of his church across the globe. His life and messages have in-

MISSIONAL REFORMATION

fluenced many in the religion sector. When he and I met for the first time in Atlanta, Georgia, my life was also positively influenced by his message on Kingdom principles.

One of the attendees at the fifteenth anniversary from Canada shared with me his testimony of how Pastor Sunday  has influenced his life. Derek's father, Doug Schneider, pastors a community Pentecostal church in Oshawa, Canada. In 2003, Derek accompanied his father to a conference where he had the opportunity to listen to Pastor Sunday's sermon. After the sermon, Derek walked to Sunday and said: *"Pastor Sunday, we need this in Canada; will you pray for me?"* When he returned to Canada, he was hired to replace the Youth Pastor of the church where his father pastors. The previous Youth Pastor had a moral breakdown which paved the way for Derek. In 2004, Derek wrote to Sunday Adelaja giving testimony of how his life had been transformed listening to his tapes and CDs. Since then, Pastor Sunday became his mentor. Derek was invited to the 12th anniversary in 2006 and has been attending the anniversaries and fasting programs at the Embassy of God since then. Derek has been implementing Churchshift ministries in Canada, such as Singles ministry and "feed the poor". Derek has named the Youth Ministries "Embassy of this generation".

Dr. George Annadorai, a prominent pastor in Asia, declared that God is using Pastor Sunday Adelaja and the Embassy of God Church for this generation. Pastor George An-

nadorai, the founder and senior pastor of the Lord's Family

Church, is also the founder of Shalom Singapore. He is known as Singapore's prayer warrior, carrying on his shoulders the burden of the Lord for the nation (Chua). Pastor Annadorai had visited Ukraine in 2004 for the second time at the 10th anniversary of the Embassy of God Church and received his revelation for Ukraine. He has been attending the Embassy of God's programs since then. In 2008, a team of 75 people from Singapore and Indonesia, led by Pastor George Annadorai, attended the Embassy of God Church anniversary. Pastor Annadorai has been establishing Churchshift ministries in Asia. In September 2008, he led a delegation of Singapore's Club 1000 to the Embassy of God in Ukraine.

EDUCATION

As mentioned earlier, each sphere at the Embassy of God has an educational section. For the educational section of this sphere, the Church has established Bible schools and Transformation Centers in many countries, including China, USA, Nigeria, UK, Russia, Holland, France, and many others.

Institute for National Transformation

  Professor Vincent Anigbogu (left) is the Director General while Pastor John Enemalah (right) is the Deputy Director General of the Institute. The Institute for National Transformation, which now has Centers located in Kenya, Uganda, Burundi, Gambia, and Nigeria, was established with a vision to develop value-grounded leaders that will transform their organizations, communities and nations. The Institute was conceptualized in November 2005; the first Institute officially started in Nigeria in February 2008.

History Makers Bible School

The History Makers Bible School (HMBS) is established in most of the countries where the Embassy of God daughter churches are planted. In the USA for example, the HMBS started in Philadelphia, Pennsylvania, in September 2006

 with Pastor Alex Mykhaylyk as the Dean. The school has since expanded to other states such as Mississippi, New York, California, and Washington. Pastor Alex Mykhaylyk, a former Dean of the Joshua Bible Institute in Kiev, left Ukraine for the first time as a missionary to India on October 9, 2002. He established the Embassy of God Church and preached in India. After having had impact on the life of several people through

Churchshift ministries, he moved to the USA as the Dean of the HMBS.

International Bible Training School

Pastor Tope Omotoye started the Stephania Soup Kitchen (in

the Family sphere) and was a Pastor of a daughter church before he moved to Germany as a missionary of the Embassy of God to start the International Bible Training Center in October 2006 in Reichenbach with his wife, Lola. In the first year, the enrollment was about 300 students. Most of the students are pastors, university students, workers, business people, housewives, and people who are involved in one ministry or the other; believers are hungry to learn about God. The school has two-level leadership training programs. Each level lasts for nine months. The session starts in October and runs till June; lessons are given every second Saturday of each month from 10 am till 7 pm.

The first set of students graduated on June 9, 2007 in Frankfurt, Germany. The senior Pastor of the Embassy of God, Sunday Adelaja, handed out diplomas to the graduates.

MISSIONAL REFORMATION

DISTRIBUTION AND MEDIA

The Press Center of the Embassy of God Church is a church ministry that provides indirect services to the church. By the time of writing of this book, the Press Center was planning several media Churchshift ministries that would include television and radio programs, Internet ministry, and publications. Currently the Center publishes two magazines. The activities of the center have been covered under church ministries in Chapter 13.

Lika Roman repented at Uzhgorad in Ukraine at a charismatic German church in 1992 when she was 8 years old. She took a decision then never to kiss any man until she is married.  Lika started to listen to Pastor Sunday's sermons in 1994; when a daughter church of the Embassy of God was planted in Uzhgorad in 2006, she immediately joined the church. Lika prays a lot and had made difficult decisions in her life; for example, she had to give up some friends to serve God. At 17, she was invited trice to be a model and travel all over the world; money was advanced to her and the contract ready to be signed. She prayed about it and she knew it was not God's will for her life; she had peace in her mind for not taking the job. Lika was in college between 2002 and 2006 to study International Relations; she worked at a hair dressing saloon at the same time. It was at this saloon a lady spotted her in January 2007 as a good candidate for Miss Ukraine pageant contest; she found her beautiful not only at the outside, but also in the inside. Lika prayed about it and sought her mother's opinion. She was surprised that her mother gave consent. Without much time for preparation and with intensive practice and training, Lika participated in the contest and won as Miss Ukraine 2007 at the age of 23. The organizers were shocked when she told them she reserves her self for her husband. Lika is still a virgin and no one has ever kissed her. After winning the contest, many rich men have approached her for marriage and she always tells them to meet her in church; sometimes she asks them to talk to Pastor Sunday because she knows whoever talks to him will not be the same after. She knew many of them were players.

Lika worked with the Education program of Silver Ring Youth Ministry (as will be discussed under education) and she plans to have a ministry in the media sphere; she plans to have a magazine for the secular world with Christian principles. She is also planning to have a television program and to write a book. Lika relocated to Kiev in March 2008.

MISSIONAL REFORMATION

EDUCATION

As mentioned earlier, the education sphere is the most distributed. By definition, the primary purpose of the education sphere is to evangelize to people in the education sphere, such as students, teachers, and researchers. However, the sphere is expanded to include providing education in each sphere of the society, because those who provide the education are teachers. We shall look at both scenarios at the Embassy of God. Some of the ministries in the Education sphere are Teachers Ministry, Drugs Education, and School Education Ministry.

EVANGELIZING

Evangelism in the education sphere is to win people in education to Christ. Ministers from different ministries go to schools to educate students and teachers on different aspects of life. They do not talk about God or Jesus at school. They use real life experiences to educate and those that are touched by the real life stories contact them after.

Prostitution Education

Tatiana Galusko started the school education programs. She was on the street at the age of 12 prostituting and using hard drugs. The Lord brought her to the Embassy of God in 1999 where she repented and got rehabilitated. She had no high school education when she came to the church, but by 2009, she had a Masters degree and she was already enrolled as a Ph.D. student. Tatiana's story is detailed in Chapter 15.

Tatiana started her Churchshift ministry in 2002 by speaking to teens at schools about the consequences of prostitution and drugs. By 2003, all schools in Kiev opened their doors to her program. By 2004, she gained access to all schools in Kiev region and by 2005, she had become influential in all of Ukraine; she was granted permission by the government of Ukraine to educate the teens against the use of drugs and prostitution. Tatiana has written government approved educational reforms which are being used in Ukrainian schools. Tatiana became the Head of all Churchshift programs at the Embassy of God.

Social Education

The picture below shows Valeriya Mashchenko educating about 200 students in a school program.

MISSIONAL REFORMATION

Many hunger for this education and invite them to come to their schools. They teach about love, relations before marriage, HIV, and other social matters. The team tells true stories about life, drugs, and addictions. This program is executed every week at different schools when schools resume. The program is very effective when they go with people whose life have been affected by wrong decisions. Students prefer their method than other social organizations that do the same. These classes are organized by Pastor Sergey Kushniruk.

Abstinence Education

The Silver Ring Youth Ministry does school education on abstinence before marriage. Lika Roman, a virgin and Miss Ukraine in 2007, worked with the Education program of this Ministry to visit high schools and colleges, to talk about purity, choices, and the future, using her life experience as an example. She is still learning and developing her skills on how to present her case because she can't talk about God at schools. The Silver Ring Youth Ministry also sponsored her on various trips; she visited five States in the USA for a month.

EDUCATING

As stated earlier, all the spheres have educational programs. Some of the educational programs are designed to develop people in that sphere. Some of these educational programs are History Makers Bible School in the Religion sphere, Business Center in the Business sphere, and Fatherhood Institute in the Family sphere.

Center for Personality Rehabilitation

The Social and Personality Rehabilitation Ministry is the first ministry to open a central school that serves all ministries.  The school started by providing education in the family ministry on rehabilitation, but has since expanded to providing education in other spheres. Victoria Melnik, the founder of the ministry, had a MA degree (1999) in Political Science before she joined the church in 2001; she was a smoker. She had never given her life to Christ and her friend invited her to the Embassy of God Church. They entered in the middle of praise and worship and immediately she noticed how exuberant the people were. Her impression was that they were crazy, but when the altar call was made for people to repent, she didn't know what pushed her to respond. Since that moment she felt joy in her spirit and stopped smoking. After joining the church, Victoria served at a rehabilitation center for 3 years. She identified her sphere when Pastor Sunday shared his vision about social problems. In September 2003, she started the Center for Personality Rehabilitation and Society Transformation (CPRST) with about 300 enrollments. Before the end of that year, another center was opened. She moved around to recruit people into the program; she also registered for a Ph.D. program. Year by year, the program is expanded and today, the program includes all round rehabilitation and development: socially, spiritually, intellectually, emotionally, and physically. In 2004, about 1,500 people enrolled in the program. Victoria was ordained in 2005 as a Social Pastor after finishing her pastoral training. In 2006, she obtained her Ph.D. degree in Anthropology. By 2008, the ministry had opened 50 centers in 9 countries.

Movement Against Drugs

The education section of Love Rehabilitation Center is being  led by Sergey Kushniruk, a Family Pastor. He joined the Embassy of God in 1997. He was addicted to drugs before then; he used hard drugs including heroine for several years and no one could convince him that he would, one day, be free from drugs. He was never in church but knew that the Orthodox Church existed. Somehow, he couldn't explain what led him, but he found himself attending the Embassy of God daughter church at Right Bank. When he came to church people prayed for him and assured him that Jesus would take control. Initially, he didn't believe that he would be free from drugs, but he was surprised that he was set free. The second day after the prayer, he felt peace in him and vowed not to use drugs again. He then became interested in church; he started to read the Bible and knew the story of Jesus for the first time in his life. "When people get rehabilitated, some go to the church, some don't, and some even go back to drugs or alcohol. Not all of them come to God", says Sergey. He started to attend church regularly to develop in Christ. After rehabilitation, he started to serve at the Love Rehabilitation Center. Sergey graduated from Joshua Bible Institute and became a Social Pastor.

In 2004, Sergey started to work with others at the Center on educational programs. They created social programs with 14 lessons on social ills and how to achieve goals. The team started aggressive campaigns and education against drugs. They visited schools to educate teens on the consequences of drug usage. They obtained government permits to track drug traffickers and give them in to the police. For economic reasons, this program is being undermined by pharmacies that sell alternative drugs, and even by some police officers who are drug users themselves. Below is an extract from an article, "Cheap drug addiction rising", published by Alexandra Magdik in Kyiv Post on April 10, 2008:

MISSIONAL REFORMATION

> Addiction to a cheap, widely available prescription pain killer is on the rise, and the government has no plan to stop it, experts said... Ukraine produces 90 million packages of Tramadol annually, said Vitaliy Kravchenko, a former officer at the State Security Service of Ukraine... At a March 18 roundtable addressing drug policy problems and addiction rehabilitation, participants effectively shrugged their shoulders on the fight against pharmacies illegally circulating drugs. Kravchenko suggested the problem has escalated because top officials have a financial interest. Many government officials themselves use drugs, Kravchenko added.

Sergey's team has developed audio and video education materials for the media. Pastor Roman Trokhin is one of the  leaders of the movement against peddling illegal (and even legal) substitute drugs. They meet with government officials. Roman's story is detailed in Chapter 15. Substitution therapy is a problem in the Ukraine. Like in some other countries, the government approves certain drugs as replacement for drug addicts, sometimes called Opiate Replacement Therapy (ORT). There are restrictions though; the drugs can only be purchased at certain establishments and the dose is limited to once a day. Many people on this program are finding the government approved substitute not strong enough and this has led to the peddling of illegal drugs by some pharmacies. Pavel Kutsev, who is on this substitution therapy program, has this to say (Reshetnyak):

> To tell the truth, I had started feeling better for a while. My daily dose was 180 mg. In a week my old problems returned... tolerance, shortness of breath, insomnia...
>
> It's been almost a year now since my wife and I started "adjusting" to methadone. To tell the truth, we still need to take antidepressants as the medication just does not suit patients like us well. We are not talking now about the side effects. We just feel that there is no reason for us to increase the daily dose more and more...It does not matter how large your dose is if the active substance will be excreted from the body in 12-16 hours. The only alternative that would work in this case is to consume the medication at least twice a day.
>
> Almost all 400 people from our methadone site consume other drugs along with the provided medications. Every third person still shoots up. Others take various pills. This is because in the morning you have such a severe feeling of cold turkey that you just need another drug. You cannot call this a treatment! Please understand! If you are a drug addict and every morning you have abstinence syndrome you just do not feel the effect of therapy.

In spite of frustrations of the Movement Against Drugs (MAD) in some cities, their campaign influences some others. Some Ukrainian cities are banning substitution therapy program altogether in municipal medical establishments. They reason with MAD that an addiction to one drug cannot be treated with another drug. More on Ukrainian drug problem will be covered in the Family sphere.

FAMILY AND HOME

With over 300 Embassy of God Family ministries in the Ukraine, this sphere is definitely the largest and it is expected to be so. Kuyper said *"family is the foundation of human society and it retains its position as the primordial sphere"*. The Family Ministries provide welfare and humanitarian services to any member of a family. Some of the ministries are: rehabilitation centers (217 in Ukraine), children, marriage (several), orphanage (several), handicapped, senior citizens, health, refugees, homeless, pre-marriage, pregnant women, abortion prevention, adoption, abandoned children, prison, social morals, Stephania soup kitchen, and youth ministries (several). We can only discuss a few of them.

REHABILITATION CENTERS

Drug and alcohol rehabilitation center is the first Churchshift ministry at the Embassy of God. Since then, it has become the most developed and available ministry; almost every daughter church has at least a rehabilitation center attached to it. Members of the Embassy of God have established rehabilitation programs in 10 different directions, including:

- Drug and alcohol addiction
- Food addiction
- Relatives of addicts
- Phobic and schizophrenias

- Out of jails
- HIV infected
- Unusual sexual habits (gays, transsexual, etc.)
- People in the sex business
- Computer addiction
- Games addiction

Love Rehabilitation Center

The Love Rehabilitation Center is the first drug and alcohol rehabilitation center at the Embassy of God; it was founded in 1994 by Natalia Potopayeva. The Center is now named after Natalia. In 14 years of its existence, Love Center rehabilitated over 5000 people, of which 60% were rehabilitated completely. Some went back to the streets. The government offers substitute drugs so they try to undermine their program; pharmacies too. The government doesn't support the Center financially; the Center gets funding from private citizens, mostly church members. More than 15 of those who passed through the rehabilitation center are now members of Club 1000.

Facts

According to a 2008 release by the Joint United Nations Programme on HIV/AIDS (UNAIDS), Ukraine is experiencing one of the fastest growing HIV/AIDS epidemics in the world. Figure 14.1 shows the progressive rise of the number of newly infected people year by year from the data provided by the UNAIDS report.

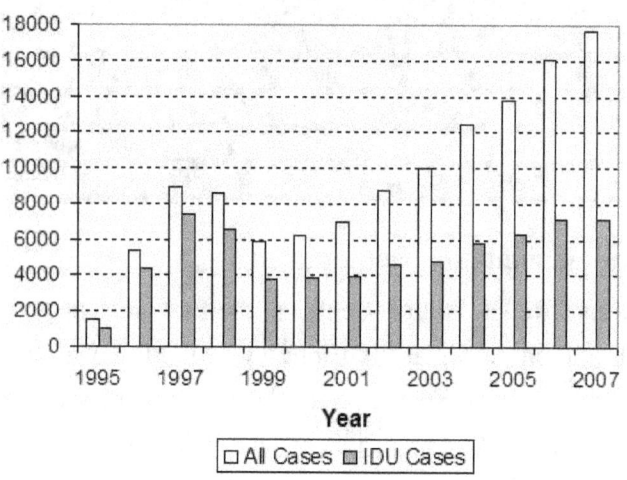

Figure 14.1: Registered News Cases of HIV-infection in Ukraine
IDU = Injection Drug User

According to UNAIDS and World Health Organization (WHO), the actual number of people infected is considerably higher than the official statistics shown in the Figure. Also, in the Figure, the number of HIV-infected among Injection Drug Users (IDUs) is compared with all infected. IDU cases are prevalent in the number of infected. For example, the UNAIDS data show that in 2007, about 40% of new HIV cases were among IDUs. Heterosexual transmission accounted for 38%, and children born to HIV-positive mothers accounted for 19%. These three cases are the principal source of HIV-infection.

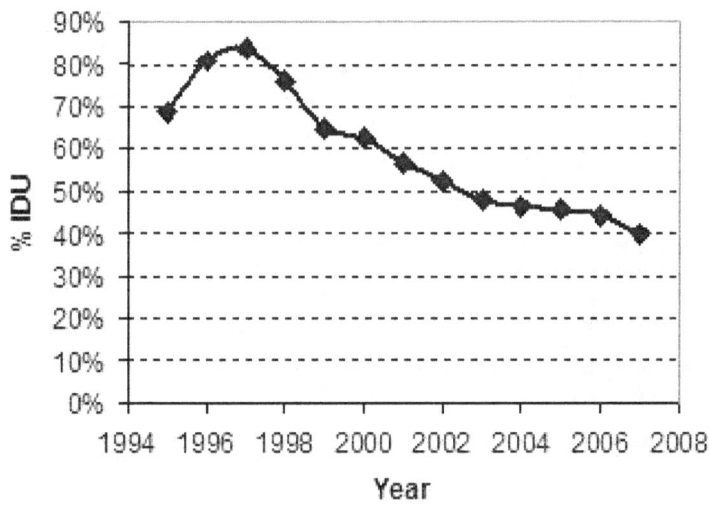

Figure 14.2: Percentage of Injection Drug users (IDUs) among newly infected people with HIV in Ukraine

Figure 14.2 shows the percent of IDU cases among all HIV infected people. The Figure shows a peak of 84% of IDU cases in 1997 which gradually reduces to 40% in 2007. Two inferences can be drawn from the data:

MISSIONAL REFORMATION

1. Drug addicts transmit HIV epidemic the most; in fact according to Krivosheev, 60-80% of all Ukrainian illicit drug-users are HIV-positive.
2. Although the percentage of IDUs is still relatively high, the steady decrease is encouraging. Of course, there are other government programs and non-government organizations that might have been factors to the steady reduction; however, the Embassy of God's rehabilitation programs and the activities of the movement against drugs certainly contribute to the relative percentage decrease in drug addicts.

STEPHANIA SOUP KITCHEN

Tope Omotoye repented in 1992 at Word of Life Church in Kiev. He watched Pastor Sunday Adelaja on TV in 1993 and was really motivated to serve God. He joined the Embassy of God Church in 1994 and worked at a rehabilitation center. In 1997, Tope was ordained as a Pastor and he started a daughter church that was meeting at a park in the cold winter of that year. Like most daughter churches in that era, his church was persecuted and denied to conduct services in a hall. He supernaturally heard a voice that gave him the name of an abandoned factory; he was able to locate the factory. He then prayed for God to send people to his church but God asked him to rather help people and gave him the idea of the "feast of love". When he announced this program to his church in 1998, more people started to come, bringing food. The church that started with less than 100 people grew to having three services. The church then needed to separate the "feast of love" ministry from the church. By the end of 1998, Leonid Chernovetskyi, the owner of the abandoned property, granted the use of the canteen (which had been abandoned for 10 years). Leonid was unknown to the Embassy of God then but he was running for the Senate. Many volunteers participated in the program. They were shocked when Leonid started to give them money in addition to his property that was being used. The homeless people spread the news around and by 1999, about 2,000 people were coming to the center everyday. The first director named the center "Stephania". In that year, the church introduced everyday church service, a Bible school, and night prayer (10pm to 2am). The everyday program and night prayers kept the homeless away from the streets.

During the winter, more and more homeless people migrated to the woods in the outskirts of Kiev, as finding shelter in the big city was becoming more difficult (Kabachenko); according to Pastor Tope, it seemed that the state was helping them in the migration. The government could not take care of all the homeless people; they would rather have many of them gathered and driven to somewhere about 100 km outside the city.

MISSIONAL REFORMATION

> "The housing and utilities administrations of different cities in Ukraine have for the past several years been locking up basements in residential buildings. There will soon be no open basements in Kyiv," Housing Ministry of Ukraine reported to Weekly.ua. (Kabachenko)

So the Stephania center became like a refugee camp with people bringing tents. The neighbors and nearby factories started to complain and the government became intolerant. The night meeting was canceled in 2004. Pastor Tope Omotoye is a member of the Apostolic Council; he relocated to Germany in 2006 to start the International Bible School.

Leonid Chernovetsky, who later became the mayor of Kiev, joined the church. He decided to take over the ministry, donating $1 million every year. The organization was registered and Lubov Razina was appointed its President. Lubov has since become a financial Partner of this Center. The Center has evolved to include other services such as health, legal, rehabilitation, Spiritual, and charity. With the assistance of Leonid Chernovetsky and his wife Alina Ayvazova, the Stephania Soup Kitchen, from 1998 to 2006, had served over 800,000 meals including 40,000 to children.

Igor Svyatec, the leader of the Ushers at Stephania Center,

used to be on drugs and felt emptiness in his spirit. He attended a church service for the first time in a protestant church in 1994. Soon after that he attended different other denominations such as Orthodox and Baptist. But all the while

Igor never stopped smoking while attending church service and he eventually went back to the streets in 1996. Igor came to Stephania Center in 2004 for regular meals and spiritual uplifting. All of a sudden, his life changed and he stopped using drugs and smoking. He is now serving other people at the center and has evolved as the head of the about 20 Ushers. In the picture below, homeless people at the center listened to a sermon on "Love and Salvation" by the head of dinning room for the center, Nadegda Rud, before the dinner is being served.

Nadegda is a widow who became a member of the church in 1994; she was a member of Pastor Tope's home group. Nadedga joined the church when she ran into serious problem of debt after the death of her husband. She is now financially free and dedicated to serving God.

MISSIONAL REFORMATION

There is a health center at Stephania Center. Many of the homeless have bad sore on their legs due to the cold weather during the winter. In the picture below, a homeless patient was receiving treatment for sore on his legs.

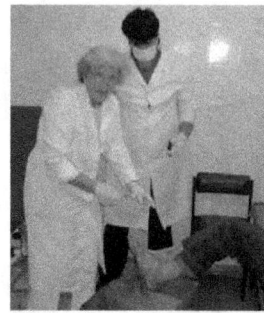
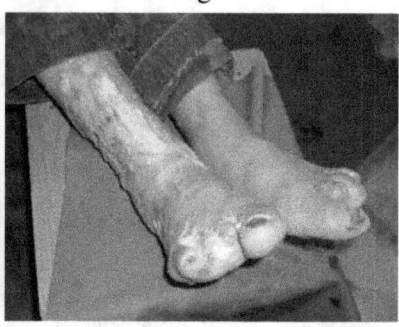

Clothing (left) donated to the center is given to the homeless people.

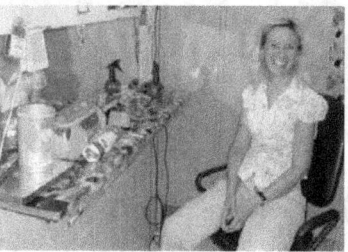

In the above picture on the right, volunteer Natasha serves as the hair dresser and barber for the homeless at the center.

Attorney Nina Shevchenko (sitting right in the picture below) and volunteer assistant, Ulia Dmitrenko comes to the Stephania center every Tuesdays for three hours to help the homeless solve problems with passports, lost IDs, documents, and other legal matters with the police and State. They are not being paid for this. It is the ministry they chose to serve in. The main problem of homeless people in Ukraine is the loss of passport, and they have difficulties in obtaining new passports because of inability to provide an address. All kinds of social services, assistance, privilege, pension registration in the Unemployment Centre, medical, and other services are only available to a person in possession of a passport.

Facts

The Ukrainian government has a homeless program. Under the state homeless program, free hot meals are served during the winter months. During the spring and summer the homeless are fed by charity and religious organizations mainly located in the larger cities (http://en.proua.com).

It is difficult to get an accurate figure of the number of homeless people in Ukraine. The official number of homeless people in Ukraine in 2005 is over 40,000 (Tipple), of which 43% are ex-prisoners. The statistics on the homeless

MISSIONAL REFORMATION

in Ukraine are based only on the data provided by the Ministry of Internal Affairs (the Police). Usually, they collected the data on the number of persons who were detained all around Ukraine. But recently, the number of detention centers, located only in a few large cities of Ukraine, declined sharply to just over 40. Besides that, the official statistics only include people who attracted attention of the militia officers by their behaviour and those people kept in detention due to judges' orders. Other homeless people whose behaviour did not give any reasons for detention and homeless women far exceed the official statistics.

> Militia officers mention that they arrest people who do vagrancy, mendicancy or begging. But as a rule they do not detain those with signs of severe illnesses, elderly people and women who don't demonstrate asocial behaviour. (Kabachenko)

In separate efforts, city councils established registration centers to estimate the number of homeless people in their cities.

> However, this is a difficult task as registration at the center is voluntary and not many vagrants will agree to register there. "Around half of these wanderers are ex-convicts that do not want their name in any database. They prefer to remain inconspicuous and feed off of charity and religious organizations rather than the state," says Oksana Kiselyova, a representative of the Happy Life charity organization. (Kabachenko)

The following statistics were reported:

- The average age of the homeless is 35-45 years, a person's most productive age.
- The Kiev City Council estimates that there are 14,000 homeless people in Kiev in 2006;

A survey was conducted by a Charitable Foundation, "A Road Home", in 2004 in 16 Ukrainian cities on a sample of 1205 homeless people who were found on the street, shelter, detention, hospital, market, and railway station. The survey revealed the following:
- About 60% of homeless people are 30-49 year old.
- More than 60% are men
- About 30% have infectious skin diseases
- About 13% have tuberculosis and hepatitis
- About 40% reported their alcohol addiction.

EMBASSY OF LIFE ORPHANAGE

In 1998, Alexander Roganov founded the Embassy of Life ministry by going to the streets to feed the homeless kids. That was the life God laid on his heart; he even took the kids to his home. Alex was a member of the Embassy of God Church that was inspired by Pastor Sunday Adelaja. Alex died in 2003. The ministry got fired up and started two orphanage homes. I visited the one in Hotov in 2008.

Homeless children are many in Ukraine. Cases have even been reported of women dropping toddlers as young as 2 years old on the streets. The orphanage home at Hotov

MISSIONAL REFORMATION

showed pictures of little children on the streets, using drugs and forming gangs. It is especially hard for them during cold winters with no shelter.

Olga Omelchenko, the Vice Chairperson of the board of directors of the Embassy of Life Ministry, came from Russia and joined the Embassy of God in 2006. Olga had met a Pastor of the Embassy of God in Russia while she was there. She joined the Embassy of Life ministry the same year. Olga does administrative jobs, looks for sponsorships, and participates in all directions of this Churchshift ministry. The ministry went through difficult times before gaining stability. The ministry operates in 10 directions with 50 volunteers.

1. Boys rehabilitation; 60 were rehabilitated in 2008; they work with a maximum of 15 at a time;
2. Working directly with children on the street;
3. Adaptation for people aged 18-20;
4. Employment agency for the orphans; business men, especially from the Embassy of God, come their to tutor;
5. Girls rehabilitation;
6. State orphanage; they work with 5 orphanage homes in Ukraine; they organize common events (three times a year) involving about 800 kids for them to interact;
7. Senior citizens care; this ministry started in 2008; they work with abandoned poor senior citizens; the ministry redeemed 155 and 80 abandoned in hospitals in 2008;

8. Crisis homes; the ministry works with government organizations and dysfunctional homes which are usually the root cause of kids running away from home;
9. Organization of summer and winter camps;
10. Taking care of families who adopt children, including psychological support and legal consultations.

The manager of the orphanage center located at Hotov, a town in Kiev region, is Marina Dyachenko. The goal of this ministry is to rehabilitate homeless children and return them to their families. Many of the kids are brought there because their parents are drug addicted; the parents have to consent to the child being taken to the orphanage. Some of the kids ran away from home. The kids go to school from the center; the center works with them on their homework and on their habits. They pray together and are taught lessons from the Bible.

MISSIONAL REFORMATION

Sergey Korakov (see picture below) was 10 years old when he was brought to the orphanage home in the year 2000. He comes from a dysfunctional family. His father is in jail and his mother has been on drugs for 15 years; she lives with another drug addict. Sergey is the youngest in his family. His brother has been to jail six times, always stealing; the second sister is handicapped, and another sister is a prostitute in Moscow.

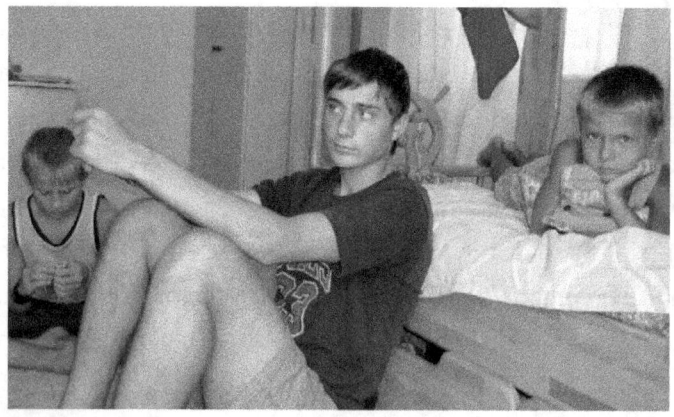

Sergey was on the streets since 8 years old; he was brought to the orphanage from there. He used to sleep in basements of apartment buildings, moving from one to another during winter. He too used drugs from age 8 to 10. When he first came to the Center, he ran away because he didn't have the freedom he had on the streets. Soon after, he came back by himself. At 17, he became a leader in the orphanage and serves others. Now, he is completely rehabilitated and is a member of a home group at the Embassy of God. He doesn't want to go back to the streets or to the bad habits again. He has been visited by his mother and he has been talking to her about rehabilitation and repentance.

Facts

According to a United Nations Children's Fund (UNICEF) 2005 Report, of the 9 million children in Ukraine, over 100,000 of them are orphans; 10% of these are orphaned due to death of a parent; the rest (over 90,000) are social orphans due to alcoholism, abandonment, or imprisonment of parents (worldorphanproject.com). UNICEF also reports that 65,000 of the orphans live in the overpopulated state-run institutions such as orphanages, boarding schools and shelters.

> Family poverty, unemployment, alcoholism and drug use are the main reasons for children being abandoned. Thousands of children also choose to run away from violence in their homes. They find refuge on the streets where they run the risk of contracting tuberculosis and HIV through injecting drugs. (unicef.org)

Epidemiological Fact Sheet on HIV and AIDS in Ukraine, released in July 2008 by World Health Organization, estimates that 10,000 children (0-14) were infected with HIV in 2007. Young girls below 14 get impregnated by young boys without any plans for the future.

The following additional statistics, provided by *The Gazetta of Music Missions Kiev* in May, 2005, are taken from www.colkerfamily.org.

MISSIONAL REFORMATION

- The older an orphan gets, the chances for his/her adoption drastically decrease.
- About 10% of them will commit suicide after leaving the orphanage before their 18th birthday;
- 60% of the girls will end up in prostitution;
- 70% of the boys will enter a life of crime;
- Only 27% of these youth will find work;
- There are presently 6,000 adoptions a year (almost all foreigners adopting);
- Only 10% of orphans are in orphanages because of death of a parent, 90% are social orphans - due to alcoholism, abandonment, or imprisonment of parents;
- There are 450 orphanages or orphan homes in Ukraine. Of these 50 are baby houses, 100 are regular orphanages for ages 8-17, 100 are boarding schools for specialized needs, 100 are shelters where 30,000 children live temporarily between leaving home and being assigned to an orphanage, and 100 are private institutions, housing a total of 1,000 children, mostly Christian efforts.

HANDICAPPED MINISTRY

Peter Buznickiy

Peter grew up in a healthy family. He is educated and was well paid. He has a home, cars, fame, and he never used drugs; however, he served alcohol to other people for 40 years. Pastor Sunday was passing by him in the year 2000 and just said "Hi". He felt the anointing of God and decided to visit the church. He started to listen to the Pastor and bought his books. He was so touched that he sells Pastor's books and gives some out freely. God completely transformed his life. Peter attended the Joshua Bible Institute and was baptized in 2004; he was ordained as a Pastor in 2006. Peter started a ministry with handicapped people. He ministers to up to 200 members in his ministry. *"There are over 500 million handicaps in the world; we need to reach out to them"*, he says soberly. There are 5,000 in Kiev and he aims at reaching out to them all. His ministry has a vision to start a school to prepare servants for taking care of the disabled people. He is proud to be part of Pastor Sunday's ministry.

> There are over 500 million handicaps in the world. We need to reach out to them.
> - Peter

Facts

According to an International Labour Office (ILO) estimates, 14% of the Ukrainian population (about 8 million people), are disabled (www.ilo.org); the official estimates in 2006 by the Ukrainian government is 2.67 million (www.un.org.ua), which is about 5.2% of the population. It was underestimated since many of the people did not register. However, this estimate is still almost twice the average for the industrialized countries. Many of the Ukrainian disabled are from these sources (which may account for the high figures):

- Veterans of the Afghanistan war;
- Victims of the Chernobyl nuclear disaster;
- Frequent accidents in the mines, such as of the Donbass.

According to the United Nations:
- About 10% of the world's population (650 million people) live with a disability; they are the world's largest minority; 80% of the disabled live in developing countries;
- 20% of the world's poorest people have some kind of disability, and tend to be regarded in their own communities as the most disadvantaged;

> Unfortunately, in Ukraine, people with disabilities are just not considered "normal." They don't have a chance for respect or equal rights in society. (Alina)

An organization that includes 49 NGOs, called "*National Assembly of Disabled of Ukraine (NADU)*" was founded on September 22, 2001. NADU participates in state policy making on the issues of socio-economic, political and various other problems of people with disabilities. It contributes to the prevention of all forms of discrimination, against people with disabilities, helps their integration in the society, and increases public awareness regarding problems that exist among people with disabilities in Ukraine (http://v1.dpi.org).

Notable deeds by various other organizations:
- The Wheelchair Foundation (in conjunction with the Church of Jesus Christ of Latter-day Saints) was to distribute 250 wheelchairs on March 26 and March 27, 2004

to physically disabled Ukrainians. (PR Newswire, Mar 26, 2004, www.highbeam.com);
- All-Ukrainian Centre for the Vocational Rehabilitation of the Disabled was set up in Lutizh, about 40 km from Kiev. The centre, located in the middle of a wood, can accommodate 130 handicapped people at a time. Various skills are taught there. Their tuition, lodging, and medical expenses are covered. The Ukrainian government and ILO are bearing the running costs (Grumiau);
- There are other NGOs, such as *God's Hidden Treasures* (godshiddentreasures.org), which reach out to the disabled in Ukraine.

YOUTH MINISTRIES

Youth Skeemans – Olga Potyzailo

Olga Potyzailo, who holds a M.Sc. degree from Kiev Economic University, is the leader of a youth ministry. She gave her life to Christ at the Embassy of God Church in 1997 when she met Pastor Sunday. A church member whose child received healing invited her; she was barren. She and her husband had been living together since 1990 and they had incurred a debt of $2,000 (USD) before they joined the church in 1997. They started a medical equipment business in 1998; they are now the leader in Ukraine in the supply of medical equipment; they have 150 staff members. Furthermore, the Lord opened her womb and she had a daughter in 2007. She is grateful to God. First, she joined a children ministry led by Konstantin Antonuk in 1998. Olga became a leader and attended the Joshua Bible Institute. She was ordained as a Pastor in April 2009.

In 1999, Olga started the Youth Skeemans (young lion) Ministry with 20 youngsters. In 2005, she added teenagers to the ministry and by 2008 she had 100 youth who joined her. They have produced teenagers who started their own businesses, best students in Ukrainian schools, three who work for television stations, and developed a musical group that has released a CD. Olga has written a book titled *"Project Turned to Life"*. She registered *"My Choice"*, an organization that covers her activities. They publish *"Success"*, a youth magazine. Youth Skeemans also works with orphanages. They use their money to finance all their activities. Sometimes they receive donations from sponsors. They meet twice a week and have created several departments including youth orphanage, abortion prevention, barrenness, media, creativity, and social adaptation. They also offer professional consultation services on women issues, career development, support, and business. They touch about 200 youth per week and affected up to 3,000 people in the first 18 months. Olga will join Club1000 soon. Website: www.vubir.in.ua.

Silver Ring – Sergey Lysak

Sergey Lysak came to Kiev in 1998 to study Economics at a University. He was already a born-again Christian from another charismatic church when he joined the Embassy of God Church in 2005. He made his intention known to Pastor Sunday that he would like to become a Youth Pastor; the Pastor said "OK, then join one of our ministries". He joined a youth gathering led by Pastor Aleksandr Safonov; Sergey didn't think it was a real ministry. He started to mobilize students who met during the weekends for training; this led to the establishment of the Silver Ring Youth Ministry. They went to schools in Kiev to teach abstinence; they teach about the consequences of HIV and Sexually Transmitted Diseases (STDs). They also organize youth concerts. Within 2 years of its debut, the ministry had educated over 10,000 students in Kiev with over 1,000 volunteers from the Embassy of God Churches in Kiev region. The over 10,000 students signed a certificate with silver rings on their fingers that they would not have sex before marriage. They are using an international AIDS Education program developed from the United Kingdom and being used in over 21 countries. The Silver Ring program has been extended to other countries; for example, it was approved in the USA. Lika Roman, Miss Ukraine in 2007, was in the USA that year to carry out the program.

Sergey Lysak completed the leadership school and graduated from the Joshua Bible institute. He was ordained as a minister in 2006.

Fatherhood – Alexander Korman

Alex, a former basketball player, gave his life to Christ in  1997 at the Embassy of God. In 1999, he became the administrative secretary at the Right Bank Church, pastored by Natalia Potopayeva, for almost 3 years. He started a theatrical ministry and later started a family ministry on fatherhood. Alex did not have a good relationship with his father. The goal of the fatherhood ministry is to improve relationships between fathers and children. There are currently 30 daughter Fatherhood Institutes established in 10 countries, including Russia, Canada, Holland, USA, and Ukraine. He started with 4 distant students in 2003 and traveled to churches to talk about the ministry. In 2004, he started 3 social programs with the government of Kiev, opening three schools: Fathering school, Pregnancy school, and Marriage school. In 2005, he was honored by the mayor of Kiev with a recognition certificate. All the wisdom and finances are the work of God, he says. He has handed the leadership of the institute to his wife; he wants to pursue other areas of ministry. He was a Postgraduate student in Sociology. Alex heads the education committee of Club 1000, heads the Living Gospel ministry (in the Arts sphere), and started a social moral movement in 2008.

CHILDREN MINISTRIES

Yuriy Grushovenko

Yuriy Grushovenko, an ex-alcoholic, was kicked out of the army because of irresponsible drinking; he lost his family and was isolated from his child. He became homeless and broke. Yuriy repented on September 15, 2003, at the Embassy of God Central Church. After about a month (before completing the leadership school), Yuriy enrolled at the Joshua Bible Institute and graduated the following year. Barely a month after graduating, a boy ran to him and said "hello" and then ran away. For three days he couldn't sleep. Something came alive inside of him.

He started to look for the boy and eventually found him at an orphanage. When he opened the door of the orphanage, about 30 kids ran to him and jumped over him and called him "daddy". A fatherhood feeling woke

> The Lord told me "if the children don't go to the church, the church should go to the children" - Yuriy

up inside of him and he then began to cry as he realized that he was not a true daddy. He walked around the orphanage home; he noticed that the playground needed to be fixed and there were so many other problems there. He asked the director why the problems were not fixed; she said because there was no man there to fix them. He then promised that he would be the man there. He began to go there everyday, to cut wood, fix the playground and furniture, and do other things. They asked him to organize Sunday school for them. He was just a baby Christian, so he had to study various Sunday school programs. He developed an interest in this and wanted to do it also for the church. At a particular church service with thousands of attendees, he noticed that there were only about 50 kids. He asked God why and God told him *"if the kids don't go to the church, the church should go to the kids"*. He began to seek where the children were and noticed that they were in school, in children prison, in the hospital, in orphanage homes, and on the streets. He had to develop the strategy to reach them. Through the direction of the Holy Spirit, he recognized that the children could be reached through education, sports, arts, summer camps, and humanitarian aids. A little over a year after repentance, Yuriy started the children ministry as the leader. Yuriy Grushovenko was later ordained as a children Pastor.

Yuriy set four developmental goals for the children: intellectual, spiritual, physical, and creative. He started with the physical development, reaching the kids through sports. He organized football (soccer) teams from about 100 orphanage homes in 4 regions of Ukraine (there were about 450 orphanage homes in Ukraine in 2005 (see facts data under orphanage); the figure was estimated at over 500 in 2008); there are around 200 teams in soccer championships. Yuriy was able to instill principles of Christ through sports. After 3 years of the program, over 50% of the children stopped smoking, stopped using bad words, stopped bad habits, found their purpose in life, and had good results at school. They have provided the right atmosphere for proper upbringing. After 3 years, Yuriy started to execute the other goals and directions. The ministry opened art groups in all of Kiev's 11 children hospitals. They also executed the intellectual development component through education. The ministry taught in schools, hospitals, and prisons. They teach financial laws and how to reach goals through Christian principles. Today, the ministry is taking care of about 25,000 children in 250 teams (each team has about 100 children).

Alexander Chvostenko

Alex and his wife, Lubov, work with families to adopt orphans. They train and prepare the interested people on how to take care of an orphan; they help them psychologically and with legal processing issues in relation to adoption licenses. They also train them on financial issues. Alex grew up with his grandmother. He never really lived with his parents because his father left home early and his mother died of cancer when he was 7. He was kept in an orphanage home. His grandmother died before he graduated from high school. When he was 18, his uncle did not accept him. So, Alex had to interrupt his collegial studies to survive by himself. He ran into serious debts; the collectors were always after him. He began to sleep outside public buildings, to drink and to smoke heavily. For the first time, he sought God in 1993 and attended a church, but he was eventually kicked out of the church. Between 1993 and 1997, he was kicked out of 4 churches because of his bad habits. He was not honest, he lied a lot, stole, and had bad odor. *"Those churches were more concerned about their reputation"* says Alex. Alex joined the Embassy of God Church on February 4, 1997; since then, he has remained there since nobody kicked him out. He stopped drinking immediately and stopped smoking after 6 months. He got married to Lubov at the Embassy of God Church. When Alex was in an orphanage home, he knew he would help children. In the year 2000, he received a revelation that the future of the children are in families. He started his ministry in 2005; the ministry was officially registered in 2008. He is the leader of a missional home group in which all the 8 of them work in his ministry. There are also 80 volunteers

working with him. By the time of the 15th anniversary of the Embassy of God Church in 2009, the ministry had worked with different families to adopt 18 children. Alex and his wife, themselves, adopted 2 children.

The picture above shows some of the team and family sharing their testimonies at the 2009 anniversary.

FAMILY MINISTRIES

Happy Family Center – Ludmila Leshchenko

Ludmila Leshchenko joined the Embassy of God in 1994 (one of the first 49). She came to the church out of curiosity but the Holy Spirit arrested her. She started the Family Center in 1995 at the Central Church. Ludmila was ordained as a Family Pastor in 1998. She ran this ministry at the Central Church until 2005 when she started a daughter church with 7 people; by 2008, attendance grew to about 150 through home groups. Ludmila had family problems in her personal life but

MISSIONAL REFORMATION

she was able to overcome them with God's help; this provided the initial experience to run the family center. By 2006, the counselors in the family ministry had counseled over 5,000 married couples. Over 2,000 church members went through the marriage preparation school and fifty couples were joined in marriage. The family center now has several directions, some of which are:
1. The school of marriage preparation;
2. The school of marriage for family couples;
3. The school of parental preparation;
4. The International Ministry, "Married for Life";
5. Homeless children and their adoption.

Marriage Ministry – Nataliya Konchenko

Nataliya Konchenko, with a B.A in Journalism and Master of

Theology, repented in 1993 at a Pentecostal church; she was baptized and served in the children ministry. She started attending an Embassy of God daughter church "Word of Faith" in 1998. She joined the children ministry at the right time they needed someone to teach kids. The previous leader moved to the Central Church and she became the leader. She came to the Central Church in 2002. She started the Marriage Ministry at the Central Church when Pastor Ludmila Leshchenko moved to pastor a daughter church. Nataliya focuses in eight family directions including counseling on pre-marriage relationships, abortion, prostitution, and children. There are several steps a couple must go through before engagement or marriage at the Embassy of God. In particular, the couple must attend the Pre-marriage School, answer 70 questions, and test for HIV and Hepatitis B at the hospital.

HEALING

Nikolay Garasayan, a rocket engineer, left the army because of various diseases; he had a stomach ulcer, hernia, fibroma, kidney problems, high blood pressure, and a heart disease. *"I was a living dead person"*, he says. His bladder was cut and one of his kidneys was going to be removed. He refused the kidney surgery and started to study the Bible. In September 1998, the Holy Spirit told him in a dream that he had been healed but requested that he served God. Nikolay repented at the Embassy of God Church on October 11, 1998. In 1999, Nikolay started to be healed gradually. He graduated from the Joshua Bible Institute that year. In December 1999, he had a health crisis and an ambulance took him to the hospital; the stones in his kidney had become sand. After two months, the sand disappeared; his kidney had become clean. After another six months, his heart disease was cured, the ulcer disappeared, and his blood pressure had dropped from 220 to 120. In 2001, Nikolay participated in the development of the Leadership Ladder School (Chapter 9 of Volume 1); he became the director of the beginners' ministry until 2004. In 2005, Nikolay was ordained as a Pastor. Together with Sunday Adelaja and Sophia Zhukatanskaya, Nikolay received an honorary Ph.D in Theology from California in 2005. In August of that year, he started the healing ministry. They pray and receive revelations. They visit homes, hospitals, metro areas, villages, and hold a healing service at the Central Church every Sunday at 6 pm. They invite people from the society to their services. By 2009, over 7,000 people have received healing through this ministry, besides those in the hospitals that they visit. After praying for people in the hospitals, some repent on their own and others kick them out. The ministry publishes testimonies in their quarterly gazette. All 12 members of Nikolay's home group are members of his ministry. That is another example of a *missional* cell group. There are other 33 leaders of the church that are in the healing ministry.

Nikolay's grandfather lived 125 years, but his father died in World War 2 at 41 when he was only 1 year old. In 2009, Nikolay turned 70. He published a book, *"Healing is Real"*.

TRUST HOTLINE MINISTRY

There was an initial hesitation to classify this ministry as "church" or "Churchshift". On one hand, the ministry is operated from the church; on the other hand, the ministry does not provide service to church members but to the society. Moreover, the ministry is run by unpaid volunteers. The 24-hour crisis telephone hotline has been operating since March 1999 and it offers round-the-clock counseling for various questions and problems from people outside the church. From 1999 to 2003, the Hotline workers counseled about 70,000 people in 44 main categories; the data for 1999 and 2001 are shown in Table 14.1. Each call is placed in only one category.

Table 14.1 Crisis Hotline Calls

	Category	1999	2001
1	11-16 years old	91	42
2	Abortion	14	12
3	Acquaintance	73	34
4	AIDS & HIV	16	16
5	Alcohol Addiction	267	325
6	Apostasy / Regeneration		69
7	Bad Habits	22	56
8	Breaking laws	21	11
9	Death of relatives	35	27
10	Debts	149	100
11	Depression	220	305
12	Disease	569	1224
13	Divorce	55	38
14	Drug Addiction	126	154
15	Family problems	322	1149
16	Fear	52	104
17	Fornication and Adultery	142	284
18	General Info	1545	9526
19	Homeless	110	13

MISSIONAL REFORMATION

	Category	1999	2001
20	Homeless Children	9	1
21	Humiliation	32	3
22	Internal problems	60	670
23	Job problems	64	177
24	Legal questions	181	102
25	Loneliness	162	166
26	Many Children	28	2
27	Ministries info	125	
28	Occultism	28	53
29	Other Questions	432	1563
30	Parents and Children	149	305
31	Perversion	57	173
32	Pregnancy	14	27
33	Pre-marriage Relation	80	72
34	Rape	11	7
35	Refugee	4	
36	Relatives of Alcohol Addicts	315	494
37	Relatives of Drug Addicts	223	571
38	Relatives of sick	282	656
39	Religious questions	216	280
40	Sexual questions	115	157
41	Soul disease	104	108
42	Suicide	70	25
43	Unemployed	373	344
44	Unforgiveness	34	48
45	Not Categorized	188	384
	TOTAL	**7185**	**19877**

It should be noted that not all calls were tracked because of the strength of the staff. The ministry tracks calls by initial faith and those who eventually joined the Embassy of God

Church. Table 14.2 shows the breakdown of the calls by faith.

Table 14.2: Breakdown of Calls by Faith

Year	Christian	Non Christian	Total	Repented	Joined	%
1999			7185	1028	297	4.1
2000	10048	3539	13587	1552	207	1.5
2001	15314	4563	19877	2039	390	2.0
2002	16166	4154	20320	1723	258	1.3
2003	12128	8119	20247	2100	360	1.8
2004	15329	4466	19795	1915	420	2.1

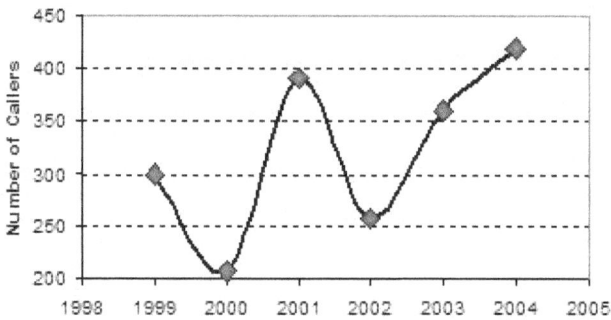

Figure 14.3: Church membership increase through Trust Hotline

Figure 14.3 emanates from these data; it shows the number of callers who eventually joined the Embassy of God. The primary purpose of the ministry is to provide help to the society, not to recruit members. Those who joined the church joined voluntarily without solicitation from the Hotline staff.

Pastor Vitaliy Sergeiko is a member of the Apostolic Coun-

cil. He pastors the first service at the Central Church and works with the Missions Department; he started many ministries, one of which is the Trust Hotline Ministry. Vitaliy gave his life to Jesus in 1992 in an Orthodox church, was baptized, spoke in tongues, and was excommunicated. He started an American Presbyterian church in 1993, which he pastored until 1996; he was ordained in 1994. By the time he left in 1996, there were 70 people attending the church. He left to establish another church which grew to 200 people in 1999. He disliked and persecuted those who attended the Embassy of God Church from the outside before joining the fold in 1999. He started the Hotline ministry immediately. He was re-ordained at the Embassy of God in 2000. In 2001, he became Pastor Sunday's assistant. He also started other ministries such as Beginners, Solomon School, Daniel School, the Press Center, and the Leadership Ladder School. Vitaliy prepared the program for the "System of 12" when it was established in the year 2000.

GOVERNMENT AND LAW

The government sphere at the Embassy of God Church started with individual politicians, such as Mayor Leonid

Chernovetskyi of Kiev, and those who work with the government. The church has realized that *"you cannot run away from the nation"* (Adelaja). Pastor Sophia Zhukatanskaya, who works with the government, established a monospherical daughter church in the political sphere; Club 1000 has recently created a political committee and Vladimir Yeremenko is running a ministry in the government sphere called "Organized Righteousness".

ORGANIZED RIGHTEOUSNESS

Vladimir Yeremenko, a teacher, joined the Embassy of God Church in 2005 after an invitation by Pastor Sunday. He has been teaching Christians since then about the need to get involved in government. He has created an Institute for this purpose. Some receive lectures through distance learning. Vladimir conducts seminars in Russia, Belarus, and Ukraine on this subject. Referring to Christians, in general, in his book *"Organized Righteousness"*, Vladimir writes:

> We have been convinced and politely advised not to get involved with politics. Some people having experienced politics have become more and more convinced that it is a "dirty" business. People who have not had such experiences don't hurry into this dirty business in order to avoid getting dirty themselves. This sphere of man's life and society has always been "dirty" and "dirk". I believe

> the time has come for God's people to understand the Lord's view on politics and His vision on this matter.

Vladimir started the Righteousness Movement in February 2006. On January 18, 2008, the movement made the decision to start a political party. They are moving towards this step by step according to Ukrainian legislation. The movement is going to naturally metamorphosize into a political party named "righteousness". Vladimir has been sharing this revelation to people across the Ukraine.

ORANGE REVOLUTION

Demonstrators, wearing something in the orange color, gathered at the Independence Square in Kiev in the brutal cold winter in November 2004; the demonstration lasted for several weeks up till January 2005. In spite of the freezing temperatures, the number of protesters reached over 200,000 people on November 25. Some reports give up to 700,000 people on November 27. Kiev's Independence Square became the epicenter and rallying point for the democratic struggle in Ukraine. The masses of Ukraine took their future into their own hands. The protests were prompted in the aftermath of the run-off vote of November 21, 2004 of the Ukrainian presidential election, between Viktor Yushchenko and Viktor Yanukovych, which was claimed to be massively rigged by the Moscow-backed authorities; there were claims of corruption, voter intimidation and direct electoral fraud.

After days of massive protests in Kiev and other Ukrainian cities, the Supreme Court overturned the election results and ordered a re-vote of the run-off election for December 26. The opposition candidate, Viktor Yushchenko, won. This was a victory, not just for him, but for Ukrainian democracy. There are several articles on the Orange Revolution.

The participation of the Embassy of God at the historical event could be counted for the church as implementing the Gospel of Peace (see Chapters 4 and 5 of Volume 1). The church erected a tent chapel for spiritual motivation and church members offered food, warm clothing, and medication to thousands of protesters at the freezing Independence Square in Kiev.

POINTS IN CHAPTER 14

Churchshift ministries are promised lands for individual believers. The ministries engage the society, both believers and non believers. They are intended to impart Kingdom principles on the society and to win souls for Christ.

Churchshift ministries at the Embassy of God are run like Parachurch organizations.

At the Embassy of God, there are several hundreds of ministries in all the seven spheres.

Ministers of Churchshift ministries are ordained as social pastors.

15. TESTIMONIES

GOD has used the Embassy of God Church in Kiev to demonstrate that we can receive miracles not only through the Gospel of Salvation, but also through good works. In the former we receive miracles principally by special grace and in the latter we receive miracles principally by our deeds through the universal grace. Almost every member of the church has a story to tell, but we cannot cover thousands of testimonies in this book. However, there is a trend in almost all the testimonies: dejection or rejection, pessimism, Holy Spirit upliftment, and then dedication to service. Many people who would have been written off in life as "nobody" became "somebody". The Senior Pastor too, Sunday Adelaja, had the same kind of story to tell. The Lord has used this church as a model to tell the world that He created us all equal and to prove that to everyone is given a gift. We need the right mindset, environment, and teaching to reach our promised land. The Lord has greatly used Pastor Sunday and the Embassy of God Church to permanently transform lives. No wonder all persecutions against Sunday Adelaja and the Embassy of God by racists, Orthodox Church, and the government has failed. Those whose lives have been transformed and who recognize the importance of the Kingdom of God, stand firmly behind Pastor Sunday irrespective of various slanders.

The testimonies given can be grouped into two types: *life transformation* and *miraculous healing*. Many of those who testify are now pastors; they became zealous for Christ and went all the way to become ministers. Hundreds of testimonies have been published by Fares Publishing in "*Look at what the Lord has done*" in three volumes. There are thousands of church members who have testimonies, but we can only cover a few samples in the two categories.

TRANSFORMATION

In spite of several miraculous healings at the Embassy of God, life transformation is what the church is really known for. It is a church where a "nobody" enters and becomes a "somebody". Life transformation is actually the commission that was given to us by the Lord; miraculous healings are bonuses. Many of the testimonies at the Embassy of God are given by those who got off the streets to become somebody in life; those who dropped out of elementary school and became Ph.D. holders, people who had nothing to eat and later feed others. Great transformations take place at the Embassy of God. It is the Lord's doing. Hundreds of those people would have died as destitute without taking such a step to give their life to Christ; they eventually came back to life, some of them as millionaires. The church proves that there is no one destined to be poor, one just needs to discover his purpose in life and his area of God-given gifts to excel.

OFF PROSTITUTION

At one session of the Embassy of God anniversary in 2009, after Yulia Donets gave her testimony, a call was made for those who God delivered from prostitution to come to the stage. It was surprising to see close to a hundred people who came up front. Those were the people present at that particular moment, not including those who might still be timid to step out. A cross section of some of them is shown below.

Some of them, including Yulia Donets (third from left), gave testimonies. Yulia was the first to boldly come out to give testimony of her deliverance from prostitution. Her testimony propelled many others to step out and also give their own testimonies.

Yulia Donets

Yulia grew up in Kiev. In 1992, when she was 16, her friend introduced her to prostitution; she was a bright student in high school then. They would travel to a Turkish community in Ukraine to prostitute. Yulia got involved in this business because her brother was in debt to a gang. After she paid the debts, they decided to make her continue with the business and they fed from her. They harassed and threatened her. Yulia's parents did not know that she was involved in prostitution until she became rich. Yulia was involved with a billionaire who took her to Malta. Although it was her dream, Yulia had to relocate to Kiev with a heart problem developed in Malta in 1997; God supernaturally interrupted the relationship and her lifestyle. She felt strong pain in her heart and medical diagnoses failed to reveal the problem. After about a month in Kiev, Yulia was brought, by her friend, to the Embassy of God Church where she met Christ. After joining the church, neighbours prayed for her and her heart problem varnished. Yulia became so excited about Jesus, that she immediately joined the praise and worship team. She also started to visit rehabilitation centers to teach. She enrolled and graduated from the

Joshua Bible Institute in 2002. Doctors eventually found out that she had many problems with her organs. She was not fearful; she was fired up and moved by the love of God. Yulia started a ministry that works with people who have sexual problems.

During one of her visits in 2006 to a rehabilitation center to teach, Yulia met Slava Donets who was under drug reha-bilitation. Slava was a drug addict for 18 years. He came to the Embassy of God in 2006. He was in jail between 2000 and 2003. When he got out of jail, he returned to his criminal activities. He was on the "wanted list" in South Ukraine, so he came to Kiev in 2006. After about a month in Kiev (just like Yulia), he found himself at an Embassy of God Church in Borispol, founded by Alex Dzuba. Slava also attended all the Embassy of God schools and graduated from Joshua Bible Institute. On October 26, 2007, Slava and Yulia got married at another Embassy of God daughter church pastored by Yuriy Kravchenko. Slava and Yulia are happily married and they do everything together. They believe that God had prepared them through their past activities for their Churchshift ministry. In their ministry, they rehabilitate gays, prostitutes, transsexuals, sexually abused victims, fornicators, incest, and all unusual sex habits. They evangelize and look for such people. They distribute flyers, broadcast through radio and television programs. They also work on the Internet. They

MISSIONAL REFORMATION

started the ministry with their own money but now they receive funding from benevolent people. They run a real estate business and other businesses together to help fund their Churchshift ministries.

Tatiana Galusko

Tatiana's testimony was given before the 2009 anniversary. I was informed that when she first gave her testimony in church, almost everybody had tears dropping from their eyes. It was so intense; she published a book about her experience, *"When You can't Live and Yet You can't Die"*. The book contains documents to prove some of her ordeals in life. Tatiana traveled through hell to get to be a candidate of the Kingdom. When Tatiana was 11, her step father wanted to rape her but she refused him. He then asked her mother to choose to live with one of them; her mother chose to live with him. So, at the age of 12, Tatiana found herself on the streets of Kiev because her mother rejected her story. On the streets, she took to drugs almost immediately; she was addicted to drugs and alcohol for 11 years and pros-

tituted for 4 years. Tatiana grew up with alcohol addicted parents before she left. She started to smoke at the age of 11 while still with her parents; she started to drink alcohol at the age of 12 and graduated to using drugs at 14. She used all kinds of hard drugs including Meth. At one point, she had only one desire, and that was to die. At 14, three men raped her. She worked as a prostitute in Moscow. She was treated like trash; several times men wanted to kill her. One wanted to throw her down from the eighth floor of a building. Tatiana became pregnant at 16 while living with two drug addicted men; by that time her step father had died and her mother came to look for her in Moscow. Tatiana had a daughter at the age of 17 and she could not tell who the father was between her two partners. After Tatiana nursed the baby for a while, the daughter lived with Tatiana's mother in Kiev. Tatiana's mother wanted a better life for the little girl and thought that a church environment would do it. She began to search for a church with good Sunday school program for little kids and someone directed her to the Embassy of God, then known as "Word of Faith". So, on one Sunday morning in 1998, Tatiana's mother came to the Embassy of God Church; she registered the child and went to a bar to drink. When she came back to the Sunday school, an usher noticed her and led her to the main sanctuary. As mentioned in Chapter 10, worship service in the main sanctuary is always Holy Ghost charged. Tatiana's mother could not resist giving her life to Christ. This was very helpful because it paved the way for Tatiana's salvation; she started to pray for her.

Early in 1999, Tatiana's mother and 7 year old daughter came to see Tatiana in Moscow; she had fever then. Her daughter told her about God and Jesus; they convinced her to come to Kiev. Tatiana reluctantly agreed because she was waiting for another dose of Meth. *"But the stories about Jesus were quieting me"* says Tatiana. She came to the Embassy of God for the first time on March 6, 1999 but she did not yield; her body wrestled with the soul. Several weeks after, a lingering inflammation wound on her arm threatened her life; she was dying of blood poisoning and the doctor told her she had few weeks to live. *"My mother had to drag me to Pastor Sunday like a stubborn cow"* she says. Two days later, she examined her arm to find a good spot to inject with drugs, but she was astonished that the inflammation had disappeared. She thought *"Maybe there is a God after all"*, but that was not convincing enough for her. Later, she got into police custody for drugs. Fear gripped her and she did not know when she uttered this prayer: *"Lord, please get me out of here; I will serve you all my life"*. Truly, her prayer was answered but she soon forgot the promise in her prayer. However, a thought which re-

> When I met Pastor Sunday, I couldn't comprehend a word that the Pastor was saying, but his touch was like a flame eating up my wound. My head went dizzy with energy pouring into me.
> - Tatiana

strained her from further drug use, kept bothering her soul, saying: "You need to go to church". It was on September 21, 1999. Myles Munroe was visiting and preaching in the church. It was on this day that she decided to voluntarily go to church without anyone persuading her. In the entire service she was standing on her feet appreciating God. She sincerely repented and gave her life to Christ. She was immediately delivered from drug addiction; she wept for joy. She had just become a new Tatiana Galusko. She was 25.

The story of Tatiana shows how the universal grace of God works a person into salvation. Without the universal grace, Tatiana could possibly not have received salvation. It was divine favor that got her out of police custody, it was divine restraint that prevented her from further drug use, and it was the universal grace that worked her conscience into repentance. Universal grace is discussed in Chapter 4 of Volume 1 and in *Grace Theology* (Olowe 2009).

After repentance, Tatiana passed through Natalia's Love Rehabilitation Center. There was fire in her bones; she enrolled at Joshua Bible Institute in 2001. By February 2002, she had become a leader of a home group and served teenagers at schools. In 2003, all Kiev schools left their doors widely opened to her. Her story became a good educational template for getting youth out of drugs. The youth love to hear her speak to them; the school principals also want her to come to their schools and speak to the teens. Tatiana went back to school in 2002 for intensive education and completed

High School in 2004. By 2005, she had become influential in all of Ukraine working for the government; her educational program had become known and all Ukrainian schools opened their doors to her. Tatiana has written government approved educational programs for Ukrainian schools. After her secondary education, she went to the University in 2004 to study sociology and psychology; she graduated in 2008. By the year 2009, Tatiana enrolled for a Ph.D. program.

Tatiana Galusko was ordained as a Pastor at the Embassy of God in 2005 and she became the Head coordinator of all Churchshift ministries of the Embassy of God; a new structure was put in place in 2009.

OFF GANG

Bachuke Banchulidze

Bachuke Banchulidze and his brother, Georgiy, were in the Russian mafia since 1982 doing all sorts of racketeering and other criminal activities. Georgiy moved to Kiev and repented at the Embassy of God on February 23, 1999. He went through one of the rehabilitation centers of the church. On a Saturday in 2001, Bachuke came from Russia to Kiev and saw that his brother had a different lifestyle. He was unhappy with him for this and had a serious argument with him. During the hot argument, Bachuke had a heart attack; his heart stopped momentarily. He decided to get rid of Pastor Sunday, who he considered was the root cause of their problems. He felt Pastor Sunday led his brother to a cult. The following day, he decided to carry out his mission; so, he headed towards the Embassy of God Church; on getting to the entrance, he collapsed. The ushers and members around called an ambulance and he was rushed to the hospital. Evidently, God stopped him from attempting to kill Pastor Sunday. When he regained conscience, he regretted his actions and came to the church the following Sunday; he gave his life to Christ. For eight months he was just attending service. He stopped using drugs and left the mafia; he had used hard drugs for 12 years. He joined the new members' class and passed through the Leadership Ladder School and the Joshua Bible Institute. His wife, a Muslim, also repented in 2002. His entire family attends the Embassy of God Church. Bachuke was ordained as a Pastor in 2005; he currently pastors a daughter church in Fastov district. He started the church in 2006 with 2 people; by 2008, the membership had risen to 150. The church has various Churchshift ministries in the Family and Arts spheres. The media was initially hostile to the church and was denied using a public building; but they built their own church. Bachuke now is in business; he owns a construction company. He made a vow to God that if He blesses him, he would use 50 percent of his income to establish rehabilitation centers. God answered his prayers and he has now established five rehabilitation centers so far.

MISSIONAL REFORMATION

Nicholay Khnanisho

Nicholay started to drink alcohol and smoke in 1958 when he was 18. He graduated successfully from high school in 1967; but then, he found himself on the street. He had two younger brothers and two younger sisters. It was difficult during the Soviet time for a poor family to take care of such a large family. His mother was on government support and they knew not Christ. Nicholay had too much free time to wander around. He got into a pick pocketing gang. He got used to it and did it for 40 years. He stole people's wallets and, in recent time, cell phones. Nicholay started to smoke marijuana in 1968 and graduated to using hard drugs in 1970. Between 1967 and 1994, he went to jail 5 times, first serving a total of 17 years. Nicholay got married in 1973; 5 months after, he went to jail. By the time he got out in 1975, his wife left him because of his deception and moved to Brooklyn, New York, with his son in 1986. That year, Nicholay moved from Kiev to Latvia and then to Moscow in 1996; his main profession was stealing. He came back to Kiev in 2007 after his second wife left him. His two younger brothers had died of drugs. The fear of God began to manifest in his life. In January 2008, he got himself mingled in a criminal act; he was to go to jail in 5 days for an offence he didn't commit this time. A man was assaulted to a state of being in a comma. The fear of God gripped him; he was 57 and did not want to go to jail anymore. He was invited to the Embassy of God by a friend. For the first time, he prayed to

God to save him and promised to serve Him. He was taken into police custody but he was later released. On the following Sunday, January 20, 2008, he rushed to the church to give his life to Christ. Nicholay went for the rehabilitation program and attended the leadership school. In September 2008, he enrolled to study at the Joshua Bible Institute. He now has a regular job in a security company. He attends a home group; he does not lead any yet. He plans to start a Churchshift ministry.

OFF ADDICTION

Former drug and alcohol addicts are the real history makers at the Embassy of God Church. The church started with them and they have become a major movement in Ukraine. There are now over 200 rehabilitation centers established by church members in the Ukraine, and several thousands of addicts have been rehabilitated. At the fifteenth anniversary in 2009, hundreds of former addicts gave testimonies of how their lives have been transformed from drug addiction of various degrees ranging from 3 to 30 years of addiction. Some were depressed and were at the point of committing suicide, some became homeless and penniless, many dropped out of school early, and nearly all of them stole and went to jail. Some of these people are now Pastors, in Club 1000, in the choir, business executives, and so on. Sergey Pyshnny, a former penniless drug addict may be the next mayor of his city by the time this book is published. The picture below shows some of those who gave testimonies at the 15th anniversary.

It is not to say that the rehabilitation centers achieve 100% of success; a fraction of them fell back to the streets. However, many of them are well rehabilitated and have formed an army of God against drugs in Ukraine. This movement campaigns against the selling of substitute drugs. They made an excellent presentation of their activities during the anniversary. In the picture below, some members of the movement are photographed with Apostle Tuff.

The movement, led by Sergey Kushniruk, Roman Trokhin, and Ludmila Gannoha, confronts the pharmacies and the government agents to stop and destroy substitute drugs. This is, perhaps, one of the reasons that Pastor Sunday Adelaja and the church are going through some times of persecution. Some officers in the government have financial interests in the selling of substitute drugs.

Roman Trokhin

Roman did not grow up with his father. He used to be a sportsman and became a sports trainer at age 14. However, he had a heart problem and a doctor advised him to stop his activities in sports. He became disillusioned because he believed that his dream had been shattered. There was no one to help him in the crisis and he lost interest in life. He started to smoke and soon graduated to using drugs. At 16, he was already addicted, and he told his mother. He was a drug addict for 11 years; he tried to stop but he couldn't. He tried different medications and no one was there to help him. In 1988, he started to get into trouble and eventually was put in a drug treatment jail. He got out of jail in 1989 only to resume using drugs. He started to steal to get drugs. He was arrested and went to jail for another year. This time, he contracted long-lasting tuberculosis in prison. After his release, Roman resumed on drugs again. Soon he had problems with his organs, his legs, and his veins. He understood that he was going to die of drugs. Whenever he saw his friends dying one after the other, he thought he was going to be the next.

MISSIONAL REFORMATION

In 1994, Roman's mother came to the Embassy of God (Word of Faith) in response to Natalia Potopayeva's TV invitation to parents of drug addicts. She took Roman to the rehabilitation center and to the church, but he soon returned to his drugs. After watching a Christian TV program one day, his flesh began to struggle with the promptings of the Holy Spirit. He continued with his business as usual, but his soul sought to fellowship with believers. In 1996, his mother sold her apartment in Kiev and moved to the village with Roman's brother. Roman refused to follow them because he knew he wouldn't get his drugs there. He began to wander around in Kiev with no particular place to stay; he lived with drug addicted people, moving from one family to another. On top of that, his documents were stolen. His friends disserted him and he became lonely. One day in February 1997, Roman needed drugs so badly that he went to an area where he usually got drugs, but the suppliers had all been arrested. Dejected, Roman stayed in the corridor for a while; it was a cold winter. He started to seriously reflect on his life. Coincidentally, his mother came to visit her friend in Kiev around that time. The following morning, Roman made the decision to take his life. He called his mother but she made him to come over to her friend's house. It was then his mother advised him to call the rehabilitation center, which he did just

> I understood that if God had worked those so many miracles in my life, then I was called to become an answer for many. - Roman

to satisfy her. It was on February 24, 1997. To his surprise, in less than an hour, a delegate of former drug addicts from the Love Center appeared at the apartment and prayed with him; instantly Roman received Jesus Christ as his Lord and Savior and was filled with joy. The next day, Roman went to start his rehabilitation program. They gave him love and demanded nothing from him. He was able to spot some of his friends at the center. Roman has a strong personality; two months after rehabilitation, he was already a leader at the rehabilitation center. His passion for Christ developed rapidly and he became a very active member of the church. In September 1997, Roman enrolled at Joshua Bible Institute; he graduated in 1998. In 2000, he became the director of Love Rehabilitation Center and in April of 2002, he was ordained as a Pastor. In May of 2002, Roman started to pastor a daughter church established by Natalia Potopayeva in Vinogradar district of Kiev. There were 152 members at the first service; the church grew to about 400 active members.

Anya was a light drug user. She came to the church in April 1997 and met Roman at the rehabilitation center when he was the leader. Roman encouraged her to enroll at Joshua Bible Institute; *"he is a good leader"*, she says. In March 1998, Roman proposed to Anya and they got married. Anya was ordained as a Pastor in 2007; she is now the assistant Pastor to Pastor Roman Troklin. Today, Roman Troklin leads a strong anti-drug campaign against the pharmacies and the government. The movement has released documen-

MISSIONAL REFORMATION

tary videos, met with officials of the national government, has instigated the arrest of drug peddlers, and has led to the destruction of substitute drugs in some pharmacies. In the picture below of the movement taken at the fifteenth anniversary, Roman is seen with the microphone.

It was there Roman lamented, in a serious tone, about the unfortunate persecution of the church and of the senior Pastor, Sunday Adelaja.

Radion Bakanov

Radion Bakanov repented at a charismatic church in the city of Dnibropetrovsk in 1998. The Pastor of this young church was killed by a gun shot in 1999 on the street after a night prayer meeting; he was trying to save someone injured during by fireworks shootout. The church then came under the spiritual coverage of Pastor Sunday and the Embassy of God Church. Radion became the administrator of the church for 3 years. In 2000, Pastor Natalia Potopayeva was invited to preach at this church. In 2003, Natalia also invited Radion to preach at her church in Kiev. In 2004, Radion relocated to Kiev. By then, the church at Dnibropetrovsk had grown to 500 attendees and was even sending missionaries to Armenia. Radion started to attend the Right Bank Church, first daughter church of the Embassy of God, pastored by Natalia Potopayeva and he became the central administrator of all daughter churches planted by Natalia in Kiev. From 2007, Radion started to go to Germany as a missionary off and on; Natalia had moved to Germany as a church planter since 2005. In 2008, Radion was ordained as a Pastor after graduating from the Joshua Bible Institute; he plans to finally relocate to Germany as a missionary Pastor.

Radion started to use drugs in High School and by 1991 he became addicted to them; he was addicted until 1998 for 7 years. He was in jail twice during those 7 years; first for gang robbery and the second time for document fraud. The judge told him he was a social danger. His parents were not poor; his father was a deputy regional administrator and his mother was a judge. After getting out of jail the second time, his father refused to let him come to his house because he was very angry for the bad reputation. Radion came to Christ because a friend invited him to a home group. His father is now proud of him. His parents were happily married but his mother passed away in 2004.

MISSIONAL REFORMATION

OFF JAIL

With thousands coming off the streets from prostitution or from drug addiction, it is obvious that thousands of the Embassy of God members had been to jail before for one thing or the other. At the fifteenth anniversary, when those who had been to jail were called to give testimonies, the stage was packed full. There were testimonies from those who had served up to thirty-five years in prison; some of them are shown in the picture below.

Vladimir Popov

Vladimir Popov served two terms in jail, first in 1989-1996 and then in 1999-2004. He comes from a well-to-do family. His father left home when he was 1 year old and his mother remarried. His step father was a composer. When he was 6, Vladimir asked her mother who God is; his mother responded in affirmative that there is no God.

15. TESTIMONIES

Vladimir lived with his grandmother for three years before moving to Kiev in the fourth grade. His mother did not really pay attention to him so he ended up in an orphanage because of his bad habits; he had started smoking and drinking Vodka as early as the third grade. The orphanage home didn't help much either; he made some friends and was not studying well; they always took to the streets. In the sixth grade, he started to abdicate from school and was always being sought by the police for criminal offenses. At 15, he was on parole for stealing a motorcycle. After, he started to work at a shoe factory but he was fired for not showing up several times. Psychologists and other people tried to help him, but all efforts were in vain. In 1987, he went to a government-paid technical school, but he was too undisciplined to get anything out of it as he was always on the streets. He was looking for the quickest way to get wealth without working. He joined a gang that everyone was scared of; they stole cars and valuable items. He was first arrested in 1989 for stealing a car and the police found out in his records that he had once been on parole, but he was released because his mother was influential in the city. Not too long after, he was part of an armed robbery and was arrested again. This time, no influence could save him; he was sentenced to 11 years in prison which was reduced to 7 years because he was not of ripe age.

> There was no God in the former Soviet Union. None of my family knew who He is. The devil shows you that the world is yours. - Vladimir

MISSIONAL REFORMATION

It was in jail that Vladimir started to hear about God through some Baptist Evangelists. When he got out of jail in 1996, he went back to his former mafia life style. In 1999, he was arrested again for assault and spent another 5 years in jail.

After Vladimir had served the second jail term in 2004, he became a realtor and met a lady who talked to him about the Embassy of God and Pastor Sunday. The lady insisted that if he wanted her friendship, he should give his life to Christ and attend church for at least 2 years. He really wanted her friendship, so he was obliged to give his life to Christ as she said even though he didn't really mean it. However, in October 2004 at a Men Conference with Apostle Tuff, Vladimir felt the Holy Spirit and continued to praise God for the baptism. After the leadership school, he entered the Joshua Bible Institute in 2005. Today, Vladimir is grateful to the lady (now his wife) for being a radical Christian; they got married in 2006 after graduating from the Institute. While Vladimir was at the Joshua Bible Institute, he left realty and became a cab driver. After graduating, he went back to real estate and made investments. In 2007, Vladimir became an active member of Club 1000 and started to teach others in business development. He is in shock that he was already in the Club of millionaires in 3 years through his hard work and service to God. He has a well expanded business in building, security, hotels, sports, and he is going international.

HEALING

Due to vast testimonies of transformations, miraculous healings at the Embassy of God have been overlooked by many people. The fact is, there are hundreds of miraculous healings that happen unnoticed. Reading through Chapters 11 to 14, we notice that some of the personalities witnessed miraculous healings in their lives. Testimonies abound on physical healings, healings from barrenness, tumors, cancer, and HIV/AIDS.

BLOOD DISEASE

Anna Sargon was in the military in the Soviet Union over 20 years ago. While in the army, she was exposed to the Chernobyl Nuclear Power Plant disaster of April 26, 1986. She had a disease of the blood and the doctor said it was incurable and that she could not have children; the doctor further warned that if she did, her child would be handicapped. Anna now has three healthy children and she is an ordained Pastor at the Embassy of God Church.

CANCER AND TUMORS

At the fifteenth anniversary of the Embassy of God Church in April 2009, four people came forward to give testimonies of miraculous healings in their lives; one especially gave an

MISSIONAL REFORMATION

emotional testimony of how the Lord healed her of a long lasting cancer problem. The testimony pushed the senior pastor to ask the attendees if any other person had a testimony of healing from cancer or tumors. Surprisingly, over 100 people came to the stage to give testimonies of miraculous healings from cancer and tumors. The pictures below show cross sections of some of those who gave testimonies.

HIV/AIDS

Liliya Kislova

Pastor Liliya Kislova was separated from her husband before joining the church. Her husband was an alcoholic and a non-believer; her son was a drug addict and was in jail with AIDS. The Lord has rejoined her family together, and the son is healed of AIDS. Both wife and husband are Pastors in the church and the son is also an active member. The daughter is a member of an Embassy of God daughter church in Russia

POINTS IN CHAPTER 15

We can receive miracles not only through the Gospel of Salvation, but also through the Gospel of Good Works.

Thousands of members of the Embassy of God have testimonies on their lips; most of the testimonies are from those God took away from the streets and made to be somebody in life.

Many of those who testify are pastors because when they got saved they became zealous for Christ and went all the way to become ministers.

CONCLUSION

The recommended way of carrying out the Great Commission is through stewardship in the area of your gifting. This makes the concept of spheres important in evangelism.

After the writing of this book to almost the conclusion, I stumbled over an article which mentions the possibility of "Gospel of works". I have also stumbled on articles that stress the importance of good works and the rewards. What I have written in this book is led by the Holy Spirit. If God has revealed this to other people, it goes a long way to show that God tells us what He wants us to know at the right moment. It is really amazing how God works. The Gospel of good works is real.

MISSIONAL REFORMATION

The Embassy of God Church, with its Central Church in Kiev, Ukraine is a model Missional Church. The church executes the Churchshift reformation which involves discipling by stewardship. Thousands of people have been transformed through their various programs.

BIBLIOGRAPHY

Adelaja, Sunday; Accessing Divine Wisdom, Fares Publishing House, 2006

Adelaja, Sunday; Spearheading a National Transformation, Fares Publishing House, 2006

Adelaja, Sunday; Victorious despite the devil, Bright Star Publishing House, 2006

Adelaja, Sunday; Church Shift, Charisma house, 2008

Adelaja, Sunday; Money Won't Make You Rich, Charisma house, 2009

Alina, Rudya; Handicapped, by our attitudes, KyivPost, April 21, 2006, www.kyivpost.com/blogs

Anderson, Allan; The Azusa Street Revival and Global Pentecostalism, Assemblies of God, enrichment journal, Spring 2006, www.ag.org/enrichmentjournal/200602/200602_164_AllPoints.cfm

MISSIONAL REFORMATION

Annadorai, George; sermon: You have filled the city with teaching - Acts 5:28, 2007, www.kumyan.org/sermons/sermon_14Oct2007.pdf

Avery, William O.; A Brief History of American Stewardship, Lutheran Laity Movement, 1995.
www.stewardshipoflife.org/Resources/LLM_Archives/LLM-History_stew_preface.htm

Babalola, J.A.; Eto Adura Lent ti Odun 1959 (Prayer Schedule for 1959 Lent), 1959

Bacote, Vincent and Pylman, Daniel; A Neo-Kuyperian Assist to the Emergent Church, Wheaton College, 2008,
www.vanguardchurch.com

Bainton, Roland; The Age of the Reformation. Princeton, NJ: D. Van Nostrand Company, Inc., 1956

Bainton, Roland; Here I Stand: A Life of Martin Luther. Nashville: Abingdon, 1978

Baker, Robert A.; A Summary of Christian History. Revised by John M. Landers. Nashville: Broadman and Holman Publishers, 1994

Barlow, Fred; William Carey: Missionary-Evangelist, 1976,
www.wholesomewords.org/missions/biocarey.html

Barna, George; The second coming of the Church: A blue print for survival, Word Publishing Nashville, 1998

Barrett, David; World Christian Encyclopedia, 2001

Barrett, David and Johnson, Todd M.; International Bulletin of Missionary Research, January 2009

Barrett, Lois Y. and Walter C. Hobbs; Treasure in Clay Jars: Patterns in Missional Faithfulness. Eerdmans, 2004

Bavinck, Herman; Our Reasonable Faith, Wm. B. Eerdmans Publishing Co. (Grand Rapids), 1956

Becerra, Ricardo; Adquiera libros y recursos de las celulas y del G12, www.apologeticsindex.org/633-g12

Beebe, David Lewis; Learning from History: The Roots of Stewardship, Stewardship Council UCC, 1994

Bi, Yantao; China: Religious demography and house churches, February 18, 2009, www.globalvoicesonline.org

Billings, J. Todd; What Makes a Church Missional?, 2008, www.christianitytoday.com

Block, Peter; Stewardship: Choosing Service Over Self Interest, Berrett-Koehler Publishers, 1993

Bosco, Peters (2007); Anglican Liturgy, liturgy.co.nz/spirituality/anglican.html

Bouma, Jake; Toward a Postmodern Youth Ministry: An Examination of Postmodern Youth Culture in Conversation with the Emerging Church, 2007, www.precipicemagazine.com/postmodern-youth-ministry.html

Branding, Ronice; Peacemaking: The journey from fear to love, Chalice Publisher, 1987, ISBN: 9780827229402

Brown, Dale; Brethren and Pacifism, Brethren Press, 1970. ISBN : B000JFP1FK

Brown, Dayo; www.wordablazeministry.org

Brown, Peter; Augustine of Hippo: A Biography. Berkeley and Los Angeles: Univ. of California Press, 1969.

Buckle, Palmer, in Press release; Public debate on Slavery in History and New Slaveries at the International Catholic Conference on Migration in Liverpool, Issued by the Catholic Communications Network, 23/11/2008

Burkholder J. R.; On the Gospel of Peace and becoming a peace church, 1994, peace.mennolink.org/articles/jrtheolo.html

Carey, William; An enquiry into the obligations of Christians, 1792

Chilcote, Paul W., Laceye C. Warner, eds.; The Study of Evangelism: Exploring A Missional Practice of the Church. Eerdmans, 2008.

Chua, Edmond; George Annadorai: Bringing Singapore's Vision into Its Fullness, http://sg.christianpost.com/dbase/ministries/1148//1.htm, Sep. 5, 2008

Cleenewerck, Laurent; His Broken Body: Understanding and Healing the Schism between the Catholic and Eastern Orthodox Churches. Washington, DC: EUC Press (2008)

Cole, Neil; Organic Church: Growing Faith Where Life Happens, Jossey Bass, 2005

Comiskey, Joel; Cell-based Ministry: A positive factor for church growth in Latin America, Ph.D. Dissertation in Intercultural Studies, The School of World Mission and Institute of Church Growth, Fuller Theological Seminary, June 1997

Comiskey, Joel; Leadership Explosion: Multiplying Cell Group Leaders for the Harvest

Comiskey, Joel; Ten Largest Cell Churches, Cell Group Journal, Dec. 2000, joelcomiskeygroup.com/articles/worldwide/tenLargest.htm

Comiskey, Joel; What is a Cell Group, www.joelcomiskeygroup.com, Jan 2002

Comiskey, Joel; Concerns about the G12 Movement, 2002, members.tripod.com/celycecomiskey

Conder, Tim and Dan B. Allender; The Church in Transition: The Journey of Existing Churches Into the Emerging Culture. Zondervan, 2006.

Cope, Landa; An Introduction to The Old Testament Template, http://readingsandreflections.blogspot.com/2007/12/introduction-to-old-testament-template.html

Cope, Landa; The Old Testament Template, Template Institute, 2007

Crann, Alice; Brownsville Revival similar to one in Toronto, The Pensacola News Journal, November 19, 1997

Cunningham, Loren; Winning God's Way, YWAM Publishing, 1988

Cunningham, William; Historical Theology. Edinburgh: The Banner of Truth Trust, 1979. Two volumes. Reprint of 1862 edition.

Dager, Al; Vengeance Is Ours, Sword, 1990

Davis, Paul; Pastor Sunday Adelaja: Incredible, Humble and Phenomenal, www.ezinearticles.com

Dodson, Jonathan; Two Kinds of Simple Church, dreamstime.com

Fares Publishing House; Look What The Lord Has Done, A Handbook of Societal Reformation from The Embassy of God Church, Kiev, 2005

Galushko, Tatyana; When you can't live and yet you can't die, Kiev Fares, 2005

George, Carl; Prepare Your Church For The Future. Grand Rapids, MI: Baker Book House, 1991

George, Carl; The Coming Church Revolution. Grand Rapids, MI: Fleming H. Revell, 1994

Grant, Michael; Jesus: An Historian's Review of the Gospels, 1995

Grumiau, Samuel; New Hope for Ukraine's Disabled Workers, Disability World, no. 18, April-May 2003, www.disabilityworld.org

Guder, Darrell L. (Editor); Missional Church: A Vision for the Sending of the Church in North America, Wm. B. Eerdmans Publishing Co., 1998

Hadden, Jeffrey; Pentecostalism, Lecture Notes, Department of Sociology, University of Virginia

Ham, Ken; Beemer, Britt; and Hillard, Todd; Already Gone: Why your kids will quit church and what you can do to stop it, Master Books, 2009

Hammond, Peter; How the reformation changed the Church, www.frontline.org.za/articles/

Hanko, Herman C.; Is General Revelation a matter of Common Grace?, October 14, 2009, common-grace-considered.blogspot.com

Hastie, Peter; Editorial, Australian Presbyterian, September 2008

Hornor, Noel; Why Don't People Understand the Kingdom of God?, The Good News, www.gnmagazine.org/issues/gn18/understandKingdom.htm

Horton, Michael; Christless Christianity: The Alternative Gospel of the American Church, Baker Book House, 2008

Iuliano, John; Church Planting Manual, www.christian-faith.com/evangelism/churchplantingmanual.html

Jenkins, Philip; The Next Christendom, Oxford University Press, 2002

Kabachenko N., The Problem of Homelessness in Ukraine, www.inclusionexclusion.nl/Ereader/Homelessness_in_Ukraine%20Dubrovnik.doc

Kalu, Ogbu U.; A Trail of Ferment in African Christianity: Ethiopianism, Prophetism and Pentecostalism

Keller, Tim; The Missional Church, June 2001

Keller, Timothy; Proverbs: True Wisdom for Living, Sermon preached at Redeemer Presbyterian Church, New York, October 31, 2004, www.generousgiving.org

Kimball, Dan; The Emerging Church: Vintage Christianity for New Generations, Zondervan, 2003

Kimball, Dan; The Emerging Church: 5 years later - The definition has changed, www.dankimball.com/vintage_faith/2008/09/the-emerging-ch.html

Kimball, Dan; Emerging and Emergent Distinctions, www.dankimball.com/vintage_faith/2008/09/emerging-and-em.html

Krivosheev E; Implementation of social strategies of countering HIV/AIDS and drug-use epidemics, International Conference on AIDS, Jul 2004

Kuyper, Abraham; Lectures on Calvinism: The Stone Lectures of 1898, Six Lectures Delivered at Princeton University, 1898 under the auspices of the L. P. Stone Foundation

Kuzminov, V. N.; Epidemiological situation in drug diseases spread in Ukraine and Kharkiv region, *Youth and Drugs (sociology of narcotism)* (eds. V. A. Sobolev and I. P. Rushchenko), 2000, pp. 159–193

Ladd, George Eldon; The Gospel of the Kingdom, 1978 (ISBN 9780802812803)

Leslie, Sarah; Dominionism and the Rise of Christian Imperialism, www.discernment-ministries.org/ChristianImperialism.htm

Liardon, Roberts; God's Generals, Albury Publishing (1996) ISBN:188008-947-5

Lloyd-Jones, D. Martyn; The Puritans: Their Origins and Successors. Edinburgh: The Banner of Truth Trust, 1987

Long, Jimmy; Generating Hope: A strategy for reaching the postmodern generation, in Telling The Truth, Zondervan Publishing House, 2000

Long, Jimmy; Emerging Hope: A Strategy for Reaching Postmodern Generations, InterVarsity Press, 2004, ISBN 9780830832170

Magdik, Alexandra; Cheap drug addiction rising, Kyiv Post, April 10 2008, www.wiserearth.org

McCallum, Dennis; Watchman Nee, 1986,
www.xenos.org/essays/neeframe.htm

McCarthy, Emmanuel; Sacerdotal Flagism: Should the Flag Be Permanently Displayed in Church Sanctuaries Or Other Explicitly Christian Environments?,
http://centerforchristiannonviolence.org/downloads/Sacerdotal_Flagism_01c.pdf

Madden, Roger; Gladly Will I Spend and Be Spent: A Brief History of the National Catholic Stewardship Council, 1997

Magdik, Alexandra; Cheap drug addiction rising, Kyiv Post, Apr 10 2008; http://www.kyivpost.com/nation/28813/

Masselink, William; General Revelation and Common Grace, W. B. Eerdmans Pub. Co. (Grand Rapids), 1953

Mathewes-Green, Frederica; Facing East: A Pilgrim's Journey Into The Mysteries of Orthodoxy. Harper San Francisco, 1997.

Mauser, Ulrich; The Gospel of Peace

McGee Gary B.; Systematic Theology, Logion Press, 1995

Murdock, Mike; 365 Wisdom Keys,
www.thoughts.com/bubbles22/blog/365-wisdom-keys-of-mike-murdock-137103

Munroe, Myles; Pursuit of purpose, www.youtube.com/

Munroe, Myles; Rediscovering the Kingdom

Neighbour, Ralph, Where Do We Go From Here: A Guidebook for the Cell Group Church, Houston: Touch Publications, 1990

Olowe, Abi; Great Revivals, Great Revivalist – Joseph Ayo Babalola, Omega Publishers, 2007

Olowe, Abi; Grace Theology for Missional Church, Omega Publishers, 2009

Parsley, Rod; Culturally Incorrect, 2007, ISBN: 978-1-5995-1013-2

Pegues, Beverly J.; The Persecuted Church Prayer Devotional- Interceding for the Suffering Church, 2007, ISBN 978-1-932805-90-7

Pfeifer, Mark; Theology of Reclaiming 7 Mountains,

PhilVaz; The Facts and Stats on 33,000 Denominations, www.bringyou.to/apologetics/a106.htm

Poludenko, Anna; Ukraine losing HIV/AIDS fight, Kyiv Post, posted 7 May 2008

Quinn-Judge, Paul and Zarakhovich; The Orange Revolution, Time Europe, November 6, 2004, www.time.com/time/europe/html/041206/story.html

Ritchie, Mark S.; The story of the Church, notes from the Church History classes taught in 1997-1999 at Community Bible Chapel, 2005

Richardson; Texas http://www.ritchies.net/churchhi.htm

Reshetnyak, Maryna; Drop-In Center: The Work Continues, posted on Jul 03, 2009, rising.globalvoicesonline.org, (accessed on Jul 4, 2009)

Rushdoony, R.J.; The Institute of Biblical Law, Nutley, NJ, Craig Press, 1973

Rushdoony, R.J.; Law and Society: Volume 2 of The Institute of Biblical Law, Ross House Books, 1982

Rushdoony, R.J.; The religious right: The assault on tolerance and pluralism in America, ADL

Rushdoony, R.John; Thy Kingdom Come: Studies in Daniel and Revelation, Thoburn Press, 1970

Ryken, Leland; Worldly Saints: The Puritans As They Really Were. Grand Rapids: Academie Books (Zondervan), 1986

Sanders, Oswald; Spiritual leadership, The Moody Bible Institute, 1994

Sauvaget, Bernadette; La "bonne fortune" de l'Ambassade de Dieu, www.reforme.net/archive2/article.php?num=3117&ref=352

Saw, David; See You At The Top, http://the-righteous.blogspot.com/2007/10/see-you-at-top.html, October 14, 2007

Saw, David; Seven Spheres of Society, http://avidsaw.blogspot.com/2008/01/seven-spheres-of-society.html, January 08, 2008

Scaramanga, Url; R.I.P. Emerging Church, September 19, 2008, www.outofur.com/archives/2008/09/rip_emerging_ch.html

Schaff, Philip; History of the Christian Church. 8 volumes. Grand Rapids: William B. Eerdmans Publishing Company, 1979

Sergiychuk, Valentina; Mastering Over The Time, Kiev Bright Star, 2008 (translated by T. Bugayets)

Sergiychuk, Valentina; The Way Out of Debt, Kiev Bright Star, 2008 (translated by T. Bugayets)

Simson, Wolfgang; The Top 10 Churches in the World, www.simplychurch.com

Stark, Rodney; The Truth About the Catholic Church and Slavery, 2003, ctlibrary.com/ct/2003/julyweb-only/7-14-53.0.htm

Stetzer, Ed; A Missional Church, Special to the Index, October 13, 2005

Stetzer, Ed and Putman, David; Breaking the Missional Code: Your Church Can Become a Missionary in Your Community, Broadman & Holman Publishers, 2006

Stewart, David J.; Good Works Verses Grace, www.jesus-is-savior.com/salvation_webpages/18-good_works_verses_grace.htm

Stewart, David J.; The Churchy World and The Worldly Church, www.jesus-is-savior.com

Synan, Vinson; The Origins of the Pentecostal Movement, the School of Divinity Regent University, www.oru.edu/university/library/holyspirit/pentorg1.html

Tan, David; The Transition From a Program Based Design Church to a Cell Church, D.Min. dissertation, Fuller Theological Seminary, 1994 (cited by Comiskey)

Thomas, Jim; The Missional Church, www.urbana.org

Tillin, Tricia; The Transforming Church, www.intotruth.org

Tipple, Graham and Speak, Suzanne; The Hidden Millions: Homelessness in the World's Cities,

Van Rheenen, Gailyn; Modern and postmodern syncretism in theology and missions. In The Holy Spirit and Mission Dynamics, ed. C. Douglas McConnell, 1997, 164-207. Pasadena, CA: Wm. Carey Library.

Verbitska, Anna; Who is Victory church trying to overcome?, Evening Kiev, Aug 19, 1997

Von der Recke, Marie-Noëlle; The Gospel of Peace Revisited, 1999, www.church-and-peace.org

Vu, Michelle A.; Missional Church Movement - The Next Big Thing?, www.christianpost.com

Wagner, Peter C.; Church Planting for Greater Harvest, Regal, 1991

Wagner, Peter C.; The Church in the Workplace, Regal, 2006

Wallis; Jim; The Great Awakening: Reviving Faith and Politics in a Post-Religious Right America, 2008 HarperOne, ISBN 9780060558291

Walsh, W. Pakenham; William Carey: India, 1793-1834, www.wholesomewords.org/missions/bcarey9.html

Warren, Rick; The Purpose Driven Church, Zondervan, 1995

Warren, Rick; The Purpose Driven Life, Zondervan, 2002

Webber, Robert E.; Younger Evangelicals, The: Facing the Challenges of the New World

Winter, Bruce; Culture's Challenge, Australian Presbyterian, September 2008

Yerimenko, Vladimir; Organized Righteousness: God, Politics and Us, Pekkanen, 2008

INTERNET BY SUBJECT

Almsgiving: International Standard Bible Encyclopaedia, www.blueletterBible.org

Almsgiving: Tips, www.charitywatch.org/tips.html

Children: Humanitarian Aid in Ukraine, www.whfc.org

Children: Children in Ukraine, www.unicef.org

Children: Ukraine Orphan Statistics, www.worldorphanproject.com

Church History: Accusations against Christians, chi.Gospelcom.net/GLIMPSEF/Glimpses/glmps010.shtml

Church History: Gnosticism, chi.Gospelcom.net/lives_events/more/gnosticism.shtml

Church History: Navigation and exploration: AD 1415-1460, www.historyworld.net/wrldhis/PlainTextHistories.asp?ParagraphID=gpp

Church History: Timeline, www.saintignatiuschurch.org/timeline.html

Church History: Roman Catholic Church Opposition to Slavery, medicolegal.tripod.com/catholicsvslavery.htm

Church History: Slavery and the Catholic Church, users.binary.net/polycarp/slave.html

Church Planting: Church planting on a 50/50 Gospel, Dec 19, 2008, churchplantingnovice.wordpress.com/2008/12/19/beyond-models/

Dominionism: Neo-Kuyperian Spheres, Discernment Research Group, 2007, herescope.blogspot.com/2007/06/neo-kuyperian-spheres.html

Dominionism: Seven Apostolic Spheres, Discernment Research Group, 2007, herescope.blogspot.com/2007/06/

Encyclopedia: www.encyclopedia.com/

G12: What is the G12 movement? www.gotquestions.org/g12-vision.html

G12: The Government of 12, www.letusreason.org/pent55.htm

G12 Revolution, www.g12revolution.com

God's Grace and Human Works, www.justforcatholics.org/a41.htm

Grace, Faith, and Good Works, www.acts17-11.com/grace_faith.html

Gospel of the Kingdom, www.gnmagazine.org/booklets/GK

Home Churches, Legal Victory For House Churches in India, January 15, 2009, www.cbn.com, www.indianchristians.in

Home groups: Xenos, www.xenos.org/aboutxenos/history.htm

Home groups, www.xafsu.com/index.php

Home groups, Yoido Full Gospel Church, http://english.fgtv.com

House Fellowship: RCCG, main.rccg.org

Peace: Characteristics of a Peace Church, www.church-and-peace.org

MISSIONAL REFORMATION

Postmodernism: Why are young people leaving the church?, WorldNetDaily, June 14, 2009

Simple Church: What Do We Mean By Simple Church, http://house2house.net

Spheres: The 17 Worldview Sphere Documents, Coalition on Revival, www.churchcouncil.org/Reformation_net

Stewardship: UPC, www.upc.org/stewardship.aspx?id=44

Stewardship: Adventist, www.adventiststewardship.com

Stewardship: United Church of Christ, www.ucc.org/stewardship

William Carey's Indian Mission,
www.csichurch.com/article/william_carey.htm

INDEX

A
Acacian, 52
Adeboye, 101
Adoption, 88
Afonso, 50
Alexandria, 42, 43, 47, 52, 63
Algeria, 42, 63
Annadorai, 187, 340
Anthony, 42
Anthropology, 350
Antioch, 41, 43, 52
Aquinas, 52, 54
Arian, 47, 48
Aristotle, 52
Arminianism, 49, 57, 143
Arminius, 57
Augustianism, 49, 143
Augustine, 49, 55, 56, 57, 70, 112, 143, 146, 150, 161, 204
Australia, 92
Awakening, 60
Azusa, 65, 66

B
Babalola, 67, 205
Babylas, 43
Bacote, 81, 150
Bakanov, 411
Banchulidze, 403
Banner, 302, 304
Baptist, 61, 65, 88, 109, 110, 112, 180, 287, 288, 360, 415
Beginners, 300, 306, 388
Biletsky, 246, 265, 287
Binder, 288, 289
Bogotá, 103, 107, 109
Borispol, 295, 296, 398
Bose, 246, 266, 279, 298, 301
Braide, 67
Branching, 87
Bright, 110, 113, 183, 187, 307
Buznickiy, 370
Byzantine, 53

C
Calvin, 56, 57

MISSIONAL REFORMATION

Calvinism, 49, 56, 57, 119, 122, 143, 181, 182, 199, 319
Canada, 60, 285, 288, 338, 340, 376
Cancer, 416
Carey, 61, 110, 180, 204
Carthage, 42, 43, 63
Cartwright, 60
Cassian, 49, 150
Castellanos, 103, 107
Catholic, 36, 40, 42, 47, 50, 54, 55, 58, 61, 65, 68, 70, 71, 108, 112, 114, 146, 194, 244
Chabannaya, 242, 305
Chalcedon, 47
Chapkis, 324
Charismatic, 26, 36, 40, 67, 68
Chernovetskyi, 244, 359, 389
Chernyavskaya, 320, 322
China, 62, 93, 94, 282, 341
Chvostenko, 380
Clark, 95
Clement, 41, 42
Club, 331, 332, 335, 341, 356, 377, 389, 406, 415
Columbus, 63, 95
Comiskey, 98, 99, 100, 102, 106, 107, 109, 110, 212
Commandment, 128, 130, 136, 137, 138, 208
Commission, 71, 81, 95, 108, 112, 118, 121, 124, 140, 154, 162, 184, 193, 199, 208, 209, 223, 225, 230, 242, 300, 420
Conformity, 200, 201, 206
Connecticut, 60
Consolidation, 105
Constantine, 46, 47, 48, 70, 198
Constantinople, 44, 47, 50, 52
Cope, 27, 110, 114, 134, 141, 146, 158, 180, 186, 189
Crowther, 63
Cunningham, 110, 113, 180, 183, 187
Curves, 335
Cyprian, 42, 43

D
Davir, 321, 322
Decius, 43
Dickson, 300
Discipling, 130, 138, 140, 142, 153, 193, 223, 225, 229, 234
Dnibropetrovsk, 411
Dobrovolska, 307
Dominion, 113, 119, 120
Dominionism, 81, 118, 119
Donets, 396, 397, 398
Dzuba, 281, 294, 296, 398

E
Ecumenical, 47, 116
Edwards, 60
Egocentric, 212, 213
Egypt, 42, 47, 63
Enemalah, 342
England, 34, 53, 58, 60, 63, 70, 180
Eutyches, 47
Exploration, 61

F
Fabian, 43
Fajardo, 103
Fares, 307, 308, 316, 395
Fatherhood, 349, 376
Federov, 310
Fellowship, 101, 102, 103, 110
Finley, 60
Finney, 60, 177
Fitness, 331, 335
Franchising, 92, 107

Frankfurt, 343
G
Galerius, 46
Galusko, 273, 346, 399, 402
Gannoha, 273, 407
Garasayan, 383
Gifts, 159, 160, 161, 218
Giving, 142, 164
Gnostic, 45
Grushovenko, 377
Guder, 78, 157
H
Handicapped, 370
Hastie, 25, 26
Healing, 383, 384, 416
Henry, 53, 62, 81, 267, 287
Heresies, 43, 44
Hippo, 56, 63
Hoarding, 211
Hospitality, 300
Hotline, 318, 324, 385
Hotov, 365, 367
Hus, 54
I
Iconoclasm, 45
Ignatius, 41
India, 34, 35, 61, 66, 93, 110, 157, 180, 246, 342
Irving, 65
Isolation, 211
Istanbul, 50
Iuliano, 84
J
Jerusalem, 52
Jethro, 101
Judaism, 145
Justification, 55, 175
K
Khnanisho, 405
Kimbang, 67
Kislova, 417
Konchenko, 382
Korman, 326, 376
Kornilova, 302
Kravchenko, 290, 327, 352, 398
Kubishkin, 338
Kuksenko, 267, 269, 290
Kumuyi, 101
Kushniruk, 348, 350, 407
Kutsenko, 268
Kuyper, 81, 97, 111, 114, 119, 120, 122, 126, 147, 148, 180, 199, 234, 319, 354
Kyrychenko, 307
Kyzub, 322
L
Ladder, 104, 223, 229, 230, 251, 315, 384, 388, 404
Leshchenko, 381, 383
Licinius, 46
Light, 142, 154, 175, 176
Lika, 344, 345, 348, 375
Luther, 34, 53, 144, 194
Lutsenko, 337
Lysak, 375, 376
M
Maghreb, 62
Makers, 342, 349
Maksimenko, 282
Malawi, 296, 297
Malyutina, 310
Marriage, 376, 382, 383
Martindale, 95
Mashchenko, 260, 347
Maxentius, 46
McCotter, 95
Mehmet, 50
Melchizedek, 165
Melnik, 274, 349

Meta, 98, 100, 257, 280, 300, 312
Methodist, 58, 59, 61, 88, 109
Milan, 46
Millionaire, 332
Mischenko, 242, 250
Modality, 85, 86
Mohammed, 50
Monophysites, 48
Monosphere, 88
Monotheletism, 45
Moscow, 288, 295, 368, 391, 400, 401, 405
Munroe, 163, 245, 255, 256, 308, 338, 402
Musical, 321, 322
Mykhaylyk, 342
N
Nicea, 47
Nicholas, 50
Nigeria, 62, 67, 86, 101, 109, 247, 281, 341, 342
NUGA, 294, 335, 339
O
Odessa, 288, 334
Oleg, 295
Omelchenko, 253, 366
Omotoye, 265, 284, 343, 358
Orange, 255, 303, 390, 391
Origen, 42
Orimolade, 67
Orphanage, 365
Orthodox, 45, 47, 52, 61, 70, 199, 244, 247, 264, 268, 305, 308, 334, 350, 360, 388, 395
Oznam, 66
P
Parachurch, 139, 314, 393
Parachute, 90
Parham, 65, 66

Parsley, 27, 184, 202, 230
Pastoral, 185, 202, 272
Peace, 35, 56, 135, 141, 171, 173, 174, 391
Pelagian, 49, 146
Pelagius, 49, 70, 112
Pentecostal, 26, 36, 64, 88, 110, 282, 294, 301, 320, 337, 338, 340, 382
Peresvetov, 296
Perfection, 60
Persecution, 46, 217
Perseverance, 57
Photian, 52
Pioneering, 85
Planting, 83, 85, 90, 98, 142
Polycarp, 41
Popov, 413
Portuguese, 62, 63
Postmodern, 36, 37, 40, 71, 72, 78
Potopayeva, 242, 243, 265, 273, 282, 284, 291, 294, 328, 336, 355, 376, 409, 411
Potyzailo, 373
Pozharizkiy, 334
Prayer, 249, 250, 300, 305
Presbyterian, 25, 65, 115, 388
Promised, 162, 209, 217, 220, 313
Prophetic, 66, 67
Prostitution, 346, 396
Protestant, 48, 53, 56, 68, 71, 143, 144, 199, 320
Psychology, 185, 274, 306
Puritan, 58
Pyshnny, 278, 406
R
Rehabilitation, 243, 273, 293, 318, 349, 354, 373, 402, 410

INDEX

Reichenbach, 343
Remonstrance, 57
Remonstrants, 57
Revelation, 127, 130
Revival, 26, 59, 69, 184, 204
Revolution, 255, 390, 391
Roganov, 365
Rome, 41, 43, 46, 47, 52, 54, 58
Rud, 361
Rushdoony, 119

S
Sanhedrin, 42
Sargon, 416
Satellite, 87, 109, 110
Schism, 52
Scholasticism, 51, 52
Sergeiko, 388
Sergeychuk, 315
Seymour, 65, 66
Shevchenko, 363
Silver, 345, 348, 375
Singapore, 109, 112, 332, 341
Skeemans, 373, 374
Slavery, 51
Sodality, 85, 89
Sphere, 110, 180, 231, 319
Spivakov, 337
Splitting, 101, 109
Stephania, 343, 354, 358
Stewardship, 114, 118, 130, 142, 158, 170
Stewart, 64, 65
Switzerland, 54
Syncretic, 32, 38, 76, 193, 194, 203, 206, 239
Syncretism, 33, 194, 196

T
Talent, 159, 164, 169, 170
Tertullian, 41, 43
Tithing, 165, 166
Transformation, 341, 350, 395
Treasures, 159, 373
Tree, 103, 109, 258
Trokhin, 352, 407, 408
Tuff, 243, 407, 415
Tunisia, 42, 63

U
Universal, 129, 147, 149, 151, 159, 402
Usok, 308
Uzhgorad, 344

V
Vasquez, 88
Vatutino, 294
Verhman, 329
VIGAN, 294, 335, 336

W
Wagner, 83, 112, 121
Wesley, 58, 59, 129, 150
Whitfield, 58
Wittenberg, 53, 54
Works, 88, 110, 129, 132, 134, 136, 138, 153, 178, 214, 224, 419
Worship, 109, 110, 247, 300
Wycliffe, 54

Y
Yeremenko, 323, 389
Yoido, 98, 103, 109
Yonggi, 87, 98, 101
Yushchenko, 391

Z
Zwingli, 54, 56

Similar books by the author

If you enjoyed this *Missional Reformation* book, you need to get these two books:

ISBN: 978-0-9795299-0-0   ISBN: 978-0-9795299-5-5

Useful Resources

These books:
www.missionalreformation.com
www.greatrevivals.com

To join ChurchShift movement:
www.churchshift.org
www.churchshiftusa.org

www.ingramcontent.com/pod-product-compliance
Lightning Source LLC
Chambersburg PA
CBHW060936230426
43665CB00015B/1964